ROYAL HISTORICAL SOCIETY
STUDIES IN HISTORY

New Series

# RED FLAG AND UNION JACK

D1612808

# RED FLAG AND UNION JACK

## ENGLISHNESS, PATRIOTISM
## AND THE BRITISH LEFT,
## 1881–1924

*Paul Ward*

THE ROYAL HISTORICAL SOCIETY
THE BOYDELL PRESS

First published 1998
The Royal Historical Society, London
in association with
The Boydell Press, Woodbridge
Reprinted in paperback and transferred to digital printing 2011
The Boydell Press, Woodbridge

ISBN 97 0 86193 239 9 hardback
ISBN 978 1 84383 636 0 paperback

The Boydell Press is an imprint of Boydell & Brewer Ltd
PO Box 9, Woodbridge, Suffolk IP12 3DF, UK
and of Boydell & Brewer Inc,
668 Mt Hope Avenue, Rochester, NY 14620, USA
website: www.boydellandbrewer.com

A CIP catalogue record for this book is available
from the British Library

Library of Congress Catalog Card Number 98–36316

This publication is printed on acid-free paper

# Contents

Publication of this volume was aided by a grant from the Scou-loudi foundation, in association with the Institute of Historical Research. It was further assisted by a grant from The Isobel Thornley Bequest Fund of the University of London.

For Jackie and Georgia

# Acknowledgments

Thanks must first go to John Ramsden. He supervised, with efficiency and insight, the doctoral thesis upon which this book is based. Daniel Pick and Peter Catterall commented fully on early work, and Sarah Palmer made valuable observations on the whole thesis. John Turner and Hugh Cunningham, as my PhD examiners, pointed out areas for improvement, as did Martin Daunton, my advisory editor for the Royal Historical Society. Peter Mandler read a version of chapter 2 and gave it more direction. Christine Linehan, executive editor at the Royal Historical Society, was patient and helpful throughout the preparation of the manuscript. The research for my thesis was made possible by grants from the Drapers' Company/Queen Mary and Westfield College, University of London and the British Academy.

Colleagues at Queen Mary and Westfield College, London Guildhall University, Middlesex University and, most recently, the University of Westminster and Royal Holloway, University of London, deserve mention. Brian Burden and Bradley Reynolds both read the manuscript at various stages looking for grammatical, syntax and typographical errors.

For permission to quote material, acknowledgement is made to Independent Labour Publications; the Local Studies unit, Manchester Central Library (for the Robert Blatchford Papers); RIBA British Architectural Library: Manuscript and Archives Collection (for the Raymond Unwin Papers); Mrs D. Evelyn and the University of Liverpool (for the Glasier Papers). Archivists and librarians at the University of London, the British Library, the British Library of Political and Economic Science and the Marx Memorial Library all aided my researches. The long chronological period covered by this book has involved large debts to other historians, to provide background, examples and directions for research and interpretation. It is hoped that footnotes and bibliography do justice to such indebtedness. Errors of fact or interpretation do, of course, remain my own.

Paul Ward
July 1998

# Abbreviations

| | |
|---|---|
| ASE | Amalgamated Society of Engineers |
| BSP | British Socialist Party |
| BWL | British Workers' League |
| CPGB | Communist Party of Great Britain |
| ILP | Independent Labour Party |
| ISB | International Socialist Bureau |
| LRC | Labour Representation Committee |
| NAC | National Administrative Council (ILP) |
| NCF | No Conscription Fellowship |
| NUR | National Union of Railwaymen |
| PLP | Parliamentary Labour Party |
| SDF/SDP | Social Democratic Federation/Social Democratic Party |
| SLP | Socialist Labour Party |
| SNDC | Socialist National Defence Committee |
| TUC PC | Trades Union Congress Parliamentary Committee |
| UDC | Union of Democratic Control |
| WEWNC | War Emergency Workers' National Committee |

**Journal Abbreviations**

| | |
|---|---|
| BIHR | *Bulletin of the Institute of Historical Research* |
| BSSLH | *Bulletin of the Society for the Study of Labour History* |
| EHR | *English Historical Review* |
| HJ | *Historical Journal* |
| HW | *History Workshop* |
| JBS | *Journal of British Studies* |
| JCH | *Journal of Contemporary History* |
| JICH | *Journal of Imperial and Commonwealth History* |
| JMH | *Journal of Modern History* |
| P&P | *Past and Present* |
| TRHS | *Transactions of the Royal Historical Society* |
| VS | *Victorian Studies* |

**A Note on the Text**
Where the Labour movement is in upper case it refers to the Labour Party, its affiliated trade unions and socialist societies. Where it is in lower case, labour movement, it refers to all of these and to non-affiliated groups.

# Introduction

'I am a Socialist but I love my country.'[1] So wrote Alfred Johnson to the editor of the *Clarion* in the early weeks of the Boer War. He had expressed concisely the defensiveness of socialists when discussing affection for their country. This defensiveness has rarely been overcome since the last third of the nineteenth century. It has informed most discussions by the left whether on contemporary patriotism or patriotism in the past. It has led to a vague belief that patriotism and socialism have coincided only in individuals, or accidentally due to events outside the control of socialists, such as wars. Hence when patriotism and socialism are mentioned in the same breath, one thinks of H. M. Hyndman, Robert Blatchford, J. B. Priestley, and above all, George Orwell. Alternatively, as with British Labour and socialist support for the First World War, it is seen as something of a surprise, a break with the past. It is, perhaps, this defensiveness that had made the analysis of patriotism largely the work of left-wing commentators.[2] The most obvious recent example was the History Workshop conference on patriotism in the wake of the Falklands War. As Raphael Samuel wrote in the preface to the collection of essays that resulted, 'it seemed that the country had gone mad', and hence the conference's aim was 'deconstructive, to bring patriotism within the province of rational explanation and historical enquiry'.[3]

Some involved in this historical reassessment of patriotism have brought more than historical interest to their subject. They have used their conclusions to make a plea for the left to re-embrace patriotism or to reject it once and for all. A recent example is John Schwarzmantel's *Socialism and the idea of the nation*. 'Socialists', he decided, '*need* to develop and sustain a concept of the nation, if not exactly a form of nationalism, and the idea of the nation need not and should not be the preserve of the right, as indeed often seems to be the case.'[4] Anthony Barnett provides an example of the rejection of patriotism. Instead, he argues, the left would be better served were it to 'insist upon the plurality of national allegiances . . . the diversity of regional differences; the plurality of racial and migrant strains; the importance of gender loyalties; the complexity of religious affiliations; and the conflicting alle-

---

1 *Clarion*, 18 Nov. 1899.
2 Miles Taylor, 'Patriotism, history and the left in twentieth century Britain', *HJ* xxxiii (1990), 971–87.
3 Raphael Samuel (ed.), *Patriotism: the making and unmaking of British national identity*, I: *History and politics*, London 1989, p. x.
4 John Schwarzmantel, *Socialism and the idea of the nation*, Hemel Hempstead 1991, 1.

1

giances of class'.[5] Both views share the idea that the left has at some point given up patriotism. In most instances this is not the case. It is rather that it is only individuals or small groups on the British left who have rejected patriotism altogether. For all the defensiveness, the majority of the British left has laid a claim to patriotism, not only when events such as wars have overtaken it, but most of the time. The degrees of patriotism and the weight given to patriotism and socialism across the left have differed. It is those whose patriotism has outweighed their socialism most often who are usually the subject of interest. This book, while looking at these patriot–socialists, also examines those socialists whose patriotism remained more submerged.

Patriotism cannot be separated from the question of national identity, for even taking its most basic definition, 'love of country', the object must be defined in order to be loved. The nation must be 'imagined' in some form to be worthy of affection.[6] Hence if most of the British left has expressed a form of patriotism, it follows that they have also indulged in interpretations or imaginings of the forms of the British nation and the character of its people. To use a phrase of Anthony D. Smith's, 'nationalism-in-general is merely a lazy historian's escape from the arduous task of explaining the influence of this or that particular nationalist idea in its highly specific context'.[7] This book aims to examine ideas of patriotism and Englishness in the historical context of the period that is generally accepted as comprising Labour's 'turning point' and its formative years.[8] That is, the period from the publication of H. M. Hyndman's *England for all* in 1881, which claimed socialism as an Anglo-Saxon mission, to the taking of office by the first Labour government in 1924, committed as it was to governing in what it called the national interest. Discussions of patriotism and Englishness played a greater part in shaping the British left in these years than has previously been thought.

At this point it is necessary to define further the parameters of the subject and the terms used in its discussion. The British left is taken to mean those who sought through socialist and independent labour politics the political transformation of the British Isles as a whole.[9] This excludes Scottish, Welsh and Irish socialists who aimed at change, in the first instance, only within the borders of their respective nations, even when this was combined with an internationalism that saw such change as part of a greater world

5  Anthony Barnett, 'After nationalism', in Samuel, *Patriotism*, i. 149.
6  Benedict Anderson, *Imagined communities: reflections on the origin and spread of nationalism*, London 1983
7  Anthony D. Smith, *National identity*, London 1991, 79.
8  *Labour's turning point 1880–1900*, ed. E. J. Hobsbawm, 2nd edn, Brighton 1974.
9  The Co-operative movement is excluded. While it indulged in expressions of an oppositional Englishness, using 'Merrie England' rhetoric, giving its major newspaper the decidedly rural name of *The Wheatsheaf*, and setting up the Woodcraft Folk as part of its youth movement, it did not commit itself to political representation until 1917, and its relations with the Labour Party were not institutionalised within the period covered by this book: Ross McKibbin, *The evolution of the Labour Party 1910–1924*, Oxford 1974, 178–91.

transformation. Those such as James Connolly, and John Maclean after he refused to join the Communist Party of Great Britain, are therefore excluded.[10] But included are Scottish, Welsh and Irish figures who wanted change in an all-British context. Ramsay MacDonald, Keir Hardie, Bernard Shaw and J. H. Thomas are therefore included. Largely for this reason, the term 'Englishness' has been maintained in the title, rather than the clumsier 'Britishness'. By consent, Scottish, Welsh and Irish socialists in the British labour movement accepted ideas about a single national political character which drew largely on an interpretation of British history dominated by events in England, such as the Norman Conquest, Magna Carta, the idea of a fifteenth-century golden age of labour and the English Civil War. Of course, English socialists, such as Hyndman, Blatchford and Morris, overwhelmingly reinforced this concentration on English rather than British history.[11]

This is not to say that non-English socialists gave up other identities. As Linda Colley has put it, 'identities are not hats. Human beings can and do put on several at a time.'[12] Keir Hardie could see himself as a socialist, a Scot, a Briton and an internationalist. Philip Snowden likewise saw himself as a socialist and an internationalist, but was also proud to have been reared among 'a sturdy, honest, blunt outspoken type' of people in Yorkshire.[13] It is unlikely however that those who saw themselves as 'English' saw much difference between this and being British. J. B. Priestley simply said, 'When I say "English" I really mean British.'[14]

Patriotism and national identity do not only come into play with reference to relationships to other nations. Patriotism can be inward-looking too, and this element was more prominent on the left.[15] The terms used to describe this inward-looking patriotism need some definition. Englishness is the attribution of characteristics, habits, customs and traditions to the English as a people which makes them distinctive from other groups of people. Likewise Britishness. Englishness sometimes included other Britons within its terms, at other times it did not. What constitutes these assumptions is historically,

---

[10] For both, see David Howell, A lost left: three case studies in socialism and nationalism, Manchester 1986.

[11] There are of course difficulties in such simple definitions of nationality. Robert Blatchford, who used 'England for the English' as a slogan, was the son of Georgiana Louisa Corri, an Italian. The self-identity of individuals must be taken for granted.

[12] Linda Colley, Britons: forging the nation 1707–1837, New Haven–London 1992, 6. See also E. J. Hobsbawm, 'What is the workers' country?', in Worlds of labour, London 1984, 49–65.

[13] Philip Snowden, An autobiography, I: 1864–1919, London 1934, 2.

[14] Postscripts, 1940, 2, in Stephen Yeo, 'Socialism, the state and some oppositional Englishness', in Robert Colls and Philip Dodd (eds), Englishness: politics and culture 1880–1920, London 1986, 310.

[15] For example, see E. Green and M. Taylor, 'Further thoughts on Little Englandism', in Samuel, Patriotism, i. 103–9. But also for the right and an inward-looking objective for imperialism see Bernard Semmel, Imperialism and social reform: English social–imperial thought 1895–1914, London 1960.

culturally and politically shaped. Hence they can change across the political spectrum. In this book, Englishness is usually taken to mean traditional, loyal and hegemonic views, whereas the term 'oppositional Englishness' is used where alternative assumptions, or the same assumptions leading to different conclusions, were taken up on the left.[16] This alternative view of nationalness did involve an acceptance of the historical experience, memory, traditions, customs and habits of a defined territory, assigning to the inhabitants a character that involved more than simply the accident of birth within that territory. What distinguishes oppositional Englishness is that it attempted to construct a democratic version of national identity. Two other terms require definition. Radical patriotism is used to delineate the political uses to which love of country was put by those who did not simply accept government/state as being synonymous with the nation. Radical patriotism, here, is used interchangeably with oppositional Englishness. It is the argument of this book that the mainstream of the British left, particularly the Labour Party, since they came to look on the state as the vehicle for social transformation, gave up radical patriotism while maintaining their patriotism. The definition of 'social patriotism' used here is that of Geoffrey Field: 'an inwardly focused patriotism, one that is oriented toward domestic social reform and implies some kind of new and improved Britain'.[17] The majority of the left came to accept British democracy and saw the elected government, of whatever party, as legitimate. It therefore became increasingly difficult for them to be radically patriotic, opposing nation to government, but they could remain socially patriotic; that is, they could use arguments about their attachment to the nation as a force for social reform. Again social patriotism has not been a monopoly of the left. Lloyd George's 'homes fit for heroes' is a classic social patriotic phrase.[18] In this sense, social patriotism means a reciprocal arrangement between classes where the ruling class offers social reform in return for patriotism. It was such class collaboration that Lenin attacked so bitterly.[19]

That the patriotism of socialists was mainly inward-looking allowed a tolerance of other nations' patriotisms. Indeed international socialism was often seen as the only safeguard for national differences.[20] A distinction was made between 'cosmopolitanism', which meant the disappearance of national differences, which was bad, and 'internationalism', which allowed the recognition of national differences.[21] Internationalism, it was felt, relied first on the acceptance of the idea of different nations. Internationalism did not mean

16 Oppositional Englishness is the term used by Stephen Yeo, and adopted here.
17 Geoffrey Field, 'Social patriotism and the British working class: appearance and disappearance of a tradition', *International Labor and Working Class History* xli (1992), 21n.
18 See Mark Swenarton, *Homes fit for heroes: the politics and architecture of early state housing*, London 1981.
19 See, for example, V. I. Lenin, *Selected works in three volumes*, iii, Moscow 1963, 298.
20 Part of the Webbs' answer to the question 'What is socialism?' was 'the maintenance of nationality by the growth of internationalism': *New Statesman*, 26 July 1913.
21 For example, R. C. K. Ensor's 1912 report for the Fabian Society on the general strike to

anti-nationalism.[22] However, from the mid nineteenth century international rivalry and imperialism made the idea of a plurality of patriotic nations living in peaceful coexistence seem inadequate. Ultimately, in 1914, the choice between socialism and patriotism had to be made. The attitudes of the British left to such events, and their discussion in terms of patriotism and national identity form a major part of this book.

Ideas about national character were not only components in arguments for social and political reform. H. M. Hyndman in *England for all* used ideas about Englishness to define how socialism in Britain could be achieved. Hyndman largely based *England for all* on a reading of Marx's *Capital*, but left the debt acknowledged only to 'a great and original thinker'.[23] He felt that Britons would not appreciate being taught by a German. This was no simple quirk of the xenophobic Hyndman, but only the first instalment in a continuing current on the British left of justifying their own socialism as in line with the English/British national character, history and political traditions. Against Marxism and anarchism in the 1880s and 1890s, syndicalism in the years before the First World War, and Bolshevism after 1917, British socialists used Englishness to denigrate these 'foreign' socialisms. Hence this book is also about the making of an authentic 'British socialism', which proved its worth in 1924, when for the first time Labour formed the government of the nation. Again this links together with the end of radical patriotism as British socialism came to accept the British state and its specific institutions as the sole legitimate vehicle for the (gradual) advance to socialism. The mainstream left's notions of Englishness converged with more traditional notions when it came to defence of the British parliamentary system.

While the focus of this book is the politics of the left, in terms of electoral strategy, a further theme, taken up rather tenuously, is that of cultural attitudes to Englishness among the left. This draws in attitudes to craftsmanship among the Arts and Crafts movement, influenced so thoroughly by William Morris. This to some extent involved a rejection of urban society as somehow un-English, and the real source of national identity was sought in the countryside. From Morris in the 1880s to MacDonald in the 1920s, the British left believed itself to be the guardian of rural Britain against the encroachment of urban capitalism, and with this went a belief that the left had a better claim to be preserving the sources of strength in the national character.

In recent years there has been an increasing body of writing on English/British national identity and patriotism. Gerald Newman and Linda Colley have outlined differing views on the formation of English nationalism and

prevent war: A. M. McBriar, *Fabian socialism and English politics 1884–1918*, London 1962, 136–7.
[22] For example, 'Social democracy, Hervéism, and militarism', *Justice*, 5 Oct. 1907.
[23] H. M. Hyndman, *England for all: the textbook of democracy*, Brighton 1973 (first publ. 1881), p. xxxviii.

Britishness respectively.[24] Both works, to use Newman's words, 'help to answer a modern need by investigating the process by which England's legendary "uniqueness", her "differentness" from continental society, arose from her very commonness with it'.[25] Despite uncovering differing motivations, they both show that, like foreign nationalisms, British nationalism was a contrivance with political purposes. This theme has been the subject of other work, particularly in the 'invention of tradition' mode.[26] The hidden nature of nationalness in Britain has largely been the result of the perceived oldness of the nation. Patrick Wright has addressed the question of how this perception affects contemporary Britain, concluding that the obsession with 'national heritage' is accompanied by a 'sense that history is foreclosed'.[27] Stanley Baldwin, who knew how to use this foreclosure to good effect, has been the subject of analysis.[28] While few other individuals have been so examined, parties and politics have.[29] Individual symbols of nationhood have also received much attention. John Bull, Britannia, pearly kings and queens, the monarchy, English music, the police, stately homes and the countryside have all found their historians of patriotism and national identity.[30] Much of the recent literature has also shown the variety of identities within the nation, and there has been work done on the relationship of different classes to patriotism.[31]

The recognition that patriotisms exist, rather than simply patriotism, has led to examination of left-wing patriotism. Some labour historians have discovered this while researching individuals and institutions of the left. David Howell has recognised the patriotic motive behind the naming of the

24 Gerald Newman, *The rise of English nationalism: a cultural history 1740–1830*, New York 1987; Colley, *Britons*.

25 Newman, *Rise of English nationalism*, p. xxi.

26 Eric Hobsbawm and Terence Ranger (eds), *The invention of tradition*, Cambridge 1983. See also Roy Porter (ed.), *Myths of the English*, Cambridge 1992.

27 Patrick Wright, *On living in an old country*, London 1985, 70.

28 For example, Bill Schwarz, 'The language of constitutionalism: Baldwinite Conservatism', in *Formations of nation and people*, London 1984, 1–18.

29 For example, Robert Colls, 'Englishness and political culture', and Hugh Cunningham, 'The Conservative Party and patriotism', in Colls and Dodd, *Englishness*; Hugh Cunningham, 'Jingoism in 1877–78', VS xiv (1971), 429–53; Frans Coetzee, *For party or country: nationalism and the dilemmas of popular Conservatism in Edwardian England*, Oxford 1990.

30 For example, various essays in Colls and Dodd, *Englishness*; various essays in Porter, *Myths of the English*; various essays in Raphael Samuel (ed.), *Patriotism: the making and unmaking of British national identity*, III: *National fictions*, London 1989; Tom Nairn, *The enchanted glass: Britain and its monarchy*, London 1988; Peter Mandler, *The fall and rise of the stately home*, New Haven–London, 1997; Miles Taylor, 'John Bull and the iconography of public opinion in England c. 1712–1929', *P&P* cxxxiv (1992), 93–128.

31 J. H. Grainger, *Patriotisms: Britain 1900–1939*, London 1986; Hugh Cunningham, *The Volunteer force: a political and social history 1859–1908*, London 1975; many of the essays in all three volumes of Samuel, *Patriotism*, take this approach.

Independent Labour Party.[32] Kenneth Morgan and Austen Morgan have pointed out that Keir Hardie and Ramsay MacDonald sought to establish a national form of socialism.[33] The biographers of Robert Blatchford and H. M. Hyndman could not fail to discuss their patriotism.[34]

Other historians have approached the left from the perspective of patriotism, as this book does. Christopher Hill's essay on the Norman yoke was the pioneering study in this field. He set out to analyse how English radicals framed their radicalism with reference to the Norman Conquest, how this fitted in with the idea of lost rights, but also as 'a rudimentary class theory of politics'.[35] It is this latter point that continued to give radical patriotism its resonance after the industrial revolution. It could cope with changing class structures because inequalities remained. Hugh Cunningham's essay, 'The language of patriotism', examined the survival of such language into the third quarter of the nineteenth century.[36] His analysis of the transfer of the dominance of the language of patriotism goes far to explain the left's defensiveness about its own patriotism. Cunningham's conclusion that, 'In the age of imperialism it was impossible to demarcate a patriotism of the left',[37] may be substantially correct. The left was forced to make numerous compromises, but Cunningham under-estimates the continuing and sustained efforts of many of those on the left to attempt to distinguish their own patriotism from that of conservatives. Miles Taylor has argued that the end of radical patriotism came in the wake of the Boer War, when the irrational political behaviour of the jingo crowds frightened the left away from patriotism.[38] This book argues that radical patriotism survived into the First World War.

While there have been a few works upon individual incidents of left-wing patriotism in the period between the revival of socialism and 1939,[39] the Second World War has been seen as a period in which the left once more dominated patriotism, however briefly. Patriotism became associated with a desire for social reform. At the same time, the right appeared un-patriotic because

[32] David Howell, *British workers and the Independent Labour Party 1888–1906*, Manchester 1983, 293.

[33] Kenneth O. Morgan, *Keir Hardie: radical and socialist*, London 1975, 203, 214; Austen Morgan, *J. Ramsay MacDonald*, Manchester 1987, chs i, ii.

[34] Laurence Thompson, *Robert Blatchford: portrait of an Englishman*, London 1951; Chushichi Tsuzuki, *H. M. Hyndman and British socialism*, London 1961.

[35] Christopher Hill, 'The Norman yoke', in his *Puritanism and revolution: studies in the interpretation of the English Revolution of the 17th century*, Harmondsworth 1986, 58–125. The essay was first published in 1954.

[36] Hugh Cunningham, 'The language of patriotism', in Samuel, *Patriotism*, i. 57–89.

[37] Ibid. 82.

[38] Taylor, 'Patriotism, history and the left'.

[39] For example, Richard Gott, 'Little Englanders', and Green and Taylor, 'Further thoughts on Little Englandism', in Samuel, *Patriotism*, i. 90–102, 103–9.

of its failure to prevent defeat at Dunkirk. The result was the landslide victory for the Labour Party in 1945.[40]

There has been a neglect of the question of patriotism in the formative years of the modern British left. Stephen Yeo has drawn some useful conclusions from the period in his essay 'Socialism, the state and some oppositional Englishness'. However, the strength of his essay, in its discussion of socialism and the state, also forms its weakness when it comes to the study of the left, patriotism and national identity. Yeo recognises that attitudes to the state were crucial in the relationships between the left and ideas of national identity, but since these attitudes to the state are the key point of his essay, Englishness enters mainly in its relationship to the British state. The formula that acceptance of the legitimacy of the state leads to an adherence to patriotism is axiomatic. It is also inadequate.[41] Radical patriotism could also express hostility to the state, for example in the opposition to conscription before and during the First World War expressed in a language claiming the rights of the freeborn Englishman against the imposition of a foreign yoke. Yet the strength of the formula is maintained, for as the mainstream left was drawn into the state (or gained the potential to form part of the state), radical patriotism was displaced. Patriotism remained. The Attlee cabinet agreed in October 1946 that the citizen in the welfare state had an obligation to undertake national service.[42] Having shaped the state in its own image, Labour expected that the electorate should fulfil its own side of the social patriotic bargain. Another useful area that Yeo draws attention to is the discussion of the way in which collectivist socialism 'regarded itself as quite "English" '.[43] He cites an example of the distortion by Edward Pease, the secretary of the Fabian Society, of a whole book by Thomas Kirkup, a commentator on socialism. Kirkup had criticised those socialists 'too much influenced by the Prussian type of government and theory of the state', which he said was 'entirely opposed to English ideas'.[44] Pease edited the fifth edition of Kirkup's A history of socialism in 1913. He left out Kirkup's concerns about Fabianism and the state. Kirkup's sarcastic criticism that 'It is easier to get control over existing machinery than to make machinery yourself', had its context changed to express a classic Fabian axiom on the state. Pease then privileged these ideas with the title 'the English school of socialism'.[45] This was an exceptional instance, but it was part of a wider process. It is necessary to expand greatly on this part of the process of the making and defence of a British socialism.

---

[40] Field, 'Social patriotism and the British working class'. Taking this forward is Stephen Howe's 'Labour patriotism 1939–83', in Samuel, Patriotism, i. 127–39.
[41] Yeo does of course recognise this, quoting William Morris on 'an Englishman's wholesome horror of government interference and centralisation': 'Socialism, the state and some oppositional Englishness', 349.
[42] Kenneth Harris, Attlee, London 1982, 322–3.
[43] Yeo, 'Socialism, the state and some oppositional Englishness', 358.
[44] Ibid. 347.
[45] Ibid. 356–7.

To do this while also maintaining the objective of showing and accounting for the continuing patriotic discourse on the left, it has been necessary to examine the British left over a relatively long period of time. The time-scale has meant a concentration on prominent figures on the left, journalists, pamphleteers, MPs and leaderships. This has been necessary to allow for the danger that patriotic language was simply the response to events that suited its use. When the responses to contrasting situations were framed in similar terms of reference, it is possible to say that these are representative of deeper underlying attitudes and modes of thought.

The aim of this book has been to examine the outward-looking face of left politics on the one hand, and the internal (though often inter-party or sectarian) debates on the other. Public utterances, written and spoken, whether directed to potential supporters or political opponents within the labour movement, have been the basis of the research. Some of these utterances were made with deliberation, such as those books, articles and speeches which came closest to theorising on patriotism and national identity.[46] Equally important for the purposes of this book have been more ephemeral utterances. The propagandist uses of newspapers, pamphlets and leaflets, and, for the period after 1906, parliamentary speeches, were the way in which the British left set out to present its public image.

In this public image, the nation became the arena in which left-wing politics in Britain operated. While a few Marxists agreed that the workers had no country, the majority of the British left believed, like Ramsay MacDonald, that

> the nation is not an abstraction but a real community – a community perhaps within which the relationship of classes requires constant adjustment. But it has a common life, it is an historical product, it has a law of evolution, and, regarding social agitation carried on by individuals is in reality a product of communal growth. . . . Therefore Parliament and the historical method, because they do express something deeper than class conflict, and something wider than workshop antagonisms, are the way in which the expanding life of the community creates new social states.[47]

The politics of labour in Britain, therefore, revolved around identities of nation as well as class. But the relationship between these two identities was not static, there has been constant re-definition of the relationship between the Red Flag and the Union Jack.

---

[46] European socialists were more given to theorising on nationalism and national identity. For two books that cover both European theory and, at different levels, British practice see Brian Jenkins and Gunter Minnerup, *Citizens and comrades: socialism in a world of nation states*, London 1984, and Schwarzmantel, *Socialism and the idea of the nation*.

[47] J. Ramsay MacDonald, *Syndicalism: a critical examination*, London 1912, 53.

# 1

# Patriotism and Politics before 1881

Historically, patriotism and the use of ideas of national identity have not been the monopoly of one class, party or social group, but have been the subjects of political struggle. The period from the late eighteenth to the late nineteenth century witnessed the transfer of the dominance of ideas of patriotism from radical to conservative forces. This introductory chapter examines that transfer.

## Patriotism and the French wars

In the late eighteenth century radicalism and patriotism were almost synonymous. Radical patriotism had a long history, stemming from ideas about an ancient constitution corrupted by the Norman Conquest.[1] The Norman yoke theory claimed that Britain's rulers were foreign interlopers who had crushed a democratic Anglo-Saxon constitution. This idea had a remarkable resonance in the eighteenth century as the ruling elite sought to define their domestic authority by embracing a cosmopolitan culture.[2] In 1771 Obadiah Hulme published his *Historical essay on the English constitution* in which he claimed that in Anglo-Saxon England elections for all power-holders had been annual. The *Patriot*, a radical paper, serialised the essay in 1792, and the London Corresponding Society used such arguments in its 'Address to the nation' in 1797. Thomas Paine in *Common sense* (1776) wrote of 'a French bastard landing with an armed banditti'; hence, 'The antiquity of the English monarchy will not bear looking into.'[3]

Radicals also embraced a wider patriotism. In 1769 John Wilkes was described by his supporters as 'The Father of His Country; The English David; The Beloved Patriot. . . . The Martyr of Liberty'.[4] Some members suggested that the London Corresponding Society should call itself the Patriotic Club; in Norwich in 1795 there was another radical Patriotic Society.[5] These were based on more recent historical events, in which other political forces could

---

[1]  Hill, 'The Norman yoke', 58–125. See also Asa Briggs, *Saxons, Normans and Victorians*, Hastings–Bexhill 1966.
[2]  Newman, *Rise of English nationalism*, ch. ii.
[3]  Hill, 'The Norman yoke', 99–101, 103.
[4]  Linda Colley, 'Radical patriotism in eighteenth century England', in Samuel, *Patriotism*, i. 170.
[5]  Cunningham, 'Language of patriotism', ibid. i. 62.

share. The English Civil War and the Glorious Revolution furnished ideas about God's Englishmen and the free-born Englishman. The settlement of 1688 had created a constitution of King, Lords and Commons, and this was inextricably linked with Protestantism.[6] William Cobbett wrote in 1801, while still a government supporter, that 'Our religion was that of the Church of England, to which I have ever remained attached; the more so, perhaps, as it bears the name of my country.'[7]

Religion united Britons against their Catholic neighbours, particularly France, against whom wars were fought throughout the eighteenth century. The despotic tyranny of Roman Catholicism was contrasted with the liberty of Protestant Britain.[8] This provided a broad area of agreement between government and reformers. The Laudable Association of Anti-Gallicans had impeccable radical credentials. For example, Joseph Mawbey, the MP who presented Wilkes's election petition in 1769, was a member. But the aims of the society, 'to promote British manufactures, and to extend the commerce of England and discourage the introduction of French modes', gave it little alternative but to side with the government against France when at war. Hence self-interest could play a role in blunting the radical force of patriotism.[9]

The French Revolution spread anxiety among Britain's propertied classes. Edmund Burke warned the House of Commons in 1790 and explained the totality of the threat of revolution:

> The French had shown themselves the ablest architects of ruin that had hitherto existed in the world . . . they had completely pulled down to the ground their monarchy; their church; their nobility; their law; their revenue; their army; their navy; their commerce; their arts; and their manufactures . . .[10]

When war broke out with revolutionary France, British governments were forced to seek the active participation of the people. They tried to do this both by suppressing dissent and by enlisting patriotism to the war effort. It was to the language of radical patriotism that they turned. For example, Pitt warned the nation in 1797 that it was 'against the very essence of your liberty, against the foundation of your independence, against the citadel of your happiness, against the constitution itself' that the French fought.[11] Old stereotypes of the French were remodelled. In place of Catholicism was put atheism. Both presented a threat to the Protestant religion. Rapaciousness, lawlessness, effeminacy and thinness (to contrast with John Bull's stoutness from eating roast beef and plum pudding) were key elements. Above all,

---

6  Colley, *Britons*, ch. i.
7  G. D. H. Cole, *The life of William Cobbett*, London 1924, 16.
8  Colley, *Britons*, introduction.
9  Idem, 'Radical patriotism', 172–5.
10  S. Maccoby, *English radicalism 1786–1832*, London 1955, 32.
11  Clive Emsley, *British society and the French wars 1793–1815*, London 1979, 64.

liberty was claimed as an essentially English virtue; one popular jingle ran, 'Our fig tree is freedom, our vine is content / two blessings by nature for Frenchmen not meant.'[12] With Napoleon's coming to power, such ideas gained popularity. Cobbett in 1808, by now a radical, declared, 'You must be satisfied that the French are, by nature, disqualified for the enjoyment of what we call freedom – that, in short, a Napoleon or some such master, they not only must have, but will have from choice.'[13] Hence both radical and government patriots constructed a version of Englishness in contrast to the French 'other'.

The British elite also re-made its lifestyle to emphasise that it was a part of the nation. Colley explains that:

> It needed to be able to repel suggestions that it was an exclusive and over-lavish oligarchy and legitimised its authority anew. Most of all, perhaps, its members needed to demonstrate to themselves as well as to others that they were authentically and enthusiastically British: to prove, as Edmund Burke put it, that 'a true natural aristocracy is *not* a separate interest in the state, or separable from it'.[14]

Hence Britain's elite sought to show that their homes and (mainly foreign) art collections belonged to the nation despite remaining in private ownership. French styles of address were abandoned. Functional clothing replaced wigs, powdered hair, silks and laces. Uniforms, showing the wearer's service to the nation, became popular.[15] Likewise, George III set out to become a national king. He opened up royal celebration to wider segments of the population. At his suggestion 250 sailors and marines were included in the victory parade of 1815. Royal celebration was made more sober and dignified, though more splendid. Unlike his grandfather and great-grandfather, George III spoke English as a matter of course, and had been schooled in Bolingbroke's 'idea of the Patriot King', and hence accepted the Protestant idea of kingship. This enabled him to become a symbol of Protestant Britain.[16]

War with France, and particularly the threat of invasion, allowed the government and its supporters to brand dissent as disloyal. So the *Anti-Jacobin Review* in 1798 condemned Charles James Fox, since 'While our gallant tars were employed in gathering laurels abroad, a factious demagogue was occupied in sowing the seeds of dissension at home.'[17] Further to this, governments used new laws to allow radicals' actions to be defined as treasonable or

[12] See Stella Cottrell, 'The devil on two sticks: Franco-phobia in 1803', in Samuel, *Patriotism*, i. 265, 269.
[13] Cole, *Cobbett*, 143.
[14] Colley, *Britons*, 155.
[15] Ibid. 174–93.
[16] Idem, 'The apotheosis of George III: loyalty, royalty and the British nation 1760–1820', *P&P* cii (1984), 110, 117.
[17] Maccoby, *English radicalism*, 127.

seditious.[18] Radicals were put on the defensive. Fox, in a speech in which he made a republican toast and condemned government measures in Ireland, said that he 'would be one of the first to aid in repelling any foreign enemy, under whatever government England might be'.[19] Christopher Reid has explained the dilemma facing radical patriots in the 1790s: 'To continue in a policy which could be construed as in the slightest degree pro-French was to invite accusations of disloyalty. Yet a readiness to unite with political antago-nists in the defence of the realm might be interpreted as an admission of pre-vious error and a conversion to the government's point of view.' Sheridan, the subject of Reid's essay, shifted the tone of his parliamentary speeches, dis-playing a pronounced hostility to the French Directory, an uninhibited expression of love of country and the suggestion of provisional support of the government for national defence purposes.[20]

The radical career of William Cobbett began only after the government tried to take over and monopolise patriotism. He does perhaps provide the best example of the continuing vitality of the radical patriotic tradition in the face of this attempt. In 1816, when Cobbett began publication of his *Weekly Political Pamphlet*, he hoped it would lead many a father to 'be induced to spend his evenings at home instructing his children in the history of their misery, and in warming them into acts of patriotism'.[21] He called his condem-nations of post-war repression 'John Bull's Counterbuff'; and after the gag-ging Acts of 1817 he wrote a seething pamphlet called *The history of the last hundred days of English freedom*.[22] To Cobbett this was not just a linguistic device. He embraced Englishness, championing 'manly' English sports, such as single-stick, in which 'the object is to break the opponent's head so that blood may run an inch'. His home at Botley was described as 'a farm-house, and everything was in accordance with the largest idea of a great English yeo-man of the old time'.[23] Cobbett was also at pains to look the part of a solid Englishman. Samuel Bamford described him 'dressed in blue coat, yellow swansdown waistcoat, drab jersey small-clothes, and top boots. . . . He was the perfect representation of what he always wished to be – an English gentleman-farmer.'[24]

---

18 Of course juries could not always be relied upon to convict. See E. P. Thompson, *The making of the English working class*, Harmondsworth 1980, 20–2, for the acquittal of members of the London Corresponding Society.
19 Maccoby, *English radicalism*, 125.
20 Christopher Reid, 'Patriotism and rhetorical contest in the 1790s: the context of Sheri-dan's *Pizarro*', in Elizabeth Maslen (ed.), *Comedy*, London 1993, 241.
21 Cunningham, 'Language of patriotism', 67.
22 Cole, *Cobbett*, 201, 219. The pamphlet was republished in 1921 by the Labour Publish-ing Company, with an introduction by J. L. Hammond.
23 Ibid. 102, 98.
24 Thompson, *Making of the English working class*, 829.

## Chartism and English rights

For all Cobbett's vitality, patriotism was no longer the monopoly of radicals. A plurality of patriotisms had emerged, often sharing much the same language but aiming at different ends. Colley points out that 'almost all sectional interest groups in Britain resorted to nationalist language and activism to advance their claims to wider civic recognition'.[25]

But patriotic language remained a central way of expressing radical demands. Such language was used against the Whig reforms of the 1830s. In particular it was used against the metropolitan and rural police bills. Matthew Fletcher, in a printed address to the people of Bury in 1839, urged resistance to the rural police bill, which was a 'fresh outrage on English rights and English feelings'.[26] The Chartists too used such language about the reforms of the 1830s. The Chartist General Convention of March 1839 passed a resolution suggesting that the government:

> had no other object than to carry out that vile system of centralization, which they had been gradually drawing around the country, and having deprived Englishmen, by the most insidious means, of the reality of their freedom, now to take from them even the semblance of their freedom. . . . Since the Whigs had been in power, they had struck more and deeper at the liberties of Englishmen than the Tories, throughout the whole of their career.[27]

The same kind of language was used to support a wide range of demands, from the points of the Charter,[28] to women's rights – one group of female Chartists called themselves the East London Patriotic Association[29] – to the right to take up arms in support of constitutional demands.[30]

Newspaper descriptions of Chartist demonstrations show that their banners included ideas of nationality and traditional demands. Chartist demonstrations used the British lion, the red rose of England, the harp of Erin, and the thistle of Scotland in support of radical demands. Britannia too made her appearance, often wearing the cap of liberty.[31] Another Chartist rally, this

[25] Linda Colley, 'Whose nation?: Class and national consciousness in Britain 1750–1830', *P&P* cxiii (1986), 116. See also Gerald Newman, 'Anti-French propaganda and British liberal nationalism in the early nineteenth century: suggestions towards a general interpretation', *VS* viii (1975), 385–418, which argues that the liberal middle class sought to promote their own values through anti-foreign and patriotic language.

[26] *The early Chartists*, ed. Dorothy Thompson, London–Basingstoke 1971, 73–81.

[27] *Chartism and society: an anthology of documents*, ed. F. C. Mather, London 1980, 57–62.

[28] See *Northern Star*, 5 June 1841, in Hill, 'The Norman yoke', 58, and *MacDouall's Chartist and Republican Journal*, 8 May 1841, in *Chartism and society*, 53–4.

[29] *Chartism and society*, 115. See also R. J. Richardson, *The rights of women*, in *Early Chartists*, 115–27.

[30] See *Northern Liberator*, July 1839, and *The Operative*, 10 Feb. 1839, in *Early Chartists*, 135–6, 185; *Northern Star*, 9 Apr. 1839, in *Chartism and society*, 63–7

[31] *Northern Star*, 29 Sept. 1839, in *Chartism and society*, 241–3. The cap of liberty shows the coincidence of the French Revolution as an influence alongside symbols of Britain: James

time to celebrate the release of two Chartists from prison, was well attended because 'the noble and patriotic defence made by the Doctor [MacDouall, one of those released] on his trial had won him the respect and admiration of every lover of his country'. Mr Wheeler, in his address to MacDouall, declared that 'by making you thus welcome, we would show our tyrants our love of patriotism and hatred of oppression. . . . Go on, then brave and noble patriot! Yours is no party struggle, it is a struggle to rescue our common country from a worse than Egyptian bondage.'[32]

Early Chartism therefore saw a flowering of radical patriotic language, since it fitted with the experiences of the politically excluded.[33] But after the early years of Chartism such language competed with a new discourse of class,[34] for as Hugh Cunningham has explained, an economic analysis of poverty replaced the political analysis of 'Old Corruption' and some Chartists became 'more determined to dwell on the peculiarities of industrial capitalism rather than the peculiarities of the English'.[35] At the same time, the perception that the 1832 Reform Act had marked the triumph of the middle class added the language of class to politics. Michael Brock, historian of the Reform Act, while showing that the act maintained the landed interest's influence, points out that 'a measure drawing a line between voters and voteless was bound to increase the class consciousness of the latter'.[36]

The weakening of the radical hold on language of patriotism allowed other political forces to enter the vacated space, establishing a dominance which the left subsequently would not be able to overcome, except in a few rare instances. One major difficulty was that these other forces used much the same vocabulary as the radicals, as they had done in the 1790s. As Cunningham has shown, it was the radicals' own internationalism that allowed ideas of English liberty to be taken over by governing forces.[37] Palmerston shared with such groups as the People's International League the idea that English

Epstein, 'Understanding the cap of liberty: symbolic practice and social conflict in early nineteenth century England', P&P cxxii (1989), 75–118. For the balance of class, national and international identities in the mid and late Victorian periods see Margot Finn, *After Chartism: class and nation in English radical politics 1848–1874*, Cambridge 1993, and Patrick Joyce, *Visions of the people: industrial England and the question of class 1840–1914*, Cambridge 1991.

[32] *Early Chartists*, 139–74. See also Hugh Cunningham, 'The nature of Chartism', *Modern History Review* i (1990), 22, for a discussion of the Englishness of the banquet celebrating the release of these men.

[33] Gareth Stedman Jones, 'Rethinking Chartism', in *Languages of class: studies in English working class history 1832–1982*, Cambridge 1983, 90–178.

[34] Asa Briggs, 'The language of "class" in early nineteenth century England', in Asa Briggs and John Saville (eds), *Essays in labour history in memory of G. D. H. Cole*, London–Basingstoke 1960, 43–73, remains the classic essay on this development.

[35] Cunningham, 'Language of patriotism', 70.

[36] Michael Brock, *The great Reform Act*, London 1973, 321 and ch. ix.

[37] Cunningham, 'Language of patriotism', 71.

freedom was a model for the countries of Europe to follow.[38] He took political advantage of this coincidence of belief to draw support in behind his own foreign policy in support of liberal nationalism abroad. Appealing directly to urban audiences, Palmerston stressed the idea of Britain's reputation resting on its freedom. The congratulatory motion on the Don Pacifico affair was tabled by a radical MP. Palmerston also worked the Russophobia of the radicals to his advantage during the Crimean War.[39] Government and people were drawn together sufficiently for the formation of the Volunteer Force in 1859, and the fact that large numbers of the corps wore Garibaldi-style uniforms suggests that membership could be seen as a progressive act.[40]

## After Chartism

From the 1860s governments, both Liberal and Conservative, made a concerted effort to make the nation a source of unity to overcome the divisions of class. Freda Harcourt sees the mid 1860s as a turning point not only in parliamentary history but also in social and imperial history, as governments attempted to respond to economic crisis and fear of the mob.[41] To face this crisis, governments from the late 1860s onwards began to re-promote the monarchy as a symbol of national unity and greatness. David Cannadine has shown that the public image of the monarchy from the 1820s onwards had reached a low point by the 1870s but 'Between the late 1870s and 1914 . . . there was a fundamental change in the public image of the British monarchy, as its ritual, hitherto inept, private and of limited appeal, became splendid, public and popular.'[42] Harcourt has in fact dated the moves to make political use of the monarchy to the 1860s. The visits to London by the sultan of Turkey, the viceroy of Egypt and a party of Belgian Volunteers in July 1867 had been turned into eighteen days of national pageantry and celebration. The queen's opposition to ceremonial had been overcome.[43] However the success

---

38 *Chartism and society*, 128–30.
39 E. D. Steele, *Palmerston and Liberalism 1855–1865*, Cambridge 1991, 15, 20, 21; for conflicts between Palmerston and radicals over foreign policy see Finn, *After Chartism*, 177–8, 181–2.
40 Cunningham, *The Volunteer force*, 107–8.
41 Freda Harcourt, 'Disraeli's imperialism, 1866–1868: a question of timing', *HJ* xxiii (1980), 87–109.
42 David Cannadine, 'The context, performance and meaning of ritual: the British monarchy and the "invention of tradition", c. 1820–1977', in Hobsbawm and Ranger, *The invention of tradition*, 107–19, 120. However, Roland Quinault argues that the rebuilding of the Houses of Parliament after the fire of 1834 exhibited a glorification of the monarch through architecture. For example, the Victoria Tower and the House of Lords as the chamber of the monarch: 'Westminster and the Victorian constitution', *TRHS* 6th ser. ii (1992), 79–104.
43 Freda Harcourt, 'The queen, the sultan and the viceroy: a Victorian state occasion', *London Journal* v (1979), 35–6. Further duties undertaken by the queen at Gladstone's behest

or otherwise of these events may be judged by the fact that republicanism peaked after them, with eighty-four republican clubs founded between 1871 and 1874.[44]

With the promotion of the monarchy came the use of imperialism as a measure of national unification. Domestic factors were not the only motivation. Russia and France were expanding their empires, with France beginning to build the Egyptian canal. Britain therefore had to assert itself internationally. At a cost of £9m., 12,000 troops were sent to Abyssinia in 1868 to release British captives, but the blaze of publicity that accompanied the expedition and the striking of a commemorative medal afterwards suggest its wider domestic objectives. Harcourt has pointed out that despite Gladstone's opposition to imperialism, his governments were as likely to invoke imperialism for purposes of domestic popularity. Hence Harcourt has concluded that this imperialism was the result of conscious political decisions within both Conservative and Liberal governments.[45]

Cunningham has shown how one particular event was used by the Conservative party for political advantage and to attach patriotism more firmly to itself. The jingo crowds of the early months of 1878 were organised by Conservatives.[46] Disraeli had been attempting both to assert Britain's strength in the world and to bind the concept of patriotism to his party. In a speech in July 1866 he declared that England's 'abstention from any unnecessary interference in [Europe's] affairs is the consequence, not of her decline in power, but of her increased strength. . . . There is no power, indeed, that interferes more than England. She interferes in Asia . . . in Australia, in Africa, and in New Zealand.'[47] The following year, in a speech in Edinburgh, he told his audience that 'I have always considered that the Tory party was the national party of England.'[48] He played on radical Russophobia, enabling his campaign to use the rhetoric of liberty. Hence he received the support of the *Englishman*, paper of the Magna Charta Association.[49] However unspontaneous and

are described in idem, 'Gladstone, monarchism and the "new" imperialism, 1868–74', *JICH* xiv (1985), 20–51.

[44] Idem, 'Gladstone', 27–8; Cannadine, 'British monarchy', 119.

[45] Harcourt, 'Disraeli's imperialism', 100–4, 107, 109.

[46] Cunningham, 'Jingoism in 1877–78', 429–53.

[47] Harcourt, 'Disraeli's imperialism', 96.

[48] Cunningham, 'Language of patriotism', 74. The fact that the second quoted speech was in Scotland and yet referred to England and not to Britain was not intended as a conscious snub to the Scottish. England was often used when Britain was meant, and Scotland was often called North Britain or even abbreviated to N. B., especially in postal addresses. While this Anglo-centrism may have been unconscious it was felt wise during the First World War for an advertisement in *The Times* to urge 'Englishmen! Please use "Britain", "British", and "Briton", when the United Kingdom or the Empire is in question – at least during the war': Hugh Cunningham, 'The Conservative party and patriotism', in Colls and Dodd, *Englishness*, 294.

[49] Cunningham, 'Jingoism', 444.

ephemeral jingoism was in 1877–8, it did succeed in frightening Liberals by investing patriotism with an irrational force.

This should not be taken to mean that radical patriotism was totally eclipsed. Conservative forces achieved a dominance of the language of patriotism rather than a monopoly. Historians have recently sought to rescue mid nineteenth-century radicalism from obscurity, and have uncovered a rich vein of popular radicalism.[50] The most interesting of these currents is that of the Tichborne case.[51] In 1865 Tomas Castro, from Wagga Wagga in Australia, claimed to be Sir Roger Tichborne, heir to the estates of a Hampshire family, who had last been seen in 1854. In 1867 Castro met Dowager Lady Tichborne, who recognised him as her son. When she died the following year, the rest of the family disputed Castro's claim, and when one of Sir Roger's former friends suddenly claimed to have tattooed Sir Roger, Castro was tried for perjury and sentenced to fourteen years imprisonment. Castro's lawyer started a paper to argue the case. He chose the name the *Englishman* and the organisation formed to defend the claimant called itself the Magna Charta Association. McWilliam has called this the largest single agitation between Chartism and the revival of independent labour politics, and the *Englishman's* circulation of about 70,000 in 1875 supports his view.[52] The agitation drew upon the tradition of the ideas of the free-born Englishman and independence, invoking the names of Hampden and Milton; its key concept was of 'fair play'.

Yet despite the Tichborne case, by the late 1870s the language of patriotism had become dominated by conservative political forces, and parties saw the advantages of taking up such language. The late nineteenth century was the age of 'new' imperialism, and patriotism and ideas of Englishness came to be used to justify the territorial 'expansion of England'. This language bore a striking resemblance to the radical patriotic vocabulary, stressing the benefits of exporting English liberty. From the late nineteenth century the output of patriotic propaganda from governments, political parties, imperial and military publicists and voluntary organisations of all sorts was massive.[53] It was into this situation that socialist and independent labour politics re-emerged.

---

[50] See Eugenio Biagini and Alistair J. Reid (eds), *Currents of radicalism: popular radicalism, organised labour and party politics in Britain 1850–1914*, Cambridge 1991; Joyce, *Visions of the people*; Jon Lawrence, 'Popular radicalism and the socialist revival in Britain', JBS xxxi (1992), 163–86.

[51] Rohan McWilliam, 'Radicalism and popular culture: the Tichborne case and the politics of "fair play", 1867–1886', in Biagini and Reid, *Currents of radicalism*, 44–64.

[52] Ibid. 44–5, 50.

[53] See, particularly, J. M. MacKenzie, *Propaganda and empire: the manipulation of British public opinion, 1880–1960*, Manchester 1984; J. M. MacKenzie (ed.), *Imperialism and popular culture*, Manchester 1986; Grainger, *Patriotisms*.

# 2

# Socialists and Oppositional Englishness, 1881–1906

England arise! the long night is over,
Faint in the east behold the dawn appear,
Out of your evil dream of toil and sorrow
A-rise O England, for the day is here
From your fields and hills,
Hark! the answer swells
A-rise O England, for the day is here!

. . . People of England! all your valleys call you,
High in the rising sun the lark sings clear,
Will you dream on, let shameful slumber thrall you?
Will you disown your native land so dear?
Shall it die unheard –
That sweet pleading word?
A-rise O England, for the day is here!

. . . Forth, then, ye heroes, patriots, and lovers!
Comrades of danger, poverty, and scorn!
Mighty in faith of freedom your great mother!
Giants refreshed in joy's new rising morn!
Come and swell the song,
Silent now so long;
England is risen! – and the day is here.'[1]

From its establishment in the early 1880s, modern British socialism has concerned itself with ideas about national character and a 'real' England. 'England, arise!', Philip Snowden recalled, was one of the favourite 'hymns' sung
at early Independent Labour Party meetings. It was sung at the first Labour
Church service in 1891. It was sung at the celebration for the twenty-nine
Labour MPs elected in 1906. It was sung to welcome Keir Hardie home from
his world tour of 1907–8.[2] 'England, arise!' had as its central theme the need
for a social transformation to improve the condition of the vast majority of

[1] Edward Carpenter (ed.), *Chants of labour: a song book of the people*, London 1888, 18–19.
[2] Snowden, *Autobiography*, i. 73; Thompson, *Robert Blatchford*, 79–80; *Programme for the
reception of Labour MPs*, 15 Feb. 1906, Royal Horticultural Hall, Westminster, London n.d.;
*Souvenir of the welcome home demonstration to greet J. Keir Hardie MP, on his return from his
world tour*, Royal Albert Hall, 5 Apr. 1908, London n.d.

the English people. It was a socialist song, a product of the revival of socialism in the 1880s. Yet it sought to appeal to people to rise because they were English, because they were patriots.

It was written by Edward Carpenter, who had left the University of Cambridge and the Church of England to settle in Sheffield as a university extension lecturer. There he came into contact with a strong radical tradition, for example, meeting the freethinker and ex-Chartist, Joseph Sharpe.[3] These links with an older radical tradition were almost certainly a major source of British socialists' espousal of radical patriotism. The Social Democratic Federation (SDF) had direct links with radicalism. Its forerunner, the Democratic Federation, was a radical organisation. Its programme had been approved by the Magna Charta Association.[4] Prominent figures in the SDF had links with the radical tradition. Jack Williams, one of the 'old guard' of the SDF, had been involved in the Tichborne agitation. Harry Quelch had been in the Southwark Radical Club.[5] Many prominent figures in the ILP and Labour Party had come through Liberal radicalism. George Lansbury was a Liberal election agent before taking most of Bow and Bromley Liberal and Radical Association into the SDF and later into the Labour Party.[6]

But 'England, arise!' also reveals another element in early British socialism that had a profound effect upon the tone of radical patriotism. This was the idea of socialism as a new life.[7] This formed a break with mid century radicalism, for it no longer accepted industrial capitalism as inevitable and sought instead to offer a whole new system of life. This qualitative change was extremely powerful. Even *Fabian essays*, supposed bible of gradualism, contained conjectures about what a socialist society would be like.[8] John Bruce Glasier noted the 'frequency of the use of the metaphors, "dawn", "morning", "day", and the like, in these pages, as emblematic of the promise of socialism'.[9] Socialism was discussed in millenarian or providentialist terms. Snowden called it 'the Christ that is to be' and Carpenter described the process of history under this belief: 'It can hardly be doubted that the tendency will be

[3] For Carpenter see Sheila Rowbotham and Jeffrey Weeks, *Socialism and the new life: the personal and sexual politics of Edward Carpenter and Havelock Ellis*, London 1977, as well as Carpenter's autobiography, *My days and dreams*, London 1916.
[4] M. S. Wilkins, 'The non-socialist origins of Britain's first important socialist organisation', *International Review of Social History* iv (1959), 199–207. See also Lawrence, 'Popular radicalism and socialist revival in Britain', and Finn, *After Chartism*.
[5] Harry Quelch (ed.), *How I became a socialist*, London n.d. [1902], 37, 72, 28–9. See also McWilliam, 'Radicalism and popular culture', 62.
[6] Jonathan Schneer, *George Lansbury*, Manchester 1990, 7–20.
[7] Stephen Yeo, 'A new life: the religion of socialism in Britain, 1883–1896', HW iv (1977), 5–56.
[8] See, for example, Annie Besant's essay, 'Industry under socialism', Fabian Society, *Fabian essays in socialism*, London 1920, first publ. 1889.
[9] J. Bruce Glasier (ed.), *Socialist songs*, Glasgow 1893, 3.

... towards a return to nature and community of human life. This is the way back to the lost Eden, or rather forward to the New Eden, of which the old was only a figure.'[10]

## Merrie England in the past

Socialists were therefore in search of this New Eden, and the past seemed to be the most likely source for a prefiguration of future socialist society. Socialism's objective was to overthrow industrial capitalism which was seen as the cause of the misery of the working class. It seemed sensible, therefore, to look for the origins of the transition to this 'new' economic system and tackle the problem of social transformation at its roots. Hence while elsewhere there was an 'expiry of historical politics' due to constitutional change and the professionalisation of history, socialists were coming anew to the past as a tool in the struggle for the future.[11]

For early socialists the study of the past and the search for a new life combined. Largely based on John Ruskin's Romantic critique of industrialisation and the research of the radical historian Thorold Rogers, socialists came to see capitalism as bringing an absolute decline in the standard of living of the English people.[12] The time before capitalism was seen in terms of a golden age. Hyndman's *England for all*, written in 1881 and handed out to delegates at the founding conference of the Democratic Federation, looked back to the fifteenth century as an age of English glory, when 'the mass of the people of these islands were in their most prosperous and wholesome condition'. Hyndman argued that 'sober, hardworking yeomen' owned the soil, and that therefore 'The fifteenth century was the golden age of agricultural England.' Even day-labourers 'lived in perfect freedom, owned plots of land themselves, and shared in the enormous common land which then lay free and open to all'. Men enjoyed 'a sturdy freedom . . . based on property and good living. . . . This was merrie England, in short – merrie, that is for Englishmen as a whole,

---

10 Philip Snowden, *The Christ that is to be*, London n.d. [1905]; Edward Carpenter, *Civilisation: its cause and cure*, 5th edn, London 1897, first publ. 1889, 35

11 The phrase is R. J. Smith's, *The gothic bequest: medieval institutions in British thought, 1688–1863*, Cambridge 1987, 171. Smith argues that the visionary and the scholar were taking over the gothic bequest from politicians; socialists can perhaps be seen as visionaries as well as politicians. For further discussion of alternative uses of the past see J. W. Burrow, *A liberal descent: Victorian historians and the English past*, Cambridge 1981, and A. Dwight Culler, *The Victorian mirror of history*, New Haven–London 1985, though both confine themselves to elite histories.

12 It was an interpretation of the history of England rather than Britain, partly because it drew on events in England, such as Magna Carta, the idea of a golden age of English labour, and the English Civil War. James D. Young has described this as a 'really rather counterfeit concept of "the British radical–democratic tradition" ': 'A very English socialism and the Celtic fringe 1880–1991', *HW* xxxv (1993), 137. Ruskin's influence is discussed further later in this chapter.

not merely for the landlords and capitalists at the top.'[13] With William Morris, Hyndman described fourteenth-century England as 'inhabited by perhaps the most vigorous, freedom-loving set of men the world ever saw'.[14] Morris contrasted the medieval workman, who worked in his own time, determining and designing what he himself would make with the nineteenth-century workman who, if a master chose that he worked at all, had to be at the factory when the bell rang, and lived in a 'sweltering dog-hole, with miles and miles of similar dog-holes between him and the fair fields of the country, which in grim mockery is called "his" '.[15] Capitalism and industrialism, Morris argued, had changed England and the English completely. Morris argued that

> gradual as the change in England has been since the time of Edward III, it has been complete; that in spite of our counties and cities being called by the same names, and that although not one new parish has been added to the English parishes since the time of the heptarchy, though there is seeming continuity in our history, yet it fares with us as with the Irishman's knife, the same knife but with new blades and a new handle: in morals and aspirations, in manners of work and life, the English people of to-day are totally different from what they were in the fifteenth century; 300 years has made them another people with little sympathy for the virtues, and no understanding of the vices of their ancestors.[16]

Hyndman and Morris set the tone for discussion of the fifteenth century by socialists. T. D. Benson and Keir Hardie described that century as the 'golden age of labour', with Hardie calling 'every departure of whatever kind from the pastoral simplicity which characterised the even tones of the lives of the men of old' as 'a burden and a curse'.[17]

Socialists had therefore found in the past an England that was 'merrie'. And they had an explanation as to why this was no longer the case. Blatchford used radical patriotic language to explain: 'At present Britain does not belong to the British: it belongs to a few of the British. . . . It is because Britain does not belong to the British that a few are very rich and the many are very

---

13 Hyndman, *England for all*, 7–9. See also H. M. Hyndman, *The historical basis of socialism in England*, London 1883, 2. The phrase 'merrie England' dates back to about 1300, when it was already being used to signify a world that had passed. John Caius, physician to Edward VI and founder of the Cambridge college, used it in 1552, referring to 'the old world when this countrie was called Merry England'. Spenser in *The faerie queene* wrote of 'Saint George of mery England': *The Oxford dictionary of proverbs*, 3rd edn, Oxford 1970.
14 H. M. Hyndman and William Morris, *A summary of the principles of socialism*, London 1884, 13.
15 'Architecture and history', in *The collected works of William Morris*, xxiii, London 1915, 312–13.
16 'At a picture show', in May Morris, *William Morris, artist, writer, socialist*, ii, Oxford 1936.
17 T. D. Benson, *A socialist's view of the Reformation*, London–Glasgow, n.d. (c. 1902), 4; Keir Hardie, *Young men in a hurry*, London–Glasgow n.d. (c. 1896) 5. See also idem, *From serfdom to socialism*, London 1907, ch. v.

poor.'[18] The question of the ownership of land remained a live issue for socialists. It explained the continuing poverty of the working class. Glasier asked 'who owns the land?',[19] and 'Casey' (Walter Hampson) asked the same question in different words, 'Who are the bloodsuckers?' He included 'a list of the principle ones'.[20] Socialists drew the conclusion that 'A robber band has seized the land,/ And we are exiles here.'[21]

In some cases socialists still held to the Norman yoke theory that the Conquest had subverted the true course of English history. The *Clarion* on 14 September 1895 published a verse called 'To the Farmers of England by One of Them':

> The Norman came to England to take our land away;
> We fought him, but he conquered. Alack, the woeful day!
> He took our land and gave it to his soldiers fierce and bold,
> And ever since they've held it, and still they mean to hold . . .
> And the sons of English freemen have toiled for lord and earl,
> And still the Norman claims the rent, and the Saxon is the churl.
> 'Tis time the memory perished of the Conqueror's wicked laws,
> 'Tis time the English nation did rule the English cause,
> 'Tis time the Norman's heavy hand were lifted from our head,
> And England for the English were the English law instead.

Blatchford had also drawn attention to the Conquest: 'They claim the land as theirs', he wrote of the landowners, 'because eight hundred years ago their fathers took it from the English people.'[22] But in effect the Norman yoke theory had been negated by Thorold Rogers, Hyndman and others. For if the fourteenth and fifteenth centuries had been a golden age because the people were organically attached to the soil, the land must have been stolen since. William Morris argued that the Conquest had turned England aside from developing 'her' own laws, language and literature as 'a great homogenous Teutonic people infused usefully with a mixture of Celtic blood', but that while for a time England was a 'piece of France . . . in time she did grow into another England again'.[23] Socialists wanted to find the cause of England's

---

18  Robert Blatchford, *Britain for the British*, 3rd edn, London 1910, first publ. 1902, 1. It is likely that the book would have been called 'England for the English' had not J. Fyrie-Mayo written, 'I cannot help noting the word "England", as if Scotland, Ireland, and Wales were not in existence!' Leonard Hall replied for the *Clarion*: 'I find it necessary to explain for the mollification of some Clarionettes, that by the phrase, "England for the English", we, of course, mean, "The British Isles for the British" ': *Clarion*, 9 Nov., 7 Dec. 1895

19  J. Bruce Glasier, *Who owns the land?*, London 1908.

20  'Casey', *Who are the bloodsuckers?*, London n.d. (c. 1907).

21  Carpenter, 'The people to their land', in his *Chants of labour*, 50–1.

22  Blatchford, *Britain for the British*, 53–4. See also Tom Mann, *Memoirs*, London 1967, first publ. 1923, 121–3; verse entitled 'Saxon grit': *Labour Prophet*, Mar. 1892, and *Clarion*, 16 Sept. 1904. Hill, 'The Norman yoke', cites further examples of late nineteenth-century socialists continuing to use the theory.

23  Morris, 'Feudal England', in *Works*, xxiii. 41.

social problems in the advent of capitalism, which implicitly involved refuting the Norman yoke theory. Instead they found the alienation of the people from the land in the transition to commercial farming. Hyndman argued that 'between the fifteenth and beginning of the seventeenth century the whole face of England had been changed. . . . The fine old yeoman class fell more and more into decrepitude. . . . By the middle of the eighteenth century there was scarcely a yeomen of the old type left.' There had been, he said, a 'long series of robberies from the people'. Morris and E. Belfort Bax described the result of the enclosures:

> The tenants were rack-rented, the yeomen were expropriated, the hinds were driven off the land into the towns, there to work as 'free' labourers. England thus contributed her share to commerce, paying for it with nothing more important than the loss of the rough joviality, plenty, and independence of spirit, which once attracted the admiration of foreigners more crushed by the feudal system and by its abuses than were the English.[24]

Socialists had therefore proved in their own terms that the onset of capitalism in the countryside had diverted the course of English history, and had reduced the standard of living of the English people. Of course, anti-landlordism and land agitation were by no means the monopoly of socialists. Henry George's *Progress and poverty* had sold 100,000 copies, and had a much wider influence than just those who had become socialists through reading it. Radical politics had a long history of land agitation before George's speaking tours in the early 1880s and the publication of John Bateman's *The landowners of Great Britain and Ireland* in 1876 had invigorated anti-landlordism. Indeed, it was this previous agitation that resulted in the remarkable receptiveness to George's land tax ideas. The Land Nationalisation Society and English Land Restoration League were radical Liberal organisations, and Joseph Chamberlain made the slogan 'three acres and a cow' central to his 'unauthorised programme' of the mid 1880s. Down to the First World War Liberals dominated the land reform movement.[25] It often seemed that socialists were simply echoing radical Liberal language. Their problem was to make themselves distinctive.

The major way of achieving this was to stress that their programme for change was complete. The radicals could offer only a reform of land ownership; capitalism would remain untouched. The socialists provided a vision of

---

[24] Hyndman, *England for all*, 16, 17; William Morris and E. Belfort Bax, *Socialism: its growth and outcome*, London 1893, 122. See also William C. Anderson, *Socialism, the dukes and the land*, Manchester–London n.d. (c. 1907), 11.

[25] John Saville, 'Henry George and the British labour movement; a select bibliography with commentary', *BSSLH* v (1962), 18–19; Roy Douglas, *Land, people and politics: a history of the land question in the United Kingdom, 1878–1952*, London 1976; Avner Offer, *Property and politics 1870–1914: landownership, law, ideology and urban development in England*, Cambridge 1981.

a totally new society – a new life. When picturing this future socialist society, the socialists looked back to the England of the past, which they saw as preferable to foreign countries, and certainly superior to industrialised England. Combined with ideas of fellowship and the new life, the English past went towards producing a vision of socialist England, most particularly in William Morris's *News from nowhere*.[26]

## Merrie England in the future

Morris had been interested by the relationship between the people and art in pre-industrial society, and saw that relationship torn asunder by capitalism (rather than industrialism). He saw England as unspectacular, loving 'the common-place English landscape' made beautiful by 'the little grey church' and the 'little grey house' that 'makes an English village a thing apart'. He believed that the choice before England was the restoration of the close relationship of the people to their art, or capitalist industrialism – 'art or dirt?' as he put it.[27]

E. P. Thompson has described Morris as 'a pioneer of constructive thought as to the organization of the social life within Communist society', and while this was not achieved solely in *News from nowhere*, this book was the single most influential of his works among socialists.[28] It describes a dream of a future English communist society. The world into which William Guest awakes is almost the England of the fourteenth century described by Morris, Hyndman and others in their more historical works:

> The highway ran through wide sunny meadows and garden-like tillage. . . .
> There were houses about, some on the road, some amongst the fields with pleasant lanes leading down to them, and each surrounded by a teeming garden. They were all pretty in design, and as solid as might be, but countrified in appearance, like yeomen's dwellings; some of red brick . . . but more of timber and plaster, which were by necessity of their construction so like medieval houses of the same materials that I fairly felt as if I were alive in the fourteenth century

According to Morris, what had once existed could come again. The condition of England was described to Guest thus:

> This is how we stand. England was once a country of clearings amongst the woods and wastes, with a few towns interspersed, which were fortresses for the feudal army, markets for the folk, gathering places for the craftsmen. It then became a country of huge and foul workshops and fouler gambling-dens, sur-

---

[26] William Morris, *News from nowhere*, London 1908, first publ. 1890.
[27] Morris, *Works*, xxiii. 41, 172.
[28] E. P. Thompson, *William Morris: romantic to revolutionary*, 2nd edn, London 1977, 682.

rounded by an ill-kept poverty strickened farm, pillaged by the masters of the workshops. It is now a garden, where nothing is wasted and nothing is spoilt, with the necessary dwellings, sheds, and workshops scattered up and down the country, all trim and neat and pretty.[29]

In Morris's version of socialism, the best had been taken up from the past and thrust into the future. Thus Hyndman and Morris wrote of 'restitution', reclaiming for the people what was theirs, rather than of 'confiscation'.[30]

More influential than Morris was Robert Blatchford's *Merrie England*. *News from nowhere* was a novel; *Merrie England* was non-fiction and propagandist. That makes its sales of 750,000 within a year all the more impressive. 'And it has not been to a new economic theory, merely, that these converts have been introduced', John Trevor, founder of the Labour Church, wrote, 'it has been to a new life. Their eyes shine with the gladness of a new birth.'[31] The title, while unoriginal, was essential, for it identified socialism as English, happy and as a restoration of the past. It was addressed to John Smith, an Oldham cotton spinner, *Clarion's* typical modern Englishman. John Smith was unlikely to be a Liberal, and was far more likely to have been brought up in the tradition of the Lancashire Tory 'politics of beer and Britannia'.[32] Blatchford's politics were staunchly independent of the Liberals and far away from the puritanism of much of the ILP, indeed he can be seen as following the Tory radical tradition of William Cobbett.[33]

Blatchford rejected the factory system both for its impact on the environment and on morality. He argued that Britain's independence could not be secure while greed was the motivating power in society, and that greed was the outcome of industrialism.[34] His socialism aimed at securing England as a nation. A rural economy, he believed, would achieve this security by taking advantage of England's insularity. Luckily, England had two things in its favour: 'The country is fertile and fruitful . . . [and] the people are intelligent, industrious, strong, and famous for their perseverance, their inventiveness and resource.'[35] Blatchford's socialism was, above all other things, national. He appealed to the people to come over to the socialists,

> If you as a Briton are proud of your country and your race, if you as a man have any pride in your manhood, or as a worker have any pride in your class men, come over to us and help in the just and wise policy of winning Britain for the British, manhood for *all* men, womanhood for *all* women, and love to-day and

[29] Morris, *News from nowhere*, 24, 54, 80.
[30] Hyndman and Morris, *Summary of the principles of socialism*, 60.
[31] Thompson, *Robert Blatchford*, 101.
[32] Patrick Joyce, *Work, society and politics: the culture of the factory in later Victorian England*, London 1982, 292–310.
[33] For a discussion of this tradition as it affected H. M. Hyndman see Mark Bevir, 'H.M. Hyndman: a re-reading and a reassessment', *History of Political Thought* xii (1991), 125–45.
[34] Robert Blatchford, *Merrie England*, London 1894, 18, 35.
[35] Ibid. 11.

hope to-morrow for the children, whom Christ loved, but who by many Christians have unhappily been forgotten.[36]

This socialism, of Morris and Blatchford was a politics based on historical precedent, in which socialism was supported by reference to the past. The search for the restoration of Merrie England took many practical forms among early British socialists. It was part of a wider 'back to the land' and 'simple life' impulse that went further than just the socialist movement.[37] Some middle-class socialists took this quite literally, moving physically 'back to the land'. Many London Fabians took houses in the country. The Oliviers and the Peases moved to the North Downs, and Charlotte Wilson bought 'a charming and idyllic little farm'.[38] Ramsay MacDonald and his wife bought a weekend cottage in Buckinghamshire, where they grew roses and vegetables, and designed a miniature tour for visitors, 'which should display the pages of national history written in their neighbourhood', taking in Stoke Poges churchyard, where Gray wrote his 'Elegy', Milton's cottage at Chalfont St Giles, and Great Hampden Church where Puritan soldiers had buried John Hampden.[39] Carpenter, of course, bought a smallholding at Millthorpe near Sheffield.

In reaction against industrialisation and urbanisation, the countryside was coming to be seen as the source of an enduring and authentic Englishness.[40] This led to a swathe of activities in which socialists were involved that sought to rescue the English rural past from extinction. These were less concerned with improving conditions for the rural population than with turning the

[36] Blatchford, *Britain for the British*, 172–3.
[37] See Jan Marsh, *Back to the land: the pastoral impulse in Britain from 1880 to 1914*, London 1982, and Peter C. Gould, *Early green politics: back to nature, back to the land and socialism in Britain 1880–1900*, Brighton 1988.
[38] Norman MacKenzie and Jeanne MacKenzie, *The first Fabians*, London 1977, 99; Edith Nesbit, quoted in Martin J. Wiener, *English culture and the decline of the industrial spirit 1850–1980*, Cambridge 1981, 72.
[39] Lord Elton, *The life of James Ramsay MacDonald (1866–1919)*, London 1939, 126–7.
[40] Blake's 'Jerusalem' is an often cited example of this. However, it was not until Hubert Parry set it to music in 1916 (to steel the British against a premature peace) that it became a left anthem. Even then, it was not much used. James Leatham in 1894 had not even included the final verse ('I will not cease from mental fight,/ Nor shall my sword sleep in my hand/ Till we have built Jerusalem/ In England's green and pleasant land.'). It was not sung at a Labour Party conference until 1990, when Jo Richardson, chairing, said that 'those delegates who are Scottish have dispensation to insert the word Scotland, instead of England, and the same goes for Wales, leaving the rest of us to uphold the old country': Labour Party, *Conference report*, 1990, 332. For the wider application of a rural idyll as the real England see Alun Howkins, 'The discovery of rural England', in Colls and Dodd, *Englishness*, 62–88, and Philip Lowe, 'The rural idyll defended: from preservation to conservation', in G. E. Mingay (ed.), *The rural idyll*, London 1989, 113–31. For many socialists, especially those around Carpenter, American romanticism and transcendentalism were inspirations of equal importance in appreciation of the countryside: Mark Bevir, 'British socialism and American romanticism', *EHR* cx (1995), 878–901.

countryside into a physical and spiritual amenity for urban dwellers.[41] Some socialists concerned themselves with preservation of rural areas and their historic monuments. Walter Crane, a supporter of the newly founded National Trust, voiced concern about the impact of the modern economy on his rather idealised view of rural society: 'Under the . . . desperate compulsion of commercial competition, agriculture declines, and the country side is deserted. The old country life, with its festivals and picturesque customs, has disappeared. Old houses, churches, and cottages have tumbled into ruin, or have suffered worse destruction by a process of smartening up called "restoration".'[42] The *Clarion* set up its own field clubs 'to bring the town dweller more frequently into contact with the beauty of nature; to help forward the ideal of the simpler life, plain living and high thinking'.[43] The thinking behind these was very much Blatchford's rejection of urban England as the true nation.

Some socialists were enthusiasts for English music. Here again the components of radical patriotism could be drawn upon. The search for folk song involved an appreciation of 'the common people' in a national context.[44] Cecil Sharp and Vaughan Williams, who both described themselves as socialists, went in search of an authentic national music in the villages of England.[45] Sharp and Vaughan Williams were professional musicians before they were socialists, but many socialists who considered themselves only amateur musicians also drew on folk song and English music of the sixteenth and seventeenth centuries.[46]

Another area of activity in which socialists involved themselves which

[41] Lowe, 'The rural idyll defended', 117. Lowe notes that the use of the term 'the countryside' began at the end of the nineteenth century and signified this new attitude.
[42] Walter Crane, *William Morris to Whistler: papers and addresses on Art and Craft and the commonweal*, London 1911, 216. Elsewhere in the same volume he blamed Americanisation: 'Some of us appear to be trying to turn England into another America – for ever scheming railways where they are not wanted, cutting down trees, and clearing away old dwelling places, and insulting even the green fields with advertisements. Anything that interferes with extra percentages is as dust in the balance to such' (p. 77).
[43] *Scout*, 30 Mar. 1895, in David Prynn, 'The Clarion clubs, rambling and the holiday associations in Britain since the 1890s', *JCH* xi (1976), 68.
[44] Chris Waters, *British socialists and the politics of popular culture, 1884–1914*, Manchester 1990, 103, 127–8.
[45] Alun Howkins, 'Greensleeves and the idea of national music', in Samuel, *Patriotism*, iii. 89–98; Marsh, *Back to the land*, ch. v. See Dave Harker, 'May Cecil Sharp be praised?', *HW* xiv (1982), 44–62, for criticisms of Sharp's methodology (and politics). These however detract little from his motives of searching for 'our traditional songs', which would be 'a great instrument for sweetening and purifying our national life': ibid. 55.
[46] Those who took an active part in the socialist choral movement could find their socialism submerged. Waters has analysed the sheet music of the Halifax and Bradford branches of the Clarion Vocal Union. Only 4.3% of it was political, whereas 16.3% was traditional folk and 11.4% was English sixteenth- and seventeenth-century music: *British socialism and popular culture*, 122. See also Dave Russell, *Popular music in England, 1840–1914: a social history*, Manchester 1987, 52–3.

had connections to ruralism and Englishness, though not unproblematically, was in the Arts and Crafts movement. It was here that Ruskin's critique of industrialisation had most impact.[47] Ruskin had argued that under industrialisation labour had been divided to such a point that the spiritual condition of the worker was degraded. He pointed back to the Middle Ages as a period when work had provided fulfilment to the extent that man could be whole. Ruskin's view of the Middle Ages was European, and it was the wider socialist interpretation of English history and particularly that of William Morris that brought the Arts and Crafts movement to look closer to home for inspiration. Walter Crane had been instrumental in the founding of the Art Workers' Guild and the Arts and Crafts Exhibition Society. He had been apprenticed to the Chartist wood-engraver, W. J. Linton. He joined the SDF around 1884 after reading Morris's *Art and socialism*. He acknowledged Morris's contribution to his socialism and his artistic work. Morris had, he said, been responsible for 'a revival of the medieval spirit (not the letter) in design; a return to simplicity, to sincerity; to good materials and sound workmanship; to rich and suggestive surface decoration, and simple constructive forms'.[48] Crane was emphatically non-sectarian, undertaking art-work for any left-of-centre political organisation that commissioned him, making his influence widely felt across the left. His cartoons adorn the socialist journals and 'shaped the imagery of socialism on trade union banners for thirty years from the early 1880s until well into the 1920s'.[49] Crane shared the idealised view of English history:

> England was once not only 'merrie' but beautiful – her people well and picturesquely clad: her towns rich with lovely architecture – life a perpetual pageant . . . the colour and fantastic invention in costume and heraldry; the constant show and processions, such as those organised by the craft guilds, full of quaint allegory and symbolic meaning . . . gay with flaunting banners.[50]

Such a view led to an equally idealised interpretation of socialism, such as his winged and draped female figures and strong heroic labourers, surrounded by the bounty of nature. Crane was also deeply touched by the symbolism of St George, and after illustrating an edition of Spenser's *Faerie Queene*, he painted 'England's Emblem', which he described as

[47] For Ruskin's wider impact on British political thought see Jonathan Mendilow, *The Romantic tradition in British political thought*, London 1986, and Mark Swenarton, *Artisans and architects: the Ruskinian tradition in architectural thought*, Basingstoke–London 1989. Of the 45 Labour and Lib-Lab MPs elected in 1906 who responded to W. T. Stead's request for information on the books that had influenced them, Ruskin was the most popular, with 14 mentioning his works: 'The Labour Party and the books that helped to make it', *Review of Reviews* xxxiii (June 1906), 568–82.

[48] Crane, *William Morris to Whistler*, 17.

[49] John Gorman, *Images of labour*, London n.d., 18. For Crane's conversion to socialism see his autobiography, *An artist's reminiscences*, London 1907, 254–5.

[50] Gorman, *Images of labour*, 163.

Our patron saint in full armour upon a white horse with red trappings, charging the dragon, behind which was a gloomy landscape with factory chimneys dark against lurid bars of sunset, and to the left a stretch of seashore, and a neglected plough in the middle distance – perhaps not an obscure allegory.[51]

Indeed St George and the dragon was a popular allegory for the struggle between socialism and capitalism, presenting the latter as an enemy of England which the socialists could vanquish, emerging as national heroes.[52] Clearly many socialists saw themselves as patriots, out to bring 'England to her own rescue'.[53]

Other parts of the Arts and Crafts movement devoted themselves to handicrafts, such as C. R. Ashbee. Ashbee, influenced by Carpenter and Morris, established the Guild of Handicraft in the East End, but in 1902 moved it out of London to Chipping Campden in the Cotswolds. As he described the move, it was a return to the English past: 'we went right out into the little forgotten Cotswold town of the Age of Arts and Crafts where industrialism had never touched, where there was an old mill and empty cottages ready to hand, left almost as when the Arts and Crafts ended in the eighteenth century'.[54] Elsewhere Ashbee suggested it was a move 'from Whitechapel to Camelot'.[55] Ashbee and his workmen seemed to be trying to revive an entire way of life, singing folk songs and performing plays from the past.[56] In order to regain an organic attachment to the soil the craftsmen were encouraged to till the soil in allotments around their houses. The Cotswolds became a centre for those seeking to go back to the land or into the past. The Webbs, fairly unsentimental in the main, took a house near Campden in order to allow themselves peace to write their monumental history of English local government. Cecil Sharp lectured on folk song to the Guild, and other Arts and Crafts workers followed Ashbee out into rural England.[57]

It is worth pointing out that what the Arts and Crafts movement took from the English past was a method of working, of healing the division of labour. While many pieces of work had direct inspiration from medieval art, there were wider influences. As Crawford has explained: 'The Arts and Crafts was less concerned with what things look like, with style, than with

[51] Crane, An artist's reminiscences, 494.
[52] For example, Edward Carpenter, St George and the dragon: a play in three acts for children and young folk, Manchester 1895; J. Bruce Glasier, On strikes, Glasgow–Manchester n.d. (c. 1897), cover; Bradford ILP, Yearbook 1910, Bradford 1910, frontispiece. Some ILP badges showed St George and the dragon.
[53] 'England to her own rescue' was a cartoon and poem by Crane in Andrew Reid (ed.), Vox clamantium: the gospel of the people, London 1894, 162–5.
[54] Lionel Lambourne, Utopian craftsmen: the Arts and Crafts movement from the Cotswolds to Chicago, London 1980, 130. For the full range of Ashbee's work see Alan Crawford, C. R. Ashbee: architect, designer and romantic socialist, New Haven–London 1985.
[55] Fiona MacCarthy, The simple life: C. R. Ashbee in the Cotswolds, London 1981, 32.
[56] Ibid. 28, 53.
[57] Crawford, C. R. Ashbee, 121, 122.

how they were made. . . . They might be plain or elaborately decorated, homely or exotic; they took their cue from Byzantium or Berkshire, the fifth or the fifteenth century. There was no single Arts and Crafts style.'[58]

The Arts and Crafts movement did not entirely reject urban life, and an important strand believed that town and country could be reintegrated, again looking back to the medieval past for their model. This can be best illustrated by an examination of the early career of Raymond Unwin, a central figure in British town planning in the early twentieth century. Unwin was active in the Socialist League in Manchester throughout the 1880s, at first sharing its revolutionary view of how socialism could be established. At the same time, however, he worked as an architect influenced by Ruskin and Morris's loathing of the division of labour and the divorce of craft from work. With the collapse of the Socialist League and the transition of northern socialism towards a politics of gradual and pragmatic reform, Unwin, while retaining the ethical base to his socialism, came to believe that the founding of a socialist society could come piecemeal through the application of Arts and Crafts methods to architecture and town planning.[59] Unwin had previously rejected the past as a model for a future socialist society, arguing of 'the good old times, in the ages of simple life and rough surroundings' that 'violence in those time ruled the day'.[60] But by the late 1890s he had taken up a *News from nowhere* view of the English medieval past and placed it centre stage in his architectural vision. Thus he argued that the old tradition of building had led to a natural growth of towns that created an informal beauty of order. The great question, he believed, was '[h]ow far [this was] possible to reproduce under modern conditions'.[61] The opportunity to answer this question was provided by the Garden City movement. Unwin and his socialist and architectural partner, Barry Parker, were appointed architects to the first garden city at Letchworth in Hertfordshire. Unwin explained the objectives of the movement:

> The Garden City movement, as the name implies, stands for a more harmonious combination of city and country, dwelling house and garden. The rapid growth of towns and cities during the eighteenth and nineteenth centuries . . . took place without any proper regard being shown for health, convenience or beauty in the arrangement of the town, without any effort to give that combination of building with open space which is necessary to secure adequate light

58 Ibid. 208.
59 For Unwin's reformism see *Labour Leader*, 18 Jan. 1902. The preceding paragraph relies heavily on Swenarton, *Artisans and architects*, ch. v, and Standish Meacham, 'Raymond Unwin (1863–1940): designing for democracy in Edwardian England', in Susan Pedersen and Peter Mandler (eds), *After the Victorians: private conscience and public duty*, London–New York 1994, 78–102.
60 'Dawn of a happier day', Jan. 1886, Raymond Unwin papers, British Architectural Library UN.15/2. He had however shared the left-wing view that in the Middle Ages the land belonged the people and that the history of land was 'a history of the confiscation of people's rights': *Commonweal*, 23 Apr. 1887, in Swenarton, *Artisans and architects*, 162.
61 Notes on lecture on town planning, 26 Feb. 1908, Unwin papers UN.2/1.

and fresh air for health, adequate un-built on ground for convenience, or adequate parks and gardens for the beauty of the city.[62]

The Garden City movement can be seen as an attempt to apply scientific principles to the building of communities, but, as Stanley Buder has argued, it was overwhelmed by Unwin and Parker's Arts and Crafts aesthetics.[63] From his aesthetic interpretation of the English medieval past Unwin favoured a revived vernacular approach to architecture; housing had to fit into the local landscape. At Letchworth therefore:

> The promoters are convinced that the high standard of beauty which they desire to attain in the Garden City can only result from simple straightforward buildings suitably designed for their respective purposes and honestly built of simple and harmonious materials: they do not seek any artificial attempts at the picturesque, nor do they ask for any useless ornamentation.[64]

This fitted reasonably well with the other modernist influences on the Garden City movement, which had such a tremendous impact on early state housing in Britain. Through Unwin's socialism the desire to recreate the English rural past was projected forward onto the building of urban society in early twentieth-century Britain.[65]

The Arts and Crafts movement can be seen as part of a popular anti-industrialism that for many of its practitioners was an attempt to rediscover a real England in the countryside. While the movement was not socialist, many of its leading figures, such as Morris, Crane, Ashbee, Philip Webb, W. R. Lethaby, Raymond Unwin and A. J. Penty, adhered to the socialist movement. They were inspired by its fundamentally moral and Ruskinian approach to social questions and the ability they felt within it to build a cultural politics that might restore the supposed social harmony of the Middle Ages.

So far discussion has been confined to prominent figures in the socialist movement, but there is evidence for the wider popularity of such ideas of medievalism, at least among socialist activists. A whole series of fund-raising events were held throughout the country taking 'Merrie England' and its implied interpretation of history as their theme. Bradford Labour Church held 'The Champion Show of the Year – Ye Olde English Fayre' in March 1895; there was a 'Merrie England Fayre' in Liverpool City Hall opening on May Day of the same year. Bolton ILP had a 'Grand Merry England Maye Fayre' with 'old English costumes and may-pole dancing' (and rather bizarrely

---

62 Raymond Unwin, *Nothing gained by overcrowding: how the garden city type of development may benefit both owner and occupier*, London 1912, 1.
63 Stanley Buder, *Visionaries and planners: the garden city movement and the modern community*, New York–Oxford 1990, 84.
64 First Garden City Ltd, 'Suggestions for the use of those wishing to build cottage property on the estate', Unwin papers, UN.12/24.
65 Swenarton, *Artisans and architects*, 164–5.

an 'Unique Japanese Stall'!). Birmingham Labour Church held a 'Merrie England Fayre' on 31 October and 1 and 2 November 1895.[66] Gorton ILP announced a 'Merrie England Maye Fayre' with 'A "MERRIE ENGLAND" VILLAGE', changing the name of the event to 'Maye in December' as it was to be held on 4 December 1895. The Gorton event offered:

> Ann Hathaway's Cottage and Cottagers. The Bee Hive and Busy Bees. The May-pole and Villagers. The Greenwood Tree and Robin Hood and his Merry Men and Maidens. The Little Brown Jug and Potters. Poets' Corner and Bards. Titania's Bower and Faerie Belles. Ye Olde Village Inn and Matrons and Maidens. I Zingari and the Gipsy Queen.

The whole event would be, the advertisement in the *Clarion* promised, 'pretty, tasteful and jolly'.[67] At the ILP's 'Great International Bazaar' in Blackburn in March 1908 children of the Socialist Sunday School offered 'Old English Morris Dancing'; there were stalls of 'Old England' – 'an Elizabethan half-timbered house', and 'Modern England', though the description seemed remarkably similar – 'a modern English cottage with dormer windows, creepers and overhanging eaves'.[68] There was more than simply a fund-raising role for such events. A *Clarion* reporter showed their significance in his comment that 'here, in Halifax, at the ILP bazaar, we have lived and moved in "Merrie England", and it is well with us'.[69] Socialists did not teach their children to dance around may-poles solely to raise money.

The interpretation of English history therefore entered into the symbolism and language of late nineteenth-century socialists and they used it in their day-to-day propaganda. Hardie wrote that a socialist was one who sought 'to resuscitate a phase of British life which produced great and good results in the past'.[70] Socialists based many of the ideas behind their actions on historical precedent, as had earlier radical movements. Such ideas involved a belief in how things should happen in England. Thus, when events did not live up to this ideal, socialists would counterpoise the belief to the reality, as in the satirical poem, 'Not in England' in *Labour Leader* of 23 December 1899:

> Let us spin a Christmas rhyme;
> Here's to England!
> 'Rule Britannia' every time;
> I'm for England!

---

[66] *Clarion*, 2 Mar. (May Day special edition), 26 Oct., 16 Nov. 1895.
[67] Ibid. 30 Nov. 1895.
[68] ILP, *Handbook of the Great International Bazaar, Exchange Hall, Blackburn, March 1908*, n.d. For other examples see *Clarion*, 6 Mar. 1897, 11 May 1901; *Labour Leader*, 4 Mar. 1899, 22 Sept. 1900, 26 Nov. 1909.
[69] *Clarion*, 13 Oct. 1894, in Waters, *British socialists and popular culture*, 90. Waters discusses both the fund-raising role and the desire to provide improving forms of entertainment.
[70] Hardie, *From serfdom to socialism*, 18.

Wise and foolish, old and young,
Come and join and give it trung [sic].
If lives he who suffers wrong,
It's not in England.

. . . If the master be denied,
It's not in England;
If war be glorified,
It's not in England;
If yon Christmas chime denotes,
The song of peace serenely floats,
Over Christians cutting throats,
It's not in England.

More general were articles in *Clarion* headed 'Britain's glory' or 'Happy England', reporting deaths through starvation, or imprisonment for theft undertaken by the poverty-stricken.[71] One *Clarion* reader objected to such methods, calling them 'a disgrace to socialism and to you. The lowest of men have always desired their country's glory. You, by raking up accidental cases of distress to old soldiers, and belittling British pluck, are doing your best to turn the people against their own country.' A. M. Thompson replied that his intention was to do the opposite, to make people have more respect for their country by changing it so that such things could not happen.[72]

The best example of oppositional Englishness is found in the *Clarion* of 16 September 1893 following the fatal shooting of a miner at Featherstone, Yorkshire. The poem by 'Bogggs' [sic] on the front page implored:

Oh, England! veil thy haughty face,
And bow thy crest with shame;
For Englishmen, with red disgrace,
Have stained they glorious name.

How tarnished is thy glory, and
How humbled is thy pride,
Since England's arms, on English land,
With English blood are dyed . . .

'Mont Blong' (Montagu Blatchford) continued on this theme, that 'British subjects have been done to death by British soldiers, and English liberty has received a blow from which it will not recover.' An editorial in the same issue pointed out that 'this is the first time since Peterloo that free Englishmen have been shot for refusing to move off the public roads'. The *Clarion* writers saw this less as an event in a class war than as a 'shameful outrage upon the

---

71 For examples see *Clarion*, 12 Mar. 1892, 9 Dec. 1893, 6 Jan. 1894,
72 'By the way', ibid. 1 Feb. 1896.

liberties of the people'.[73] They expressed not the class nature of the situation but their outrage that this could occur in England.

As socialism emerged in the 1880s and 1890s it was invested with an ethical and moral quality, much of which was based on a socialist historiography of the English past. This was used to pre-figure a future socialist society. Across a range of activities, history for socialists became not so much a guide to the present, but to the future. This reading of the past provided not only an explanation for the fundamental shortcomings of capitalism, but also a vision of a new society in which a social equilibrium would be restored. British socialism therefore sought to combine both class and national identities in a new form of historical politics.

[73] Ibid. 23 Sept. 1893.

# 3

# Constructing British Socialism, 1881–1906

If socialists were keen to assert that they represented the true defence of the English struggle for liberty, they were especially keen to show that socialism itself was 'English', for they perceived that they were seen as 'foreign'. May Morris, looking back from 1936, was of the opinion that 'To the man in the street, in those days, socialists and revolutionaries were an importation from the continent – a legacy of the days of 1848 and the French Commune of 1871 jumbled together – all the more execrated as such.'[1] The first issue of *Justice* believed that 'Democratic socialism was everywhere spoken of as merely another name for secret assassination or dynamite outrage, and the greatest efforts were made to show plainly that no matter how rife such ideas were abroad, socialism could never take root in England.'[2] William Morris was inclined to treat the whole idea as a joke in his play, *The tables turned*. The judge claims that, from their (Cockney) accents, the 'ruffianly revolutionists . . . are foreigners of a low type'.[3]

The SDF was especially involved in trying to refute ideas that socialism was foreign to Britain, particularly in its early years. Hyndman wrote that:

> It is well known that the idea of socialism is of no foreign importation into England. Tyler, Cade, Ball, Kett, More, Bellers, Spence, Owen, read to me like sound English names: not a foreigner in the whole batch. They all held opinions which our capitalist-landlord House of Commons would denounce as direct plagiarisms from 'continental revolutionists'. We islanders have been revolutionists however, and will be again.[4]

An editorial in *Justice* in 1884 was entitled 'Socialism in '34'. It named Cobbett, Cartwright, O'Connor, Thomas Frost, Bronterre O'Brien and Ernest Jones as forebears of modern socialism, and concluded that 'English socialism then is no recent importation, it is native to the soil, and the socialists of 1884 are but continuing the work which has been handed on from previous generations.'[5] Socialists in the 1880s were keen to show that they belonged to a native tradition, and that the potential for the growth of socialism existed.

[1] Morris, *William Morris*, ii. 73
[2] *Justice*, 19 Jan. 1884
[3] Morris, *William Morris*, ii. 537, 539
[4] Hyndman, *Historical basis*, 4n. The title itself shows the attempt at national legitimisation.
[5] *Justice*, 19 Apr. 1884, editorial by R. P. B. Frost. For more English name-dropping see also H. M. Hyndman, *Socialism and slavery*, 3rd edn, London n.d. (*c.* 1892), 4.

Hyndman even stressed that 'in England . . . there was more practical socialism than in any other nation', and that he was following the Chartists by emphasising national history, for 'unlike continental revolutionists, they founded their claims upon the history of their country, and clamoured for the restoration of rights which their fathers had been deprived of'.[6] Hyndman's patriotic temperament had been combined with socialism through a 'foreigner'. He failed in *England for all* to acknowledge Marx as the source of the economic arguments presented, and Marx claimed that Hyndman had done this because 'the English don't like to be taught by foreigners'.[7] Yet Hyndman admired another foreign socialist, Ferdinand Lassalle, who was, Hyndman wrote,

> unlike Blanqui or Marx, essentially a national socialist, who wished above all things, to raise the fatherland to a high level of greatness and glory. This national turn, though a great weakness economically [because of the global capitalist economy] . . . was nevertheless a help rather than a hindrance to an agitator who wished to rouse his countrymen from a long and apparently hopeless apathy.[8]

Hyndman saw himself as an English Lassalle, combining socialism with patriotism. Hyndman believed that 'ideas vary with race and climate',[9] and explained that 'We, perhaps, alone among the peoples can carry out with peace, order and contentment those changes which continental revolutionists have sought through anarchy and bloodshed.'[10] He argued that this was possible because Britain and other Anglo-Saxon communities had already achieved political liberties such as freedom of speech denied to continental Europeans. Furthermore, 'men of our race have so far been able to work out political problems without that dangerous excitement which has attended the endeavour to solve them elsewhere'.[11] Hence, while fundamental changes were needed, they could be peacefully and rapidly achieved in Britain. Patriotism and self-restraint had been bred from an acceptance amongst even the poorest that real reform was possible without violent change.[12]

Hyndman could be inclined to use violent language; one pamphlet of his was called *The coming revolution in England*, and included the startling line: 'Revolution! What have the workers to fear from revolution!'[13] But such language from Hyndman was rhetorical. He combined a Marxist belief of 'the combination of modern prolectarians [sic]' with a belief in national character-

---

6  Hyndman, *Historical basis*, 409, 208.
7  Karl Marx and Frederick Engels, *Correspondence 1846–1896: a selection*, London 1934, 397.
8  Hyndman, *Historical basis*, 417.
9  Idem, 'The dawn of a revolutionary epoch', *Nineteenth Century*, Jan. 1881, 2.
10  Idem, *England for all*, 194.
11  Idem, 'Dawn of a revolutionary epoch', 11–12.
12  Idem, *England for all*, 5.
13  Idem, *The coming revolution in England*, London n.d. [1883], 30.

istics, for he saw such a combination as aided by the 'constructive instincts' of 'the Celto-Teutonic peoples'.[14] Such reliance on beliefs about English national character left Hyndman vulnerable to attack by more moderate socialists, who used ideas of national identity to defend their own approaches to socialism, and who could rely on the full force of the dominant ideology about the nature of the English and their political behaviour.[15]

### The Fabian Society and the normal course of English life

In 1896 the Fabian Society told the Second International congress meeting in London that:

> The Fabian Society is perfectly constitutional in its attitude; and its methods are those usual in political life in England.
> The Fabian Society accepts the conditions imposed on it by human nature and by the national character and political circumstances of the English people. It sympathises with the ordinary citizen's desire for gradual, peaceful changes as against revolution, conflict with the army and police, and martyrdom. . . .[16]

This was the finished product of Fabian policy, for ten years earlier a Fabian tract had declared that 'English socialism is not yet anarchist or collectivist, not yet definite enough in point of policy to be classified.'[17] Two years earlier still, in 1884, the Society had declared that 'we would rather face a civil war than such another century of suffering as the present one has been'.[18] Until the late 1880s the Society was unable to formulate a unified policy. Its leading members were attracted to different elements of the socialist movement; Bernard Shaw favoured the revolutionaries, Hubert Bland rejected both the SDF to the left and the Radicals to the right, Annie Besant was disposed towards ethical socialism but thought the SDF more concerned with practical politics, Charlotte Wilson was an anarchist, Sydney Olivier was drawn to the simple lifers, and Sidney Webb and Graham Wallas sought co-operation with London Radicals.[19] It was only after the unemployed riots of 1886 and Bloody Sunday in 1887, when police and soldiers violently prevented a demonstration in Trafalgar Square, that the Society totally embraced constitutionalism.

In *Fabian essays*, Sidney Webb argued that in Britain, 'important organic

---

14 Idem, *Historical basis*, 194n.
15 See Philip Dodd, 'Englishness and the national culture', and Robert Colls, 'Englishness and the political culture', in Colls and Dodd, *Englishness*.
16 Fabian Society, *Report on Fabian policy*, tract no. 70, London 1896, 4.
17 Fabian Society, *What socialism is*, tract no. 4, London 1890, in MacBriar, *Fabian socialism and English politics*, 10.
18 Fabian Society, *Manifesto*, tract no. 2, London 1884, in ibid. 4.
19 MacKenzie and MacKenzie, *The first Fabians*, 77–8.

changes' could only be achieved democratically and gradually, constitution-ally and peacefully.[20] Shaw, in the same volume, declared

> This, then, is the humdrum programme of the practical social-democrat today. There is not one new item in it. All are applications of principles already admitted, and extensions of practices already in full activity. All have on them the stamp of the vestry which is so congenial to the British mind. None of them compel the use of the words socialism or revolution: at no point do they involve guillotining, declaring the Rights of Man, swearing on the altar of the country, or anything else that is supposed to be essentially un-English.[21]

However much wit Shaw intended the last part of the statement to show off, subsequent actions by himself and other Fabians tend to suggest that there was seriousness behind the wit. Shaw had written the tract *What socialism is* in 1886, declaring for anarchism and socialism. He tried to eradicate its mem-ory; it was never reprinted. Indeed in 1890 a tract of the same name appeared without reference to anarchism. Shaw had remarked of his Hampstead debates with Philip Wicksteed on Marx that they 'ended in my education and conversion by my opponent', and added self-importantly, 'and in the disap-pearance of the Marxian theory of value from the articles of faith of British socialism'.[22] Webb called *Fabian essays* 'a complete exposition of modern English socialism in its latest and maturest phase',[23] and Edward Pease, in the official history of the Fabian Society, argued that the Society's 'first achieve-ment . . . was to break the spell of Marxism in Britain. . . . The Fabian Society freed English socialism from this intellectual bondage. . . . If German social-ism would not suit, English socialism had to be formulated to take its place. This has been the life-work of the Fabian Society.'[24]

The Society was therefore deliberately aiming to create what it saw as an authentic English socialism. One reason for this was connected with the class of person the Society aimed to recruit and influence. Permeation required that people already involved in the political parties should be converted to Fabianism. The tactic of permeation adopted by the Society required that no potential ally should be alienated. Shaw wrote of the Fabians that their 'socialism could be adopted either as a whole or by instalments by any ordi-nary respectable citizen without committing himself to any revolutionary association or detaching himself in anyway from the normal course of English life'.[25]

[20] Fabian Society, *Fabian essays*, 34–5.
[21] Ibid. 200.
[22] Michael Holroyd, *Bernard Shaw*, I: *1856–1898 the search for love*, London 1988, 182, 178.
[23] Sidney Webb, *Socialism in England*, Aldershot 1987, first publ. 1890, 38.
[24] Edward R. Pease, *The history of the Fabian Society*, London 1916, 90–1, 236, 240. It can be no accident that the book contained anti-German remarks during wartime.
[25] Bernard Shaw, preface to William Morris, *Communism*, tract no. 113, London 1903, 3. Paradoxically, for a master of paradox, Morris's pamphlet was an attack on the 'make-shift

## The *Clarion* and the Walsall anarchists

While the SDF had suggested that socialism had a tradition in England, the Fabians argued that not all socialism was English. The use of violence for political ends was also rejected as un-English. In 1892 six anarchists in Walsall were arrested for making a bomb intended for the assassination of the tsar of Russia.[26] Writers on the *Clarion* were concerned that the reputation of socialism would be damaged. They therefore condemned the methods of the anarchists as un-English, even stooping to suggest that only foreigners could be involved:

> For they are foreigners, it seems,
> And Anarchists – may be,
> Who merely hatch their violent schemes
> For export, don't you see?
>
> And as we open wide our doors
> To all who lift the latch,
> Those Anarchists, from foreign shores,
> Come here their plots to hatch. . . .

An editorial continued:

> England, at this time of day has only loathing and scorn for schemes of violent revolution. At no time were the English people enamoured of revolt, but now when all reform can be won steadily by education and constitutional means, the very mention of force excites anger and contempt. The people have the power, if they have the will, to bring about by peaceful means the emancipation of the people. . . . Even should the need for such means exist, the weapon selected by an English revolutionary would not be dynamite. Were they to fight, the English would come out into the open and fight like Englishmen. But they have no need to fight.[27]

The *Clarion* sided firmly with the British state against the anarchists, four of whom were British, as it turned out. They had been tricked by an *agent provocateur* into making a bomb for use against Europe's most despotic ruler. With this stance the *Clarion* was prepared to use both xenophobia and anti-immigrant sentiments.[28] The *Clarion* did attack the press coverage of the case, but only for suggesting that the bomb-makers were socialists.[29] The

---

alleviations' of reformist socialism, which would come to be 'looked upon as ends in themselves' (p. 11).

[26] John Quail, *The slow burning fuse: the lost history of the British anarchists*, London 1978, ch. vi.

[27] *Clarion*, 16 Jan. 1892.

[28] For the perceptions of a link between immigrants and anarchism see Haia Shpayer-Makov, 'Anarchism in British public opinion 1880–1914', VS xxxi (1988), 496.

[29] *Clarion*, 9 Apr. 1892.

following week an editorial declared that 'modern English socialism is not a violent revolutionary movement . . . *English* socialism today has nothing to say to barricades and dynamite'.[30] The anarchists received sentences of up to ten years in jail. Among prominent socialists, only Edward Carpenter, who gave evidence in their defence, supported them.[31]

## The ILP and 'British socialism'

The rejection of violence as un-English extended to revolutionary methods in general. At the inaugural conference of the Independent Labour Party in Bradford in 1893 an outburst by Ben Tillett was received with shock by the assembled delegates. He said:

> In spite of all that has been said about the socialists, he thought English trades unionism was the best sort of socialism and labourism. He wished to capture the trade unionists in this country . . . who did not shout for blood red revolution, and, when it came to revolution, sneaked under the nearest bed. . . . With his experience of unions, he was glad to say that if there were fifty such red revolutionary parties as there were in Germany, he would sooner have the solid, progressive, matter of fact, fighting trades unionism of England than all the hare-brained chatterers and magpies of continental revolutionists.[32]

Even the *Clarion* was moved to condemn Tillett. Blatchford called it 'the most regrettable incident' and reminded readers that 'the labour cause is the labour cause in Germany as in England. Justice is not a geographical idea'.[33] Tillett, in an essay written in 1895, repeated the root of his sentiments, but without the venom: the workers 'have been, it is true, temporarily led away by other and chimerical movements, but the sturdy common sense of their leaders, and the law-abiding instincts of the masses, have always brought them back to the true and constitutional line of progress'.[34]

Had he used such language at the ILP conference it is unlikely that anybody would have objected, since the leadership of the ILP shared Tillett's aim, that was to attract the trade unions to the idea of labour representation. In the discussion over the name of the new party at the conference, a delegate from Glasgow suggested the name 'Socialist Labour Party' because 'in Scotland the Labour Party had come to the conclusion that it was best to call a spade a spade'. Supporters of the Labour alternative pointed out that an electoral party must appeal to more than just socialists.[35] David Howell has

---

[30] Ibid. 16 Apr. 1892.
[31] The radical *Reynolds' Newspaper* also supported the anarchists: Shpayer-Makov, 'Anarchism in public opinion', 502.
[32] *Report of the first general conference of the Independent Labour Party*, London 1893, 3.
[33] *Clarion*, 21 Jan. 1893.
[34] Ben Tillett, 'The need for labour representation', in Frank W. Galton (ed.), *Workers on their industries*, London 1895, 219–20.
[35] ILP, *Conference report*, 1893, 3.

concluded that 'pragmatism and, perhaps, patriotism combined to give near unanimous backing to the Labour option'.[36] Leeds socialist Tom Maguire later commented on the chose name, the Independent Labour Party, that 'suddenly a name was coined that hit off the genius of the English people'.[37] Hence in the formation of Britain's most important socialist organisation of the 1890s, ideas of national identity played a role in the naming of the party.

The 1890s saw the conjunction of two elements that led to an increasing attack on non-parliamentarian socialism as foreign. First, the defeat of the wave of new unionism led many trade unionists to look towards political activity rather than industrial struggle. Hence in Bradford the defeat of the Manningham Mills strike led to the establishment of the Bradford Labour Union, which was central to the foundation of the ILP. In Leeds, where new unionism had been more successful, it was not until 1906 that an ILP councillor was elected.[38] The employers' counter-offensive of the 1890s pushed trade union leaders into greater consideration of independent labour representation, but did nothing to increase their trust of socialists. The leaders of the ILP set out to dispel this mistrust. Second, many socialists began to doubt the steady progress of socialism. Between 1893 and 1895 not a single ILP candidate was elected at a parliamentary election, and Keir Hardie lost his West Ham South seat in the 1895 general election, which saw what Howell has called 'the death of easy optimism'.[39]

Such conditions led the rank-and-file of the ILP to press for unity with the SDF, to the chagrin of the increasingly centralised leadership, which was becoming dominated by Hardie, MacDonald, Glasier and Snowden. While the leadership was looking towards a greater alliance with the trade unions, the membership seemed to be spoiling this by seeking links with the Marxists. Through using the language of Englishness (or, as will be shown, Britishness) the leadership could show the trade unions how moderate was British socialism and, at the same time, oppose fusion or federation with the SDF.

The language of Britishness provided a useful unifying point around which a labour movement still divided by nation and region could coalesce. Patrick Joyce has pointed out that a sense of labour identity was strongly rooted in particular localities, for example among textile workers in Lancashire or miners in Durham, and that in some senses the Labour Party was the creation of these particularistic senses of industry and place.[40] Socialism and labour organisation could be fragmented along regional or national lines, such as separate union and party organisation in Scotland. The early socialism of

---

36 Howell, *British workers and the ILP*, 293.
37 *Dewsbury Reporter*, 13 Oct. 1894, in E. P. Thompson, 'Homage to Tom Maguire', in Briggs and Saville, *Essays in labour history in memory of G. D. H. Cole*, 301–2.
38 Henry Pelling, *The origins of the Labour Party 1880–1900*, 2nd edn, Oxford 1966, 94–5; Thompson, 'Homage to Tom Maguire', 302–3.
39 Howell, *British workers and the ILP*, 309.
40 Joyce, *Visions of the people*, 138–9.

Philip Snowden and Robert Blatchford was strongly northern in character. The first chapters of Snowden's autobiography are a tale of a sense of loss of a distinct Yorkshire culture from which he saw his socialism emerging.[41] Blatchford differentiated between his own socialism and that of metropolitan socialists:

> When came [socialism]? What is it? If you asked a London socialist for the origin of the new movement he would refer you to Karl Marx and other German socialists. But so far as our northern people are concerned I am convinced that beyond the mere outline of state socialism Karl Marx and his countrymen have had little influence. No; the new movement here; the new religion, which is socialism, and something more than socialism, is more largely the result of the labours of Darwin, Carlyle, Ruskin, Dickens, Thoreau and Walt Whitman. It is from these men that the North has caught the message of love and justice, of liberty and peace, of culture and simplicity, and of holiness and beauty of life.[42]

In South Wales and Scotland labour activists could see themselves as distinct from the English labour movement. The socialists, Thomas Gwynn Jones, R. J. Derfel and R. Silyn Roberts, contributed significantly to the flourishing of Welsh culture at the turn of the century,[43] and in Scotland demands for home rule combined with the desire for independent labour representation.[44] 'Celtic' socialists sometimes considered the English a conservative people and despaired of their backwardness. During the Boer War, 'Marxian', who had some Welsh blood in him, complained that:

> We are on the road to complete despotism – the more complete because an ignorant democracy, inspired by unintelligent capitalist newspapers, care practically nothing for the essentials of freedom. If the English people like this sort of thing, by all means let them pay for it. The Celtic races are increasingly sick of being taxed to support the farce. And the sooner Ireland, Wales, and even dumb Scotland have national assemblies of their own, the better I shall be pleased.[45]

This is not to say that the labour movement was fragmenting or over-divided. Indeed the labour movement was playing a significant part in the 'nationalis-

---

41 Snowden, *Autobiography*, i, ch. i. Socialists could also be attached to a particular city, hence Fenner Brockway entitled his biography of Fred Jowett *Socialism over sixty years: the life of Jowett of Bradford (1864–1944)*, London 1946. J. B. Priestley wrote a preface.
42 Robert Blatchford, *The new religion*, Manchester n.d. The influences Blatchford cited were not of course northern. Joyce expands on this theme of a 'northern British democratic patriotism': *Visions of the people*, 80–4.
43 Kenneth O. Morgan, *Rebirth of a nation: Wales 1880–1980*, Oxford 1982, 97–8, 101.
44 Michael Keating and David Bleiman, *Labour and Scottish nationalism*, London–Basingstoke 1979, ch. ii.
45 *Labour Leader*, 8 Feb. 1902

ation of culture' occurring at the end of the nineteenth century.[46] This did not necessarily mean the submerging of separate national or regional identities. They existed side by side, sometimes complementing each other, and only sometimes coming into conflict.[47]

One major reason why language seeking to establish the national character of socialism in Britain became the language of Britishness rather than of Englishness was that the ILP leadership was dominated by Scots. This did not reflect the strength of the Scottish membership of the ILP. At the inaugural conference, of the 120 delegates, only eleven represented Scottish organisations, compared with twenty-two from Bradford and fourteen from London.[48] Nevertheless, Glasier, Hardie and MacDonald, of the 'big four' on the ILP NAC, were of Scottish birth.

John Bruce Glasier,[49] born in 1859 in Ayr but brought up in Glasgow, as a young man discovered Byron and Shelley and turned to poetry, sending the privately-printed 'Empire against liberty' (1879 or 1880) about Russia, to Gladstone, Disraeli, Garibaldi, William Morris and others. The poems showed a combination of love of liberty and love of country that signified radical patriotism. The choice of recipients suggest that he believed radical patriotic language could be suitable for all political positions. For example:

> Then rise ye freemen for your fellowmen –
> For Liberty! and strike the Despot down!
> Break into fragments his blood-tarnished crown;
> Let not a relic of his power remain!
>
> How grand! How glorious! Liberty appears
> When struggling in the foremost front of war!
> When patriots around their hearts' blood pour
> To gain their rights, and dry their country's tears![50]

The Eastern crisis showed how such sentiments could cross the line into support for jingoism, for Glasier joined the Volunteers and in his diary exclaimed: 'Why should not every British youth be prepared to defend the glorious privileges of his country! . . . . Shall it ever be written in history that Britons lost their rights and liberties so dearly purchased by the blood of their

---

[46] José Harris, *Private lives, public spirit: Britain 1870–1914*, London 1994, 17–23.

[47] Cf. Keith Robbins's view of the 'blending' of regional and national identities to create a British culture: *Nineteenth-century Britain: England, Scotland and Wales: the making of a nation*, Oxford 1989.

[48] Howell, *British workers and the ILP*, 291.

[49] For Glasier see Laurence Thompson, *The enthusiasts: a biography of John and Katharine Bruce Glasier*, London 1971.

[50] Ibid. 20–5; Glasier papers, University of Liverpool, Sydney Jones Library, GP/6/2/26–7. Joseph Chamberlain replied that 'The Radical party in Russia can hardly expect the sympathy of British Liberals as long as they work by such means as attempted assassination': Glasier papers, GP/1/1/4, 15 Apr. 1880.

fathers, through negligence and weakness?'[51] And it was to English symbols that Glasier was attracted, for his diary for 1878 reveals that he revered the great popular hero, Nelson. 'Dear Nelson', he wrote ' – how truly English he was. I envy Hardy kissing him – how different from your stoical Wellingtons and Napoleons, he possessed a true and almost childlike enthusiasm – Nelson and Wolfe are two heroes that ought to be dearest to the hearts of all englishmen [sic].'[52] As late as 1905, long after his conversion to socialism, Glasier could write of Nelson that there was 'something of the heroic spirit of boyish daring, enthusiasm, and supreme exultation in dashing through storm and terrible fronts of power, which is one of the high elements of the race'.[53] After a brief interlude in the Irish Land League, Scottish Land and Labour League[54] and SDF, Glasier followed another hero, Morris, into the Socialist League. He was attracted by the ethical aspects of socialism, and while being seen as a 'barricades man' in his early years, tactics were of little interest to him.[55] In 1893 he married Katharine Conway and became attracted by the ethical bent of the ILP, the Socialist League having been taken over by anarchists. After gaining prominence in the banned socialist meetings at Boggart Hole Clough, near Manchester, he was elected to the ILP National Administrative Council (NAC) in 1897. As Hardie explained, Glasier had changed. 'In [the] days when I first met him', Hardie recalled in 1903, 'he was still an idealist pouring out fiery contempt on politicians and all their works. He is still an idealist, but has come to recognise that the way by which the ideal may be reached is more prosaic than his fresh enthusiasm at one time imagined.'[56] In 1893 Glasier had written that 'Socialism gives us our highest ideal of the conduct of life, and calls from us the highest service of thought, emotion, and deed – that is our aim and prophecy, and to it is due the utmost and gladdest devotion of all our gifts and powers.' Referring to the Russian nihilists, Paris Communards and Chicago anarchists, he wrote of socialism as 'a Religion for which many of the bravest and most gifted souls of this age have offered their lives'.[57] Yet by June 1903 he wrote to Carpenter about the ILP that:

It has been the means of restoring the English tradition into our socialist agitation – a tradition which was lost by the usurpation of the Marxist and Communard. For myself, I feel as one set free now that I am able to speak and work for socialism without feeling that I belong to a different cast of beings from

---

51 Thompson, *Enthusiasts*, 30.
52 Ibid. 31. Wolfe defeated the Jacobites at Culloden, though Glasier was more likely to have been referring to his role in the capture of Quebec in 1759.
53 *Labour Leader*, 27 Oct. 1905.
54 The Scottish Land and Labour League was founded in 1884 to attempt to link socialism to the crofters' agitation: Bleiman and Keating, *Labour and Scottish nationalism*, 47.
55 Stanley Pierson, *Marxism and the origins of British socialism: the struggle for a new consciousness*, Ithaca–London 1973, 142, 144.
56 Thompson, *Enthusiasts*, 113.
57 Katharine St John Conway and J. Bruce Glasier, *The religion of socialism: two aspects*, Glasgow–Manchester n.d., 10, 16.

that of the ordinary Liberal or Tory. I feel much joy, too, now that I realise that socialism is not a thing that a few refugees and philosophers brought into the world from twenty to forty years ago, but that it is a power that began with the beginning of the world and permeates infinitude.[58]

Glasier embraced reformism, and argued that it was the real native tradition of British socialism of which the ILP was the perfect expression, and, like the Fabians, saw it as a normal part of English life.[59] But this tradition may also have suited the European socialist movement, he believed. After the 1904 meeting of the Second International in Amsterdam he wrote to Hardie that

> I am more than ever convinced that the continental movement has fallen into a species of mere radicalism, and that it is marching by mere watchwords rather than by either faith or right. The half of these bourgeois leaders abroad strike me as utterly unregenerate from our Morris, Ruskin, Burns point of view. . . . The cause of socialism not only in our own country but in the world will receive a new character of freedom if only we set our ILP or British (should I not say Scottish?) conception above all German formulas.[60]

James Keir Hardie, born in Lanarkshire in 1856, came to socialism via trades unionism. Having been a miner, he became secretary of the Ayrshire Miners' Union in 1886. Hardie drew the fury of Henry Broadhurst at the 1887 Trades Union Congress when he attacked Broadhurst for being involved in a company using sweated labour. Broadhurst rebuked him thus: 'These intolerable, un-English attacks by Mr Hardie were a new feature of the Congress. He was surprised at a man coming here for the first time and showing such bad taste (hear, hear).'[61] This shows the confusion surrounding the ideas of Englishness, for Hardie was of course a Scot, and the Congress was being held in Wales.

Hardie was proud of his Scottishness, drawing his socialism from the Covenanters, Carlyle and particularly Burns. He wrote, 'I owe more to Burns than any other man alive or dead.'[62] He remarked on having read Border tales, and how 'these took hold of my imagination and created within me a love of the tales and traditions of Scotland'.[63] During the Mid-Lanark by-election in 1888 that made him a national figure, he appealed for, and received, the support of the Scottish Home Rule Association (of which Ramsay MacDonald was London secretary). He also accused the Liberal

58 Stanley Pierson, *British socialism: the journey from fantasy to politics*, Cambridge, Mass. 1979, 60.
59 See *Labour Leader*, 2 Apr. 1904.
60 Glasier to Hardie, 2 Sept. 1904, Glasier papers, GP/1/1/704. *Clarion* (6 Feb. 1892) had suggested (with tongue in cheek) exporting Fabian lecturers 'to impart a little reason and usefulness' to European socialism.
61 Morgan, *Keir Hardie*, 19.
62 *Labour Leader*, 22 Jun. 1909, in Caroline Benn, *Keir Hardie*, London 1992, 11.
63 'The Labour Party and the books that helped to make it', 11.

candidate, a Welsh barrister, of being unable to understand Scottish issues.[64] He displayed Scotland's distinctiveness from England at the 1889 congress of the International jumping up every time a delegate said 'English'. Hardie corrected them, 'And Scots!'[65]

Hardie, like Glasier and MacDonald, accepted a notion of Scottishness, but in a Scotland divided along religious and national lines, sided with the Scottishness of the kirk. Hardie showed some hostility towards Irish immigrants, whom he claimed forced down miners' wages, describing the typical immigrant as having 'a big shovel, a strong back and a weak brain' and coming from 'a peat bog or tattie field'.[66] The ILP attempted to overcome such divisions, not least to attract the Irish vote, and Scottish labour activists tended to be strong supporters of home rule for Scotland, but also for Ireland.

Hardie was central to the formation of the ILP, and was a fairly typical specimen of a north British blend of labourism and socialism that was the root of its politics. But he revealed too the problem of nationality in a multi-national state. He shared the mainstream view of the past, of a medieval golden age, which also presented an ideal for the future.[67] This view was based more on a reading of English, rather than British or Scottish history. It was a pre-union golden age, a merrie England. Thus in July 1914, in an article called 'If I were a dictator', he declared, 'I would have England a "merrie England".'[68] Likewise before the main body of *From serfdom to socialism*, he quoted a poem that urged, 'Come ye that listen, rise and gird your swords,/ Win back the fields of England for the poor.'[69]

This in no way stopped Hardie from appealing to electors in Merthyr Tydfil through their shared Celticness. In 1898 he had decided that 'all Celts . . . are socialist by instinct'.[70] He made a point of visiting an eisteddfod and learnt to sing the Welsh national anthem in Welsh.[71] He declared 'Socialism the hope of Wales',[72] and hoped one day to see 'the red dragon . . . emblazoned on the red flag of socialism, the international emblem of the working class movement of the world'.[73]

Hardie's socialism, despite its ethical quality, was also 'practical'. 'With the speculative side of Socialism the average man with us has but small concern',

---

64 Howell, *British workers and the ILP*, 147.
65 Benn, *Keir Hardie*, 70.
66 *Ardrossan and Saltcoats Herald*, 8 Sept. 1882, in Howell, *British workers and the ILP*, 142.
67 See Hardie, *From serfdom to socialism*, ch. v.
68 *Young Man*, July 1914, in *Keir Hardie's speeches and writings*, ed. Emrys Hughes, Glasgow n.d., 162.
69 Hardie, *From serfdom to socialism*, p. xii.
70 Benn, *Keir Hardie*, 142. His pamphlets attacking Scottish employers, for example Lord Overtoun, should perhaps have suggested otherwise.
71 Ibid. 164–5.
72 Keir Hardie, *Socialism the hope of Wales*, London n.d. (c. 1908), publ. in both English and Welsh language editions.
73 Benn, *Keir Hardie*, 257.

he wrote, 'it is its common sense which appeals to him'.[74] He used Scottish-ness to defend this view of an essentially British socialism,[75] but usually he spoke more generally of the British in his rejection of the politics of the SDF. He attacked the SDF and the idea of class war as foreign. 'The propaganda by class hatred is not one which can ever take root in this country', he wrote, ' – which I regard as a most fortunate circumstance.'[76] But surprisingly he was attracted by the idea of Marxism; despite his 'Indictment of the class war' he also wrote articles claiming Marx for the ILP.[77] Morgan however puts this into context: 'Hardie claimed to be a follower of Marx. But it was clearly a very British, very respectable Marx that he presented – one quite unrecognisable to Engels. . . . Hardie was creating a Marx . . . in his own image.'[78]

James Ramsay MacDonald, born in 1886 at Lossiemouth, completes the trio of Scots dominant on the ILP executive in its first two decades.[79] In the mid 1880s MacDonald left Scotland, first for Bristol and then London. He joined the Fabian Society and became secretary of the London Committee of the Scottish Home Rule Association. In 1906 he told the *Review of Reviews* that Scott's Waverley novels and Scottish history had 'opened out the great world of national life for me'.[80] He maintained support for home rule for Scotland, calling ideas of home rule all round 'a frank recognition of the national interests of England, Ireland, Scotland, and Wales [which] would . . . tend to preserve that diversity in life which strengthens the imperial stock'.[81]

Having been rejected as Liberal parliamentary candidate for Southampton he stood as an independent labour candidate in 1895 and joined the ILP. His socialism suggested few links with labourism, which he saw as sectional. 'Our movement', he declared, 'is neither a party nor a class movement, but a national one.'[82] This was a sentiment he held throughout his career. He believed socialism should attract all the progressive forces in Britain, and saw the appeal to national interests as the most appropriate way to secure it. It also stemmed from his whole conception of socialism, which he saw as an organic movement of the whole of society which was shaped by habits, laws and customs. Since society was an organism, socialist change had to be gradual.[83]

MacDonald therefore saw any changes in society being determined by

---

74  Hardie, *From serfdom to socialism*, 34
75  See Iain MacLean, *Keir Hardie*, London 1975, 41.
76  *Labour Leader*, 17 Aug. 1901.
77  'An indictment of the class war', *Labour Leader*, 2, 9 Sept. 1904; 'A lame excuse and a libel', ibid. 26 Nov. 1909; 'Karl Marx, the man and his message', ibid. 26 Aug. 1910.
78  Morgan, *Keir Hardie*, 203.
79  Howell points out that Scottish influence in the ILP did not end with the 'big four': *British workers and the ILP*, 133.
80  'The Labour Party and the books that helped to make it', 577.
81  J. Ramsay MacDonald, *Socialism and government*, London 1909, ii. 120.
82  *Southampton Times*, 11 Aug. 1894, in David Marquand, *Ramsay MacDonald*, London 1977, 36–7.
83  J. Ramsay MacDonald, *Socialism*, New York 1970, first publ. 1907, 117.

national circumstances; the party of change had to base itself on these. Hence the failure of the SDF, who 'foreign outlook, phrases and criticisms . . . never quite fitted themselves into British conditions'. He continued:

> With the formation of the Independent Labour Party, Socialism in Great Britain entered upon a new phase. Continental shibboleths and phrases were discarded. The propaganda became British. The history which it used, the modes of thought which it adopted, the political methods which it pursued, the allies which it sought for, were all determined by British conditions.[84]

With Hardie, MacDonald used such beliefs to appeal for the formation of a progressive alliance of radicals and socialists, and the same sentiments had the advantage that they should also appeal to Liberal trade union leaders. In an article published in January 1899, Hardie and MacDonald stressed the bankruptcy of Liberalism and declared socialism as the inspiration of progressive forces in the coming century. 'The Independent Labour Party is in the true line of apostolic succession', they wrote, and went on to emphasise the 'British' character of ILP socialism:

> The spirit of British Socialism, which regards its mission to be the transformation of the whole social fabric . . . has the historical sense predominant, and that is only saying that, like all great movements nurtured under a democratic form of government, it trusts to no sudden changes, it needs no beginning afresh, it works under the conditions it has found, its constructive methods are chiefly adaptation and rearrangement, its ideals are the growths of the past, its work is to proportion and complete the present.[85]

After the formation of the Labour Representation Committee in 1900, in which the ILPers had been able to reject the SDF's motion of a party committed to the principle of class struggle, MacDonald turned once again to the Liberals, securing a secret electoral agreement which enabled the election of twenty-nine Labour MPs in 1906.[86] MacDonald was now prepared to use arguments about the nativeness of his conception against the left wing of his own party, those who were dissatisfied with the labour alliance and the parliamentary party.[87]

MacDonald, with Hardie and Glasier, were all proud of their Scottish origins, but in the last instance they were British national politicians seeking all-British measures. James D. Young has written of the 'English domination of British Socialism', seeing in this a form of 'cultural imperialism', but this tends to ignore the role of Scottish socialists in the forging of an all-British

---

[84] Ibid. 49–50.

[85] J. Keir Hardie and J. R. MacDonald, 'The Independent Labour Party's programme', *Nineteenth Century*, Jan. 1899, 25

[86] Frank Bealey and Henry Pelling, *Labour and politics 1900–1906: a history of the Labour Representation Committee*, London 1958, chs ii, vi.

[87] MacDonald, *Socialism and government*, ii. 12.

socialism.[88] To them, the English past was seen as a place and time that could provide a powerful example of a society in essential harmony. The incursion of industrial capitalism had destroyed this harmony, but the interpretation also offered its own solution. The English past was seen as a site of struggle to gain political liberties, a fight successfully won when the House of Commons had gained pre-eminence and representative government had arrived. On to the end of this struggle could be attached the struggle for social liberty, which socialists saw as their historic task. Again the site of this struggle would be the House of Commons, situated in the English (and British) capital and at the centre of English history. The mainstream of the British left accepted that the advance to socialism would come by means of parliament. The political strategy involved was therefore British. Within this strategy, Hardie could appeal for the votes of his constituents through their Welshness, but when elected he took his seat at Westminster. Hardie stood for Mid-Lanark in 1888, but none of these early leaders were elected for Scottish seats. Hardie in 1892 was elected for West Ham South, in 1900 and subsequently for Merthyr Tydfil; MacDonald was elected in 1906 for Leicester; Glasier stood unsuccessfully in a Birmingham constituency in 1906. This mattered little to them, for they saw themselves as British politicians. All three were involved in the attempt to present the ILP, and later the Labour Party, as the British form of socialism. The British labour movement overwhelmingly accepted the territorial integrity of the British nation, and hence largely used ideas about Britishness, which were dominated by English idioms. Ireland was a different matter altogether, but Shaw, operating in the context of British socialism, himself used ideas of Britishness.

Socialists in the late nineteenth century involved themselves in an attempt to prove the national legitimacy of socialism. While the early attempts had been non-sectarian, because socialism remained largely undefined in Britain, later attempts by the ILP and Fabian Society were aimed at left-wing socialists. A major part of this construction of a national form of socialism had, paradoxically, been undertaken by socialists from national minorities within the multi-national British Isles.

### Britain for the British or the World for the workers?

How then did the legitimisation of socialism through the appeal to national character, history and conditions sit alongside British socialists' professed internationalism? Internationalism was an extremely important element of their socialism. Marx and Engels's call, 'Working men of all countries, unite!', was essential to British socialists: since capitalism was global, the struggle for socialism too had to be global. In Britain there had been a long tradition of

---

88  Young, 'A very English socialism'.

radical internationalism which socialists aimed to continue. Symbolic of this was May Day, held annually from 1890. British socialists often saw May Day not only as a celebration of the international solidarity of labour, but also as a traditional English holiday. Hence Walter Crane's cartoon for May Day 1894 was called 'The workers May-pole'.[89] The SDF too tended to see May Day in such terms. H. W. Lee, the SDF secretary, wrote a pamphlet explaining its significance. He wrote about 'May Day in olden times' and asked: 'Can we look back on those festal doings without regret – nay sorrow – that they are no longer with us? Does it not prove that our ancestors, whatever drawbacks they may have suffered in some respects, were far freer from cramping, monotonous drudgeries than the mass of mankind are today?'[90] He drew attention to the May pole and sports of the fifteenth and sixteenth centuries, which the SDF would be reviving at the 1900 May Day celebrations at Crystal Palace.[91] British labour therefore often fitted their internationalism around an affection for English traditions. They did not believe that the workers had no country, but supported the idea of pluralism when it came to nationality. Hence the *Clarion* for its May Day issue for 1895 commissioned Crane's 'A garland for May Day', which included the slogan 'The cause of labour is the hope of the world', but also 'Merrie England' and 'England shall feed her own people.' The usual celebration for May Day tended to include a 'May fayre'.[92]

For most British socialists, internationalism was something desirable, but it was also something distant.[93] With few exceptions, socialists operated in a largely national (or sometimes imperial) context.[94] This could lead to socialists seeing no further than the English Channel. This was most blatant in Blatchford's socialism. Laurence Thompson points out his parochialism, and comments, 'Blatchford regarded nothing in *Merrie England* as rhetorical; but the least rhetorical thing in it was the title, which meant exactly what it said.'[95] In both *Merrie England* and *Britain for the British*, Blatchford argued for an autarkic economy. Both books contained chapters asking 'Can Britain feed herself?'[96] The answer was a resounding yes. This question was seen as a

---

89 Walter Crane, *Cartoons for the cause: designs and verses for the socialist and labour movement 1886–1896*, London 1976, cartoon ix.
90 H. W. Lee, *The first of May: the international labour day*, London 1900, 4.
91 Ibid. 5, 6.
92 See ch. 2 above.
93 See, for example, Snowden, *The Christ that is to be*, 12.
94 Work on an international level was undertaken by trade unionists, such as Tom Mann, who aimed to create an international dockers' union: Mann, *Memoirs*, ch. ix 'International labour organization, 1886–1898'. Unions such as the Amalgamated Society of Engineers had branches around the world, for example in Canada, South Africa and Australia, but these were less an expression of internationalism than of skilled workers' emigration to the dominions: Logie Barrow, 'White solidarity in 1914', in Samuel, *Patriotism*, i. 275–87.
95 Thompson, *Robert Blatchford*, 110.
96 Blatchford, *Merrie England*, ch. iv; *Britain for the British*, ch. xii. *Merrie England* actually asked 'Can England feed herself?'

selling point for *Merrie England*. 'War with America means famine in a month', declared an advertisement. 'If England could feed herself she would not be at the mercy of any foreign power. How it can be done is clearly shown in *Merrie England*.'[97]

It was to this end that he urged the improvement of agriculture; he saw it as the answer to the 'arithmetical problem' that *Merrie England* sought to solve: 'Given a country and a people, find how the people may make the best of their country and of themselves.' Hence, 'the people should make the best of their own country before attempting to trade with other people's'.[98] Blatchford became contemptuous of internationalism: 'We were out for socialism and nothing but socialism and we were Britons first and socialists next.'[99] Blatchford's slogan 'Britain for the British' was not therefore solely a statement of oppositional Englishness, but an exclusion of others, those who were, unfortunately, not British.

Blatchford was not alone in his desire to see England feed itself. Arthur Hickmott of the SDF called the dependence on foreign food 'a great source of national weakness' necessitating an expansion in the size of the Royal Navy.[100] Leonard Hall of the ILP was emphatic on the subject of foreign trade: 'What blasphemy from the point of view of patriotism! . . . It is to the opening up and development of our *home market* right here in our own country, amongst our own people, that we must turn, and turn quickly if we are to avert that national shipwreck that seems to threaten. . . .'[101]

In 1909 a 'National Labour and Socialist' conference on food supply was held in London, though by this time talk of food supply in time of war was linked to the 'German menace', so that only seven ILP branches sent delegates.[102] But even Hardie, 'more than any other Labour leader of his day . . . associated with the idea of international fraternalism',[103] declared during a by-election in Bradford in 1896 that 'in every county of merry England there was a real demand for British goods without going beyond the seas'. Morgan points out that Hardie's conclusions were usually nationalist, even mercantilist. Outlets for British products could be found in abundance at home; the competition for markets overseas was unnecessary.[104] Howell has argued that the ILP as a whole thought in terms of a national economy, though still as part of a global system.[105]

---

97  For example, *Clarion*, 4 Jan. 1896.
98  Blatchford, *Britain for the British*, 133.
99  Idem, *My eighty years*, London 1931, 199.
100  Arthur Hickmott, *Socialism and agriculture*, London 1897, 3.
101  Leonard Hall, *Land, labour and liberty, or the ABC of reform*, London 1899, 10–11.
102  *National labour and socialist conference on our food supply: official report*, London 1909. Forty-two SDF branches sent delegates.
103  Morgan, *Keir Hardie*, 178.
104  Ibid. 91, 179.
105  Howell, *British workers and the ILP*, 348. For a discussion of the emergence of a left-wing national political economy in the late nineteenth and early twentieth centuries see Frank

The Islington branch of the ILP had recommended a boycott of the *Clarion*, believing it to be printed on foreign paper; Blatchford assured readers that despite British paper being more expensive and of lower quality than foreign paper 'we feel that while so many of our own countrymen are out of work we ought to use British paper'.[106] Indeed from July 1895 the following claim was found on every issue: 'Printed by trade union labour (the eight hour day) and on English-made paper.' At the height of the South African War, J. G. Graves felt confident enough in the patriotism of *Labour Leader* readers to advertise his watches with the slogans, 'BRITISH!' and 'Sound English watch', with a picture of the British lion in front of an oversize watch.[107] Whereas many politicians and commentators saw 'splendid isolation' in terms of foreign policy, and indeed many were becoming alarmed by Britain's isolation, many on the left saw this isolation in terms of a domestic policy, and would continue to see it as splendid.[108]

## The left and immigration

One potential area of conflict between the exclusive aspects of 'Britain for the British' and the radical patriotic idea of liberty came in the area of alien immigration. Underlying the whole subject was the dominance of ideas about race at the end of the nineteenth century. Even opponents of restrictions being placed on immigration discussed the issue in terms of the possible effects on the stock of the English as a 'race'. Glasier was prepared to admit ignorance; he wrote, 'We do not know to what extent, and under what conditions, the intermixing, or even the co-operation of different races is good or bad for the physical health or social progress of nations.'[109] But the framing of the question in these terms suggested that it was a problem of race and nation, and allowed those who sought to prevent immigration on the grounds of its effect on 'the race' a head start in the arguments. Some of these were also on the left. Ben Tillett, as early as 1889, was attacking government policy which allowed 'all the dregs and scum of the continent to make foetid, putrid and congested our already overcrowded slums . . . while . . . men who would have been very good citizens, good patriots, bearing and discharging social responsibility with credit to themselves and honour and glory to their

---

Trentmann, 'Wealth versus welfare: the British left between free trade and national political economy before the First World War', *Historical Research* lxx (1997), 70–98.

[106] *Clarion*, 19 Jan. 1895.

[107] *Labour Leader*, 3 Aug. 1901.

[108] For the complex attitudes towards isolation see Christopher Howard, *Splendid isolation*, London 1967.

[109] *Labour Leader*, 30 Apr. 1904. For the background to the immigration issue see David Feldman, *Englishmen and Jews: social relations and political culture 1840–1914*, New Haven–London 1994.

country . . . are starved and driven to desperation'.[110] In 1893 the *Clarion* saw the problem in terms of immigration combined with emigration. An editorial spoke of the mismanagement of the nation which meant that 'the best of our bone and brain must seek a living in other lands, leaving their places to be filled with the mental and physical dregs of foreign peoples who did not mind serving as slaves and living as beasts'. [111]

The health of the nation was seen as the concern of the left, and in part that health was seen to be determined by the origin of its inhabitants rather than by its social organisation. At the 1903 ILP conference, which rejected a resolution proposing immigration restrictions, Glasier spoke of the decline of the nation, showing concerns not usually associated with the left:

> Our foreign trade is flagging; our internal freedom and external defence are less secure; our military glory is dimmer; our national character, our literature, our science, our inventions are in less repute; our young and virile population is quitting the country as if it were a sinking ship, and we are getting in pauper aliens and rich predatory aliens instead.[112]

The defeated resolution (submitted by Hyde branch) presented the second argument for restriction: 'That in the opinion of this conference it is necessary seeing the effect alien immigration has upon the housing problem and labour market generally, some measure should at once be passed into law restricting same.'[113] This was more normal ground for socialists and trade unionists, but it could be used to disguise blatantly racialist arguments. Tillett, leader of the dockers, amongst whom foreign labour was negligible, argued that indirectly this competition affected his members. Conditions in the docks were made worse, he argued, by the influx of English men 'ousted from their own trades by the foreigners'.[114]

Generally the left were opposed to any restriction of immigration. Support for restriction came mainly from those trades that perceived themselves to be under threat of cheap competition.[115] Trade union representatives giving evidence to the Royal Commission on Alien Immigration in 1903 included three from the National Boot and Shoe Operatives, four from the coster-

110 Jonathan Schneer, *Ben Tillett*, Chicago–London, 1982, 60.
111 *Clarion*, 4 Apr. 1893. See also *Labour Leader*, 9 June 1894, in John A. Garrard, *The English and immigration 1880–1910*, London 1971, 19.
112 J. Bruce Glasier, *Labour: its politics and ideals*, London n.d. [1903], 5. Glasier's position seems to have been to oppose restrictions on immigration because the numbers involved did not warrant it, not because of internationalism: 'The anti-alien sentiment', *Labour Leader*, 30 Apr. 1904.
113 ILP, *Nominations for officers and NAC and resolutions for the agenda, 1903 conference*, London 1903, 13.
114 Garrard, *The English and immigration*, 163–4. Garrard shows (pp. 164–5) that in effect the competition was minimal, even in the boot-making trade only 1 in 25 workers was Jewish, and the proportion was declining, yet it was the boot-makers' union which was at the forefront of resolutions to the TUC aimed at restricting immigration.
115 Colin Holmes, *Anti-Semitism in British society 1876–1939*, London 1979, 21.

mongers' unions and five from clothing unions.[116] Nevertheless, the evidence that Robert Smillie, president of the Scottish Miners' Federation and member of the ILP, gave to the Commission showed that opposition on the grounds that aliens displaced labour became linked with stereotypical views of the newcomers. Smillie said of the 1,320 Lithuanian miners working in Lanarkshire that 'we do not object to him as a foreigner at all'. Yet he could also add that 'they can live a good deal cheaper than our own people', and that 'they are a serious danger [because of language problems] indeed to themselves and our own people'. He was forced to admit that 'we have not at the present time had any single accident caused to a British workman by a foreigner'. The chairman asked him if he wanted aliens excluded until all British miners were working. Smillie hedged around the question, but the chairman pushed the point. In the end Smillie replied that 'we have reason to complain that our people should go idle while the foreigners are underground'.[117]

There were many attacks on restriction. Andreas Scheu of the Socialist League criticised the argument that alien immigration was the cause of low wages. If an aliens bill were passed into law, he wrote:

we may safely assume that poverty in the British Isles will soon be a thing of the past! . . . How easy and well-to-do the East End workman and workwomen would then become, all of a sudden. . . . For observe, that the British workmen never compete with each other, and therefore reduce their wages. . . . To Ireland, the poor foreign Jews have, as yet, not penetrated . . . and hence the standard of the Irish peasants and wage workers is almost an ideal one.[118]

Attacks on immigrants as anarchists increased the left's opposition to restrictive legislation, despite much of the British left's hostility to anarchism. Arnold White, a leader of the anti-immigration lobby, declared that 'the vast majority of these foreign Jews are anarchists and nihilists of the very worst type'. Lord Salisbury had introduced an aliens bill in July 1894 aimed at 'those who live in a perpetual conspiracy of assassination'.[119] The aliens bill of 1904, which the government withdrew, had a clause enabling the exclusion of those of 'notoriously bad character'. Such factors aroused in the left a tradition of English liberty. At the annual conference of the SDF in 1884 it was claimed that 'alone among English organisations, [the Democratic Federation in 1882] came forward to champion one of the most glorious privileges of our country', the right of asylum.[120] This was a view agreed with by Harry Snell, author of an ILP pamphlet on immigration, which can be taken as the ILP 'line' on the issue. He wrote of 'a tradition that has remained unbroken for hundreds of years; that has given us material prosperity and

116 *Royal Commission on Alien Immigration 1903 minutes of evidence*, Cd. 1742.
117 Ibid. 842–5. I owe these points to Harriet Jones.
118 *Commonweal*, 19 May 1888, in Garrard, *The English and immigration*, 186.
119 Ibid. 26, 32.
120 *Justice*, 9 Aug. 1884. See also ibid. 31 Jan., 21 Mar. 1885, and *Fabian News*, Mar. 1903.

moral strength'. Snell argued that not only would the 'notoriously bad character' clause have prevented men such as Marx, Engels, Mazzini, Stepniak
and Kropotkin from gaining entry to England, but also that Jesus was of notoriously bad character to the authorities of Jerusalem. 'If England has not lost
its spirit and forgotten its history', he continued, 'it will not allow an international police conspiracy to decide who shall be its guests.'[121] All four LRC
MPs voted against the 1905 aliens bill (which was passed), Hardie asking the
Commons about refugees from tsarist Russia, 'Are we to say to these poor
creatures that England of all lands under the sun is no resting place for them
from the conditions now prevailing in their own country?'[122]

The opposition to restrictive legislation was in large measure framed inside
ideas and language of an oppositional Englishness. Garrard concludes that
'with few notable exceptions, and with a greater or lesser degree of enthusiasm and interest, spokesmen for all the main socialist movements in Britain
condemned aliens legislation as reactionary, unbrotherly, inhuman, unde-
manded and unnecessary'.[123] The general feeling of both socialists and trade
unionists was summed up by the LRC in 1905: 'Proposals like the aliens bill
[were] misleading and calculated to divert attention from the real cause of
evil, namely the existence of monopoly and the burdens which the non-
producing sections place on the industrial classes.'[124] Garrard's conclusion
that 'the left wing finds itself defending the status quo against a Conservative
party willing and able to pose as the champion of the ordinary British
voter',[125] gives only half the story, for the defence that the left was inclined to
adopt was based less on socialist internationalism than on traditional ideas of
English tolerance and liberty. Hence socialists opposed to immigration
restrictions proudly argued that it was they who stood for English traditions,
while those holding anti-alien sentiments were being un-English.

There was an ambiguity in the internationalism of the British left. May
Day was celebrated as an international festival, but within the context of recognising it also as a celebration of Englishness. The Marxist axiom that 'workers have no country' was rejected in favour of a view of the plurality of
national identities. This did not always allow that each nationality was of
equal worth. J. R. Clynes recalled his attendance at the International congress in Zurich in 1893: 'It was difficult to co-ordinate the statements of the
stolid British delegates, abhorring armed violence, as much of the mock hero-
ics, with the inflammatory verbal orgies of the representatives of certain of
the Latin and Slavonic races.'[126] British delegates to such conferences, while

121 Harry Snell, *The foreigner in England: an examination of the problem of alien immigration*,
London n.d. [1904], 3, 6, 7. See also verse by H. Lazenby in *Labour Leader*, 13 Jan. 1905.
122 Morgan, *Keir Hardie*, 179–80.
123 Garrard, *The English and immigration*, 182.
124 Philip Poirier, *The advent of the Labour Party*, London 1958, 234.
125 Garrard, *The English and immigration*, 202. He compares the left's attitude at the turn of
the century with that of the 1960s.
126 J. R. Clynes, *Memoirs 1869–1924*, London 1937, 72.

being attracted emotionally to the international solidarity of labour, seemed determined to stress their differences from their continental comrades. To be English, or British, remained special. Much of the left approached strategies for socialism, economics and immigration in terms of their perceptions of national identity. In 1899 the Boer War was to bring such perceptions held by the left into conflict with those of a nation at war.

# 4

# The Left, England and an Imperial War

At the end of the nineteenth century Britain was the major imperialist power in the world. J. A. Hobson calculated that from 1870 to the end of the century, Britain had added 4,754,000 square miles and a population of 88 million to its empire.[1] This growth coincided with the emergence of socialist and independent labour politics in Britain. Despite a preoccupation with domestic affairs, the left had no option but to respond. The left's initial reaction was condemnation. Robert Blatchford, not well known for his anti-imperialism in later years, wrote in 1892 that while the English people had 'sound heads and hearts' and 'often meant well', nevertheless 'their history is a long roll of blunder and plunder and slaughter and oppression'.[2] *Labour Leader* on 2 February 1899 printed a verse by 'Backyard Stripling', entitled 'Progress and plunder', sarcastically celebrating the empire thus:

> O! we are the British nation, and our heaven-appointed station
> Is to make our influence felt in every clime.
> So we send our Christian traders, civilising charted raiders,
> Who keep spreading rum and gospel all the time . . .

Opposition to empire was therefore based on an awareness of British national identity in imperialism. Bernard Shaw had brought out this aspect in 'The man of destiny'. 'As the great champion of freedom and national independence, he annexes half the world, and calls it Colonization', he commented on the Englishman.[3] This chapter examines the responses to the South African War of 1899–1902, as the longest and most costly imperial military engagement between the emergence of socialism in the 1880s and the First World War. While most of the left opposed the war, they did so from positions of radical patriotism, using an oppositional notion of Englishness. Discussion of the war therefore provides an opportunity to examine the left's ideas about patriotism and national identity, from the minority of socialists who supported the British war effort on the one hand, to the minority who rejected all patriotism in favour of working-class internationalism, on the other.

---

1  J. A. Hobson, *Imperialism: a study*, London 1902, 18.
2  *Clarion*, 21 May 1892.
3  Bernard Shaw, *Plays pleasant*, Harmondsworth 1946, 225.

## Blatchford and England

Many readers of the *Clarion* felt shocked and betrayed by Blatchford's announcement on the outbreak of the war that he would be supporting the British war effort. Southampton SDF and Paisley ILP passed motions of censure upon him; in Liverpool a black cross was painted across his portrait.[4] H. Russell Smart, a member of the ILP NAC, 'confess[ed] to having read the utterances of Nunquam with distress and dismay'.[5]

Blatchford's reasoning was as follows: 'Well, my friends, I am a Socialist, and a lover of peace', he wrote,

> but I am also an Englishman. I love my fellow men of all nations . . . but I love England more than any other country. Also I am an old soldier, and I love Tommy Atkins. . . . England's enemies are my enemies. I am an Englishman. That is the point I wish to make clear. I am not a jingo, I am opposed to war. I do not approve of this present war. But I cannot go with those Socialists whose sympathies are with the enemy. My whole heart is with the British troops. . . . I am for peace and for international brotherhood. But when England is at war I'm English. I have no politics and no party. I am English.[6]

Blatchford had been one of the most clear advocates of oppositional Englishness; he was, he said, a socialist, an internationalist, an opponent of war, but he could not completely reconcile these positions with being English when England was at war. He denied being a jingo, he had refused to stand for 'Rule Britannia' at a music hall, but now, he told his readers, 'my daughter has orders to play "Rule Britannia" every night while the war lasts'.[7]

*Clarion* readers had reason to be shocked, for, while he had not been consistently anti-imperialist, Blatchford had opposed imperial expansion, often in strong terms. As late as June 1899 he had declared that 'Our Empire was built on blood, pillage, and chicanery – mixed with some cant about the word of God. I want none of it.'[8] He had asked 'What is patriotism?' and replied

> The patriot will answer 'love of country'. But we Socialists feel that such an answer is not true. The Socialist loves his country, and loves his countrymen and countrywomen; yet the Socialist will not write himself a patriot [because that] means also the desire to exalt our own country above all others, to enhance the glory or extend the power of Britain at the expense of all the other nations of the earth. If patriotism really meant true love of our native land, then I should claim that Socialists are patriots, and I should go further and claim Socialists are the only true patriots since they alone are striving for

4   *Clarion*, 18 Nov. 1899.
5   *ILP News*, Nov. 1899. Nunquam was Blatchford's pen-name.
6   *Clarion*, 21 Oct. 1899.
7   Ibid.
8   Ibid. 3 June 1899.

the real honour and the real welfare and the real advancement of their nation.[9]

His patriotism before the war had been antagonistic to the extension of empire; it had been inward-looking. The national interest could only be served within England's borders. He had seen this as compatible with internationalism, which was nobler than patriotism since it was not so narrow.[10] But Blatchford's position on the outbreak of the Boer War was not a complete reversal of his pre-war stance. He had argued that while it was better not to have an empire to start with, the empire was a reality and that had to be faced. 'We never ought to have conquered India', he wrote,

> Very well. But we *did* conquer it, and we must govern and defend it, or we must give it up. And if we are to give it up, to whom is it to be given, and *when*, and *how*? And in the meantime what? . . . . For my part, I am a sincere advocate of peace, and an unwavering opponent of war. And, being what I am, I am in favour of keeping a large and efficient fleet, of strengthening the defences of our empire, and of making our army as fit as science and discipline can make it.[11]

Blatchford saw in the Boer War a threat to the empire. He therefore supported Britain. He had also served in the army for six years and, as his biographer has pointed out, devoted seventy-six pages of his autobiography to his army years, and only sixteen pages to the period 1893 to 1910.[12] Again and again he wrote about his old regiment, the 103rd Fusiliers or 'Ramchunders'. When war broke out 'the religion of *esprit de corps*' returned to him and he could not side with the Boers against men he did not know but considered friends.[13] This combined with his almost total lack of consistent socialist theory. Neither did he have the Liberal Little England tradition to fall back upon. Blatchford had been a proponent of the 'fourth clause', stating that where no socialist or labour candidate stood in an election ILPers should abstain, which was a response to the Lancashire working class's rejection of Liberalism.[14] One further ingredient went into the recipe for Blatchford's support for the war. The failure of the ILP at the 1895 elections had resulted in much disillusionment among British socialists. Blatchford was more deeply affected than most, having backed the abortive plans for unity between the SDF and ILP. Thompson comments that Blatchford's 'former idols, Thoreau, Ruskin, Whitman, Carpenter, went toppling . . . so he came to rest more and more upon the old, sure things: Sally [his wife], the family, home, England,

9   Ibid. 27 May 1899.
10  Ibid.
11  Ibid. 4 Feb. 1899.
12  Thompson, *Robert Blatchford*, 9.
13  Blatchford, *My eighty years*, 37.
14  See Pelling, *Origins of the Labour party*, 97, 121, and Howell, *British workers and the ILP*, ch. ix.

the English-speaking peoples of the Empire. They were not perfect. But they existed. And where could one see, smell, touch the united workers of the world, the brotherhood of man?'[15]

Blatchford's socialism had become increasingly national from the late 1890s. He came to believe that the empire was necessary for the achievement of socialism in England.[16] He argued that British workers had much to lose if the empire fell: liberty, free speech, a free press and free education. To justify his support for imperialism he noted the 'fact that England is universally admitted to be the best colonising power the world has known, and the gentlest and wisest ruler over subject races'.[17] In 1899 Blatchford merged his radical patriotism with a vision of empire, and it was to be this imperial England and Englishness that he urged Britons to defend.

## Fabianism and empire

Blatchford later tried to reconcile his support for an imperialist war with socialism by denying the two were connected. The war was 'a matter of international politics and had nothing to do with Socialism'.[18] Most of the Fabian Society felt it wise to say the same. Bernard Shaw urged Edward Pease, the Society's secretary, 'Don't let us, after all these years, split the Society by declaring ourselves on a non-socialist point of policy.'[19] The executive shared his view.[20] Pease, in his role as historian of the Society, correctly stated that 'in this matter the left and right wings of the Fabians joined hands in opposition to the centre'.[21] Those with either socialist or Liberal leanings opposed the war and rejected the Society's silence, since it suggested acquiescence in a belligerent imperialism.[22]

S. G. Hobson's motion opposing the war at the Society's meeting of 8 December 1899 was put in terms of a mixture of socialism and radical patriotism. It proposed that the Society 'formally dissociates itself from the imperialism of capitalism and vainglorious nationalism' because 'the phase of imperialist passion that has over-run this country of recent years . . . has debased the conscience and lowered the democratic spirit of the English people'.[23] The outcome of the subsequent debate was that the members of the

---

15 Thompson, *Robert Blatchford*, 146–7.
16 Logie Barrow, 'The socialism of Robert Blatchford and the *Clarion* 1889–1918', unpubl. PhD diss, London 1975, 392, 394.
17 *Clarion*, 13 July 1901.
18 Blatchford, *My eighty years*, 200.
19 Michael Holroyd, *Bernard Shaw*, II: *1898–1918 the pursuit of power*, London 1989, 36.
20 See *Fabian News*, Feb. 1900.
21 Pease, *History of the Fabian Society*, 129.
22 For the chronology of the debate and referendum see ibid. 129–31, and *Fabian News*, Dec. 1899–Mar. 1900.
23 *Fabian News*, Dec. 1900.

Society voted narrowly (by 259 to 217 votes) not to make a pronouncement on the war. About fifteen members then resigned, including such prominent names as Ramsay MacDonald, J. Frederick Green (both on the executive committee), George Barnes and Pete Curran (future Labour MPs), Walter Crane, H. S. Salt, Mrs MacDonald and Mrs Pankhurst. Those remaining joked that this was 'the Boer trek'.[24]

The Fabian Society, having refused to make a pronouncement on the war, then sought to formulate its views on imperialism; Bernard Shaw drafted a 100-page pamphlet entitled *Fabianism and the empire*. It would appear at first that it was a rejection of British liberal nationalism and non-interference, which it condemned with the word most anathema to Fabianism as 'individualistic'.[25] It justified imperialism in thoroughly Fabian terms. It argued that a nation no more had the right to do what it wanted with its territory than a landlord had the right to do what he pleased. Both must take into account the interests of the rest of the world.[26] Of course, 'theoretically', the world's resources should be 'inter-nationalized', it declared, 'but until the Federation of the World becomes an accomplished fact, we must accept the most responsible Imperial federations available as a substitute for it'.[27] The Fabians proclaimed themselves the true internationalists, and the socialist opponents of the war 'ultra-nationalist, ultra Gladstonian, [and] old Liberal to the fingertips'.[28]

A. M. McBriar says of the Fabian argument that 'they did not believe England's [civilisation] was so much higher than that of her other Western neighbours – France, Germany, Italy, or America. . . . The Fabian's standard of "higher civilization" was a European standard.'[29] However, Webb's article of 1901 courting the Liberal Imperialists urged them to address 'a burning feeling of shame at the "failure" of England' and called for national, not European, efficiency and 'virility in government – virility in South Africa [and] virility in our relations with the rest of the world'.[30] Lenin, another socialist forced to examine the question of nationalism from the point of view of a socialist in an imperial nation, in a polemic against Russian socialists who rejected Poland's right to self-determination on the grounds of proletarian internationalism, accused them of echoing bourgeois chauvinism. The point was, he wrote, that 'in the capitalist state, repudiation of the right of self-determination, i.e., the right of nations to secede, means nothing more than

24 Beatrice Webb, *Our partnership*, ed. B. Drake and M. I. Cole, Cambridge 1975, 193.
25 *Fabianism and the empire: a manifesto by the Fabian Society*, London 1901, 2–3. For membership involvement in discussing Shaw's drafts see Pease, *History of the Fabian Society*, 134.
26 *Fabianism and empire*, 44–5.
27 Ibid. 24.
28 Sidney Webb, 'Lord Rosebery's escape from Houndsditch', *Nineteenth Century* l (Sept. 1901), 374.
29 A. M. McBriar, *Fabian socialism and English politics 1884–1918*, London 1962, 128–31.
30 Webb, 'Lord Rosebery's escape', 374–5, 385.

the defence of the privileges of the dominant nation'.[31] This applies to the Fabian Society; in the name of socialist internationalism, they supported British imperialism.

An extreme example of this appears in a pamphlet by J. Ernest Jones called *The case for progressive imperialism*.[32] Jones subtitled his name as 'Fabian and ILP'.[33] He supported the idea of a world-state. He rejected as individualism under other names: 'Every country speaking its own language, nationalism, national and racial sentiment, national patriotism, national freedom, national non-intervention or non-interference, insular treatment of world questions, the claim of nationality and national independence.'[34] Jones did not, however, reject English nationalism. He continued: 'It must here be shown the foolishness and futility of disloyalty to England and the English Empire. Why is it foolish? Because English civilisation and liberty, in spite of all its faults, is the best and widest and most tolerant in the world.'[35] He directed his deepest criticism at the Irish, whom he accused of Little Englandism, their nationalism being caused by their audacity in having a different religion from England and a 'useless' language.[36] The world, he declared, needed but one language; opposition to 'the stamping out of languages' would only be 'sentiment'.[37] He concluded that annexing other countries was not stealing if it was for those countries', and the world's, benefit.[38] Jones was an extreme proponent of internationalisation through British imperialism, and it was through the acceptance of many of the hegemonic ideas of imperialism, framed in language expressing the intention to civilise and take liberty to the world, that he was enabled to deny national feelings whilst in fact espousing them.

### Patriotic opposition to the war

Liberal opponents of the war certainly did not reject ideas of patriotism. Unionists in the 1900 general election urged voters to 'have nothing to do with such traitors to their countrymen fighting for Britain, but vote for the Unionist candidate!' and declared that every vote for a non-Unionist was a Boer bullet fired at British soldiers.[39] Liberal opponents of the war, however, claimed a higher patriotism. At a peace meeting some months before the war

---

31 Lenin, *Selected works in three volumes*, i. 590.
32 J. Ernest Jones, *The case for progressive imperialism*, 2nd edn, London, 1902.
33 *ILP News*, Feb. 1903, repudiated the pamphlet.
34 Jones, *Progressive imperialism*, 3.
35 Ibid. 6.
36 Ibid. 6, 8, 9. He also accused the ILP of having been 'captured' by the Irish, 7.
37 Ibid. 14.
38 Ibid. 20.
39 John S. Galbraith, 'The pamphlet campaign on the Boer War', *JMH* xxiv (1952), 1–16; Arthur Davey, *The British pro-Boers 1877–1902*, Cape Town 1978, 56

started, George W. E. Russell, of the Transvaal Committee, condemned 'The advocates of war [who] are prostituting the sacred names of freedom and justice to glorify money-getting and justify bloodshed.' He denied such people were patriots, claiming instead that 'We are the true and real patriots' since 'we stand for the fair fame of Christian England amongst the civilized nations of the world'.[40] Arthur Davey says of the pro-Boers that 'In their own elevated view they were patriots who served their country's best interests just as Burke and Chatham had done in the 18th century when they had warned against the alienation of the American colonists.'[41]

Socialists followed similar thinking. This was not novel for socialists in 1899. Elijah Copland, president of the Newcastle branch of the Democratic Federation, had declared fifteen years previously that:

> War in the defence of the liberties of a people, or in opposition to acts of aggression, whether of foreign or native foes, is justifiable – nay, it is noble, and calculated to develop some of the grandest traits in the human character – self-sacrifice, devotion, bravery, endurance, patriotism. But when have we, in England, had such a struggle? Our latter-day escapades have been onslaughts on weak and so called barbarous nations.[42]

Again and again, socialist opponents of the war took up this radical patriotic theme. As tension rose before the war, Smart in *ILP News* set the tone: 'the infamous conduct of the Government in its negotiations with the Transvaal must be a cause of rage and humiliation to every honest patriot'. And what should ILPers do? 'It concerns the honour of every self-respecting lover of his country to protest with all the power that is in him against the atrocious crime which we are apparently about to commit.'[43] The ILP NAC called the war one 'of aggression . . . especially humiliating to the democratic instincts of this country'. The following year, Glasier as conference chairman spoke of the ILP as defenders of the national honour who 'had kept inviolable the name of their native land . . . [while the government] had thrown away their good name, and their reputation for fair play and for freedom'.[44] From the nature of the sources of these utterances, it can be suggested that the official ILP policy on the war was one of radical patriotism, rather than socialism.

The ILP were not alone in using such arguments against the war. Anti-war arguments in the *Clarion* were framed in such terms.[45] Neither were the Marxist SDF immune from such utterances. F. Reginald Statham believed that 'the British Empire [had] been built up on a foundation of justice and

---

[40] *The pro-Boers: the anatomy of an anti war movement*, ed. Stephen Koss, Chicago–London 1973, 8. See also pp. xxvii–xxviii, 8, 33, 66, 94, 130.

[41] Davey, *The British pro-Boers*, 11. See also A. J. P. Taylor, *The trouble makers: dissent over foreign policy 1792–1939*, Harmondsworth 1985, 109.

[42] Elijah Copland, *Guarantees against unlawful war*, Newcastle-upon-Tyne 1884, 4.

[43] *ILP News*, Sept. 1899. See also 'Marxian', *Labour Leader*, 21 Oct. 1899.

[44] ILP, *Conference reports*, 1900, 3; 1901, 28.

[45] See, for example, *Clarion*, 13 Jan. 1900.

constitutional liberty, and we can only endanger the Empire by flying in the face of these principles'.[46] A leader in *Justice* by John Ellam, a year into the war and after the general election results, gave a sigh of despair: 'Alas! England today is not the England of our forefathers. Neither are the men of England of the same type as those who won for her a proud pre-eminence among the nations as the land of freedom and of staunch independent manhood.'[47]

The socialist pro-Boers were encouraged in their national rather than class assessment of the war by two factors. One was an idealised and mythical conception of the Boer agrarian lifestyle. The other was the proposition that the war was being fought not so much for England, as for cosmopolitan (that is, Jewish) financiers. Many socialists looked wistfully at the rural life of the Boer farmer, seeing in it both the English past before capitalism and the vision of an English future after capitalism. Hardie is best known for entertaining this sentimental view of the Boers:

> As a pastoral people the Boers doubtless have all the failings of the fine qualities which pertain to that mode of life; but whatever these failings may have been they are virtues compared to the turbid pollution and refined cruelty which is inseparable from the operations of capitalism. As socialists, our sympathies are bound to be with the Boers. Their republican form of government bespeaks freedom, and is thus hateful to tyrants, whilst their methods of production are much nearer our ideal than any form of exploitation for profit.[48]

The Boers, it was believed, had the virtues most admired by British socialists. They were fighting heroically for freedom and national independence. Hence John Lister urged the Boers to fight for the 'sturdy democratic rule of manly folk . . ./ Stand for right and freedom./ Stem the raid for gold!'[49] Arthur Hickmott gave much the same message, 'Patriots, young and old/ Forward for hearth and home!/ Down with "the tools of gold".'[50]

What made these supposed virtues of the Boers so important to British socialists was that they believed them to be lost English virtues. Willie Wright called the Boers 'a liberty-loving people like the British', and Hardie advised his readers to 'try to imagine what the free yeomen of England were 200 years ago, and you have some idea of Boer life'.[51] The virtue of the Boers, then, was that they were a pre-industrial, agrarian (and, needless to say, a white) people, far enough away to be idealised, as British socialists had idealised the English past. The Boers were unconsciously seen as fighting by proxy the war against capitalism that in England had been lost. Hardie argued that

---

[46] F. Reginald Statham, 'South Africa in the past and future', *Social-Democrat*, Feb. 1900.
[47] *Justice*, 27 Oct. 1900.
[48] *Labour Leader*, 6 Jan 1900. See also *ILP News*, Nov. 1899, Jan 1900; *Hansard*, 4th ser. lxxxviii. 7. Dec. 1900, 300–3 (Hardie), and ILP, *Conference report*, 1901, 3.
[49] *Labour Leader*, 14 Oct. 1899.
[50] *Justice*, 7 Apr. 1900.
[51] *Labour Leader*, 18 Nov. 1899; 17 Mar. 1900. See also Reginald Statham, *The South African crisis: the truth about the Transvaal*, London n.d., 5.

THE LEFT, ENGLAND AND AN IMPERIAL WAR

the Boers did not arm themselves to fight the British but to protect themselves from the 'devilish designs of Rhodes and Co'. They fought British troops not because they were British, but because they represented capitalism.[52] In this way, the issues at stake in the war were confused. The capitalism threatening the Boer republics may have been British, but that did not mean it represented the true nation.

Such arguments were reinforced by antisemitism. Hyndman was perhaps the most infamous antisemite among early socialists, his biographer maintaining that 'even at a time when anti-Semitism was not uncommon in left-wing political circles, Hyndman gave much offence'.[53] One of his lecture titles was 'The Four Internationals: the Jews, the Catholics, the monarchs, the socialists', with only the last-named being spoken of in a good light. In this list, 'the Jews' and capitalists were synonymous.[54] Hyndman's first written comment on the war described it as 'The Jew's war on the Transvaal' and blamed the 'Jew-jingo press' and the British ruling class run by 'their masters, the capitalist Jews'.[55]

The ILP seemed determined to outdo Hyndman in antisemitism.[56] ILP News of October 1899 thought it 'worth noting, by-the-bye, that the most prominent of the Jingo organs are owned and financed largely by stalwart patriots whose names have curiously foreign terminations and whose features seem to indicate they are of the circumcision'.[57] Labour Leader mocked such foreign 'patriots', printing the following alleged advertisement:

> Moses Cohen
> Patriotic Grocer
> Buy our Union Jack Safety Matches
> (made in Sweden)
> Sparkling Lump. Khaki Brand
> (pure German beet)
> 'Old England' Flour
> (finest American)
> Imperial Stove Polish
> (Swiss manufacture)[58]

Such outbursts were given a measure of respectability by the publication of J. A. Hobson's The war in South Africa: its causes and effects which seemed to back the antisemitism with empirical evidence. Hobson's thesis on

---

52 Labour Leader, 17 Mar. 1900.
53 Tsuzuki, Hyndman and British socialism, 128.
54 Justice, 10 Mar. 1900.
55 Ibid. 7 Oct. 1899, in Bill Baker, The Social Democratic Federation and the Boer War, London 1974, 5–6.
56 This is a point that Colin Holmes underestimates. In Anti-Semitism and British society, the ILP received three lines of attention, while Hyndman gets nearly a whole page (pp. 68, 69).
57 Labour Leader, 14 Oct. 1899.
58 Ibid. 19 May 1900. See also 8 Feb. 1902, 14 Dec. 1901.

imperialism was that a surplus of capital in Britain caused by under-consumption led to investors looking elsewhere for more profitable invest-ment, and he included a sub-plot within this thesis when it came to discuss-ing South Africa:

> We are fighting in order to place a small international oligarchy of mine-owners and speculators in power in Pretoria. Englishmen will surely do well to recognise that the economic and political destinies of South Africa are, and seem likely to remain, in the hands of men most of whom are foreigners by ori-gin, whose trade is finance, and whose trade interests are not chiefly British.[59]

Peter Clarke's interpretation of *The war in South Africa* suggests that 'Hobson wanted to confute twice over the patriotic claim that the interests at stake were "national": once by showing that they were sectional, and again by showing that they were cosmopolitan.'[60] The majority of the British left fol-lowed Hobson down this path, combining an element of class interpretation of the war with a left-wing, though antisemitic, nationalism, which allowed them to make claims that 'the man who is pro-Boer is the true patriot and the best friend of England'.[61] This also meant that socialists could brand those who supported the war as somehow un-English, or at least as acting in a man-ner harmful to England as a nation.

The left found the jingo mobs especially shocking, seeing them as an out-burst of irrationality.[62] Hyndman's second volume of autobiography, pub-lished ten years after the end of the Boer War, described vividly his impression of the scenes in London:

> The display of hysterical and even maniacal joy and exuberance on Mafeking night in London surpassed in unseemly indecency anything I could have imag-ined. The whole manifestation spoke of a people in decay. . . . It was nothing short of an orgy. I saw myself girls of respectable appearance, and ordinarily, no doubt, of modest demeanour, carrying on with men whom they did not know after a fashion that women of the loosest life would have hesitated to adopt. This, too, early in the day and in the open street.[63]

*Justice* at least twice described 'mafficking' as 'bestial',[64] and the SDF were not alone in looking with disgust at such scenes. Glasier noted in his diary, 'Am utterly dismayed at this fearful exhibition of rowdyism and intolerance. All our civilization seems to fall away. . . . Alas, the people seem to have gone back. The *Daily Mail* and the other great capitalist and Jewish papers have

[59] J. A. Hobson, *The war in South Africa*, London 1900, 197. For positive reviews see *Clar-ion*, 17 Mar. 1900, and *Justice*, 24 Mar. 1900.
[60] Peter Clarke, *Liberals and social democrats*, London 1978, 92. See also Feldman, *English-men and Jews*, 265–6.
[61] Keir Hardie in *Labour Leader*, 17 Mar. 1900.
[62] Taylor, 'Patriotism, history and the left'.
[63] H. M. Hyndman, *Further reminiscences*, London 1912, 172.
[64] *Justice*, 2, 30 June 1900.

excited madness among them.'[65] It is likely that he played a part as chairman in the ILP conference resolution of 1901 that declared

> That the displays of rowdyism and worse which were observable in the streets and public places after the relief of Mafeking . . . and on other occasions merit the serious attention of all who have the welfare of the nation at heart, as they seem to betoken a loss of dignity and a degeneration of the character of the race. That this conference regrets this degeneration, considering that the power to take joy and grief calmly indicated the innate stubbornness and self-control of the people and that these are among the greatest attributes of a great nation.[66]

The left responded to such irrationality not by dropping patriotism but by discussing it in terms of a stronger national identity that could be revived. And as the war dragged on, such patriotic exuberance became much less common, allowing the left to regain its confidence. *Justice* and *Labour Leader* respectively reported with relief the 'Decay of the mafficking spirit' and the absence of 'Police and patriots' from an anti-war meeting in mid 901, and the subsequent declining popularity of the Unionist government.[67]

The formation of a policy of opposition to the war on the basis of a supposed British standard of conduct meant that opposition was not necessarily based on anti-imperialism, but on opposition to imperialism as it was practised. This allowed Ramsay MacDonald to frame an imperial policy for Labour based on many of the hegemonic imperial assumptions. MacDonald did not reject imperialism, seeing in it something virtuous. '[T]he underlying spirit of imperialism', he argued, was 'a frank acceptance of national duty exercised beyond the nation's political frontiers.' In this sense 'the spirit of imperialism cannot be condemned'. What he objected to was was the 'prostituting' of such 'high purposes'.[68]

With his organicist conception of history and his deep dislike of sudden change, MacDonald was also inclined to argue that the present was so much the prisoner of the past that there was no point at all in trying to escape:

> The question of Empire cannot be decided on first principles, so far as this country is concerned. We have a history, and it is an imperial one. . . . [We cannot] re-write history, to undo evil. . . . We have gone so far in our imperial history that we can hardly look back. We can be guided in our future work; we cannot re-cut and re-carve our past.[69]

[65] Diary, 13 Mar. 1900, Glasier papers, GP/2/1/7. See also diary, 10, 14, 19 Mar. 1900.
[66] ILP, *Conference report*, 1901, 43.
[67] *Justice*, 25 May 1901; *Labour Leader*, 29 June 1901.
[68] J. Ramsay MacDonald, 'The propaganda of civilisation', *International Journal of Ethics*, July 1901, in Bernard Porter, *Critics of empire: British radical attitudes to colonialism in Africa 1895–1914*, London 1968, 185–6.
[69] *Ethical World*, 12 Nov. 1898, in ibid. 189.

But then he did not believe that Britain's past had been any obstacle to his politics. He believed Britain's rulers had been largely liberal in the past with a love of liberty and tolerance. This was the national spirit and it was also the justification for Britain's imperial role.[70] He rejected the break-up of the empire, arguing that it would lead to a greater militarism, for if Britain's army and navy were to be reduced in size,

> the burden which would be shifted from our backs would be imposed upon others, and I think we are entitled to claim that an armed Britain is as unlikely to disturb the peace of the world as any other military power. . . . The British Empire under democratic custodianship can be a powerful element in the maintenance of peace and the promotion of the international spirit.[71]

But MacDonald did want to see reform of the empire. The flagship of his proposed policy was the 'Imperial Standard', and this was very much a British standard, for

> when the expression 'British' is used in civil matters it implies something more than a mere description of racial or national origin. 'British' justice, 'British' honour, 'British' administration, carry to our minds certain qualities of justice, honour, and administration, and our imperial policy has always been commended to our people at home – whenever they troubled their heads about it – on these moral or qualitative grounds. . . . Now the task of the democratic parties of the Empire is to establish guarantees that this moral quality will be preserved untainted.[72]

This standard was to involve no slavery, untainted administration of justice, fair trials, law resting on consent – in short 'the inheritance which past experience has taught the present generation of Britons to cherish'.[73] MacDonald's vision of empire was a socialist version of Greater Britain.

The Imperial Standard effectively became Labour Party policy; it was not anti-imperialism but an alternative imperialism, framed by MacDonald and based on assumptions, if not of British superiority then at least of a British genius for government and administration that was of benefit to the colonised. In *ILP News* in January 1898, MacDonald had argued against further extensions of the empire, but had hoped that 'the most democratic country in the world' would have the most influence. He made clear elsewhere which country he believed this to be, and other socialists shared his view. 'Marxian', after condemning jingoism in a column entitled 'inebriated London', summed up thus:

---

[70] J. Ramsay MacDonald, *Labour and the empire*, Hassocks 1974, first publ. 1907, 5.
[71] Ibid. 36–7.
[72] Ibid. 49.
[73] Ibid. 50.

Yet one cannot altogether disown the country of one's language and birth, simply because it happens to be inhabited by fools under deferred sentences of death. Despite my colder reason, despite my large admixture of Welsh blood, I love the name and fame of England. If one nation must lead, let England lead the light and freedom and justice of the newer days. And so, in my English prejudice, I cannot wish South Africa lost to England.[74]

## Marxists and patriotism

It has been shown that while the ILP was united in opposition to the Boer War, the *Clarion* group and the Fabian Society were divided. The SDF were also subject to divisions, though these emanated from a left group which stood in opposition to all patriotism.

Hyndman brought ideas with him into socialism about the nature of Englishness and imperialism. *England for all* had argued for internationalism, but took a route based on race rather than class. Thus, he urged

> Surely those who are in favour of a unity of all peoples . . . cannot fail ere long to understand that the first step towards this great end must be a closer and yet closer union of peoples of the same race, language and political traditions, working together for the good of all portions of that noble federation.[75]

Hence, as the Fabians and elements in the ILP were to do, Hyndman saw a progressive role for the British in world politics. He based his ideas on a belief in the nature of the English. 'We are, or might be', Hyndman wrote, 'the leaders and protectors of freedom, independence, and true liberty in Europe.'[76] But, as Eric Hobsbawm has warned, Hyndman was not the SDF.[77] His views on race, nation and imperialism were challenged from within the SDF again and again. Thus, in 1884, as the nation discussed General Gordon in the Sudan, *Justice* declared that 'right or wrong, Gordon went to Khartoum as the envoy of the people of England, and we ought to get him out of his dangerous mission if we can'. An editorial, while condemning the sending of troops to begin with, attacked the Liberal government for the abandonment of Gordon.[78] Ernest Belfort Bax wrote a letter condemning such support for imperialism, and calling Gordon 'neither more nor less than a traitor'.[79] But such minor attacks were not enough to divert Hyndman. In September, he wrote of England's duty:

---

[74] *Labour Leader*, 29 Sept. 1900.
[75] Hyndman, *England for all*, 166.
[76] Ibid. 170–1.
[77] 'Hyndman and the SDF', in E. J. Hobsbawm, *Labouring men: studies in the history of labour*, London 1968, 233–4.
[78] *Justice*, 26 Apr., 10 May 1884.
[79] Ibid. 24 May 1884.

It is, we hold the duty of a Democratic England, having cleared herself of greed and oppression, at home and abroad, to stand before the world as the champion of the liberties of Europe. . . . Such an opportunity of international usefulness and greatness unalloyed with any mean ideas of national 'glory' lies before us in the immediate future.[80]

Hyndman's attitude to the empire played a part in the split at the end of 1884 that led to the formation of the Socialist League, which once again left Hyndman in control of the SDF. He celebrated by reprinting the final passage of *England for all* envisaging England's leading role in *Justice* under the title 'The socialist's patriotism', and he editorialised on the 'Death of a hero', as the news of Gordon's demise had reached Britain: he was, *Justice* moralised, 'butchered by the ferocious hordes of the Mahdi'.[81]

The capture of the Socialist League by anarchists in the late 1880s saw the return of the anti-imperialists to the SDF, and with rising imperial tensions the debate inside the SDF was resumed. It has been suggested that it was a speech by William Morris at the SDF's New Year's gathering in 1896 that led to outright condemnation of the Jameson Raid, though Hyndman still managed to give 'thanks to Mr Chamberlain's active interference [that meant that] we were clear . . . as a nation, of responsibility' for the raid.[82] He did not believe the raid to be the result of truly British intentions in South Africa, but 'part of a great project for the constitution of an Anglo-Hebraic Empire in Africa'.[83]

While Hyndman saw the empire as a step along the road to internationalism, with diversions from that road largely caused by a sinister Jewish International, Bax saw it as an expedient of capitalism to prolong its life. He argued that 'every new market opened up is an obstacle in the way of [working-class] emancipation. . . . It is a thing of vital importance to the early realisation of socialism to stem the tide of annexation and colonial expansion without delay.'[84]

When the Boer War broke out in 1899, Hyndman's response was again to attack Jews, provoking outrage in the SDF, particularly from East End Jewish members, as well as from Bax and Theodore Rothstein. A Jewish emigré from Russia, who joined the SDF in 1895, Rothstein was critical not only of Hyndman, who, he said, seemed to have forgotten about class in his frenzy against Jews,[85] but also of that section of the left which opposed the war on grounds of morality, but nevertheless wished for British success for reasons of liberty and democracy. Rothstein perceptively summarised the thinking of many

---

[80] Ibid. 13 Sept. 1884.

[81] Ibid. 24 Jan. (the section referred to is quoted on p. 38 above), 14 Feb. 1885.

[82] Tsuzuki, *Hyndman and British socialism*, 125; *Justice*, 11 Jan. 1896, in Baker, *The SDF and the Boer War*, 3.

[83] Baker, *The SDF and the Boer War*, 4.

[84] *Justice*, 16 June 1894, in Porter, *Critics of empire*, 100.

[85] Baker, *The SDF and the Boer War*, 6.

British socialists. He described the belief that Britain was the 'most progressive country in the world' and how British socialists saw their nation standing for 'democracy and political freedom'. This stood behind Britain's opposition to 'the aggressive despotism of Russia' but also the right of asylum in Britain. For these reasons, he argued, British socialists could do little else but wish for a British victory in South Africa, despite their moral opposition to the Boer War.[86]

This line of argument resulted in 'the cause of democracy and freedom being promoted, or even maintained, by crime and conquest'. On the contrary, he argued, the war was itself a product of growing reaction in England over the previous twenty-five years, and, were the British to win, it would only increase the reaction. He, like Bax, saw imperialism as an obstacle to socialism, hence were Britain to lose South Africa and subsequently the empire the British socialist movement would benefit by ridding itself of 'the imperialistic nightmare that has been sapping the very marrow of her bones'. Freed from this, Rothstein argued, Britain would then be in a position to 'head the movement for progress and liberty all the world over'.[87]

This was along the lines of Marx's argument that 'in relation to the Irish worker [the English worker] feels himself a member of the *ruling* nation and so turns himself into a tool of the aristocrats and capitalists *against Ireland*, thus strengthening their domination *over himself*'.[88] It was an argument that, as Rothstein outlined, most British socialists rejected. He had also foreshadowed Lenin's ideas on revolutionary defeatism, which, again, the majority of British socialist opponents of the First World War were to reject, not least because they were attached to ideas about English democracy and liberty.[89]

Bax too was critical of ideas of 'British freedom': 'There is an impression abroad among Englishmen and foreigners alike that England represents fair play in the expression of opinion and personal freedom, above all other nations.' This, he argued, was a myth that would not stand up to investigation. He argued that the difference between the British and continental ruling classes was the former's 'superior astuteness' of knowing when to allow free speech and when to suppress it, allowing other agencies such as 'British public opinion' to act when the government chose not to. He pointed out that much of the British press did not need suppressing anyway, but that the government would act when it felt it necessary, as it had done in Ireland during Queen Victoria's visit, seizing an entire edition of *United Ireland*.[90]

Bax claimed that he had no feelings of patriotism, which he saw as a new religion replacing Christianity, worked up artificially by the press and

---

86 'The war and democracy', *Social-Democrat*, Mar. 1900, 71.
87 Ibid. 72, 73.
88 Marx and Engels, *Correspondence*, 289.
89 See ch. 7 below.
90 *Justice*, 19 May 1900.

politicians.[91] States and nations were not 'real, in the sense of an essential articulation or stage of human society, but a mushroom growth dating from the close of the Middle Ages (*circa* fifteenth century)', he argued.[92] He did not see patriotism as a static phenomenon but as a historical construction, for, as he noted, 'up till quite recently to be patriotic meant to be opposed to the monarch and governing classes of your own country in the interests of the people of your country'. Yet he did not want to give encouragement to left-wing patriotism, for he concluded with

> a word of protest against any attempt to revive the word 'patriotism', or to refurbish it for democratic purposes. Let us . . . leave it to the designing rogues and beguiled fools now in possession of it. In its old sense the word has had its day . . . Social-democrats want no 'true patriotism', whatever that may mean. They want to do away with patriotism altogether and substitute in its place the 'internationalism' of the class-conscious proletariat.[93]

Of course, while Bax may have been keen to forgo patriotism, much of the left was not. The debate between Hyndman, Bax and Rothstein on patriotism and imperialism naturally had repercussions inside the SDF. Bax and Rothstein were on the safer socialist ground of internationalism, and hence when Hyndman counter-attacked he did so by declaring the war 'a struggle between two burglars. . . . The future of South Africa is, I believe, to the black man; and if I am going to agitate for the independence of anybody, it is for the independence of the splendid native tribes who are being crushed by the Boers and ourselves together.'[94] While Hyndman was genuinely concerned about the fate of subject peoples, this argument was, as Bax observed, a 'red herring'.[95] Hyndman saw the war as Jewish-inspired but he did not want Britain defeated, having expressed concern about the fate of the whole empire in such an eventuality. He therefore argued that agitation against the war was a waste of time and money, the role of the SDF being to spread socialism. While he received the backing of the SDF executive, he subsequently resigned and Rothstein was elected top of the poll in the following elections.[96]

The left in Britain was not united on the question of the imperialist war in southern Africa, even within its separate groupings, though apart from the Fabian Society, which saw some resignations and a loss of influence for the Society, there were no really damaging divisions. Thus while the editor of the *Clarion* supported 'England', his staff were mainly pro-Boers, and the newspaper remained a forum for debate on the war issue. The ILP and SDF

---

91 E. B. Bax, *Reminiscences and reflexions of a mid and late Victorian*, London 1918, 195.
92 Idem, 'Love of country', *Social-Democrat*, Sept. 1900, 272, 274.
93 Idem, 'Patriotism', *Justice*, May Day supplement 1901.
94 Ibid. 20 July 1901.
95 Ibid. 3 Aug. 1901.
96 Baker, *The SDF and the Boer War*, 10–12.

were generally against the war, though there were differences over whether a British or Boer victory should be hoped for. The majority of the British left opposed the war, and, whatever their views on the best outcome, they opposed it wholeheartedly, having to defend themselves from attack, both verbal and physical. While shocked by the irrationality of jingoism, the left refused to give up patriotism and the opposition in most cases was based on a radical version of patriotism, and again and again they stressed their loyalty to 'their' country, opposing a radical version of its interests to the official version of the 'national interest'. Traditions of radical patriotism had survived the socialist revival of the 1880s and came to be applied to contemporary events. The left shared many of the assumptions and terminology about the nature of England's role in the world with the ruling class, and this led to the strange paradox that pro-Boers often called for a swift victory by the British, thus limiting their campaigning to the nature of the post-war settlement, arguing for a magnanimous peace. Only elements within the SDF attempted to apply a socialist analysis of imperialism, and from there to patriotism and ideas about the nature of Englishness, which led them to reject such ideas. But the rise of Anglo-German antagonism in the years immediately after the war in southern Africa was to put these elements under pressure, even within the SDF.

# 5

# The Labour Party and Parliament, 1906–1914

The Labour Representation Committee was formed in February 1900 as a coalition of trade union leaders, who wanted legislative protection from employers' and legal attacks, and socialists who looked to state action to achieve socialism. These groups united against the SDF, who proposed that the new body should be based upon 'a recognition of the class war', to pass Keir Hardie's pragmatic-sounding amendment to establish:

> a distinct Labour group in Parliament, who shall have their own whips, and agree upon their policy, which must embrace a readiness to co-operate with any party which for the time being may be engaged in promoting legislation in the direct interests of labour, and be equally ready to associate themselves with any party in opposing measures having an opposite tendency.[1]

The ILP socialists, even while recognising its limitations, saw the new Labour party as the agency for socialist transformation in Britain, and it was no accident that it confined itself to parliamentary activity. This stemmed from a simple belief held by the mainstream left that the state was a neutral body entirely under the control of parliament, itself capable of being brought under the control of 'the people', once they had the vote. Generally it came to be accepted that parliament equalled the state equalled the nation (or at least the national will).

Barry Jones and Michael Keating have noted that the Labour Party and its immediate predecessors have 'rarely given any sustained attention to the form of state whose power and role [they] have pledged to extend' and have described this as 'sheer intellectual failure'.[2] Mainstream left thought in Britain rejected any theory of the state as the institution of class power, seeing it instead as a neutral body. Bernard Shaw voiced the classical exposition of reformist socialism in Britain as early as 1891:

> It is easy to say, Abolish the State; but the State will sell you up, lock you up, blow you up, knock you down, bludgeon, shoot, stab, hang – in short, abolish you, if you lift a hand against it. Fortunately, there is . . . a fine impartiality about the policeman and the soldier, who are the cutting edge of State power. They take their wages and obey their orders without asking questions. If those orders are to demolish the homestead of every peasant who refuses to take the bread out of his children's mouths in order that his landlord may have the

---

1 Pelling, *Origins of the Labour Party*, 209.
2 Barry Jones and Michael Keating, *Labour and the British state*, Oxford 1985, 2–3.

money to spend as an idle gentleman in London, the soldier obeys. But if his orders were to help the police to pitch his lordship into Holloway Gaol until he had paid an Income Tax of twenty shillings on every pound of his unearned income, the soldier would do that with equal devotion to duty. Now these orders come ultimately from the State – meaning in this country, the House of Commons.[3]

This was the theory sent out to ILP branches and meetings; as the speakers' edition of an ILP leaflet explained, 'Socialists believe in the State. It is the masses using their political power for the good of the whole.'[4] MacDonald was concerned about 'the ephemeral nature of the great bulk of the matter which we publish' compared to continental socialist theory, especially since 'the growth of British democratic institutions and the characteristics of British political methods have a special and direct bearing upon Socialist theories and tactics'.[5] Hence *Socialism and government* aimed to deal with this lack of discussion of the role of the state. Yet for all his grandiloquence, MacDonald followed Shaw; the state, he wrote, 'is the organised political personality of a sovereign people – the organisation of a community for making of its common will effectual by political means'. His claim that the state was not the same as government, parliament, Whitehall or even society, but was almost a living entity of itself, that 'thinks and feels for the whole' fitted well with Idealist thought popular among social reformers at the end of the nineteenth century.[6] The state was seen as a 'spiritual personality' with a 'moral will' that could reform not only the material living conditions of the people, but also revitalise the moral health of its citizens, in a period when industrialisation and urbanisation were dividing society. MacDonald and other ethical socialists shared such a view with New Liberals and with the national efficiency movement as state action came to be seen as an all-encompassing solution to society's ills.[7] But MacDonald's theorising added nothing to a socialist theory of the state. Elsewhere he had revealed his belief that parliament was the central institution, not only of the state but of the nation:

The most appropriate subject for the Democracy to study is history, and the most appropriate section of that study is the history of Parliament; because in the history of Parliament you are studying your own evolution. The history of

---

3  G. Bernard Shaw, *The impossibilities of anarchism*, Fabian tract no. 45, London 1893, 26. See also Hardie, *From serfdom to socialism*, 6–7, for a very similar analysis of the state.
4  *The socialist state*, ILP position leaflet, London n.d.
5  'The socialist library prospectus', Apr. 1905, in MacDonald, *Socialism and government*, i. For the case that MacDonald and others were establishing a democratic socialist theory distinct from Liberalism see Duncan Tanner, 'The development of British socialism, 1900–1918', in E. H. H. Green (ed.), *An age of transition: British politics 1880–1914*, Edinburgh 1997, 48–66.
6  MacDonald, *Socialism and government*, i. 3–4, 17.
7  For Idealist thought on the state see José Harris, 'Political thought and the welfare state 1870–1940: an intellectual framework for British social policy', *P&P* xxxv (1992), 116–41.

the British Parliament is the history of the evolution of popular liberty in this country. . . . History read by historically minded men is not the record of failures, but a record of success right through.[8]

The belief that the state was a neutral body was made possible by a rejection of any theory of class struggle as the motor for social and economic change. Hardie had declared that propaganda of class hatred was foreign. He also claimed that 'there is no "ruling and oppressed class", in the Marxian sense of the terms in England now. . . . As a matter of fact, the whole thesis upon which the class war was formulated is now antiquated and out of date.'[9] MacDonald echoed this, arguing that socialism did not come from the economic interests of a class:

> The man through whom Socialism is to come is not to be the economic man, the class-conscious man, the man toiling with the muck rake. He is to be the man of ideals, of historical spirit, the man in whose intelligence, religion and sense of what is of good report will have a dominating influence, the generous and ungrudging co-operator with his fellows.[10]

MacDonald went so far as to argue, in the midst of massive industrial unrest, that 'it is the anti-Socialist who makes class appeals'.[11]

This rejection of class war and the belief that the state was neutral meant that Labour thinkers counted on, in the first instance, numbers, and in the second, the good sense of the civil service, police and army. As shown above, an 'English' or 'British' socialism had been constructed which rejected violence and revolution. Reinforcing the idea that such methods were foreign was the belief that parliamentary democracy also made them unnecessary. Labour politicians could not, however, reject class interests altogether. As Hardie noted after the election in 1906, 'a Labour Party which did not menace Park Lane would not be worth its room in Parliament'.[12] Yet despite an Edwardian electorate that was 70 per cent working class, where there was no shortage of constituencies in which the working class formed a majority, Labour leaders believed the appeal to class was not enough.[13] Hence, Labour could make appeals to those outside the working class, as did Philip Snowden in Blackburn in 1900, assuring the electorate that 'Socialism is not merely for

---

[8] J. H. B. Masterman, *The House of Commons: its place in national history*, London 1908, 29–30. MacDonald was chairing one of the lectures upon which the book was based.

[9] 'An indictment of the class war', *Labour Leader*, 9 Sept. 1904. See also ibid. 17 Aug. 1901.

[10] MacDonald, *Socialism and government*, i, p. xxviii.

[11] J. Ramsay MacDonald, *The socialist movement*, London 1911, 149.

[12] 'The Labour Party: its aims and policy', *National Review* xlvi (Feb. 1906), 1007.

[13] A. K. Russell estimated that from half to two-thirds of seats had working-class majorities: *The Liberal landslide: the general election of 1906*, Newton Abbot–Hampden, Conn. 1973, 21. Duncan Tanner has concluded that 'the electoral framework in which Edwardian political parties operated was not overwhelmingly biased against the working class, or against parties which were based more heavily on this social group': *Political change and the Labour Party 1900–1918*, Cambridge 1990, 128.

the poor widow, it was the cause of the small capitalist, the struggling professional man, and the poor shopkeeper.'[14]

The Labour view of the state led to the belief that Labour could actually
become the state.[15] Thus Labour, by rejecting ideas of class conflict, aimed to
prove that it was a national rather than sectional party. In the same article in
which Hardie had said that Labour needed to 'menace Park Lane', he also
warned that

> The Labour Party, however, must concern itself with the wider issues of
> national life and policy. One of the claims we put forward is, that in the best
> and truest sense of the word we are a national party. We have no sectional
> interests to serve, and the things which we desire most are just those which
> would benefit the community as a whole.[16]

MacDonald was keen to show in 1905 that 'an infusion of labour class representation into the House of Commons would . . . not result in class, but in
national legislation'.[17] Unlike the Irish party, MacDonald explained, the
Labour Party 'is not at war but at peace with the nation'.[18] Such beliefs were
bound to have an effect on the way in which Labour saw its role and subsequently its behaviour in parliament.


### Labour in the House of Commons

The election of twenty-nine Labour MPs (with another MP joining Labour
after the election) in January 1906 brought great hopes to significant sections
of the working class. The socialist movement grew rapidly. The number of
SDF branches rose by 100 between 1906 and 1908, while the ILP, claiming
30,000 paid-up members, saw the establishment of 375 new branches
between 1906 and 1909. The circulation of *Clarion* reached 80,000 in 1908.[19]
The executive of the Labour Party told the annual conference held within a
month of the election:

> One thing is already clear. A new party which can place its candidate at the
> head of the poll in the historic constituency of Newcastle-on-Tyne, with one

[14] *Blackburn Times*, 29 Sept. 1900, in Keith Laybourn, *Philip Snowden: a biography
1864–1937*, Aldershot 1988, 47. See also ILP leaflet, *Socialism for shopkeepers*, Common
sense politics no. 6, London 1909.
[15] See Stephen Yeo, 'Socialism, the state, and some oppositional Englishness', especially
pp. 360–1.
[16] 'The Labour Party: aims and policy', 1007.
[17] Rodney Barker, 'Socialism and progressivism in the political thought of Ramsay Mac-
Donald', in A. J. A. Morris (ed.), *Edwardian radicalism 1900–1914: some aspects of British
radicalism*, London 1974, 123–4.
[18] MacDonald, *Socialism and government*, i, p. xxvii.
[19] Kenneth O. Morgan, 'Edwardian socialism', in Donald Read (ed.), *Edwardian England*,
London 1982, 93–111.

of the highest votes in the whole country; a party which can win seats in Bradford and Glasgow, in Dundee and London, against the nominees of both Liberals and Tories, has a future before it, it will have a hand in the making of history.[20]

Yet the executive was not laying the whole truth before the conference, for only thirty-one of the fifty LRC candidates had faced Liberal opposition, and twenty-four of the twenty-nine successful Labour MPs owed their victories to the absence of Liberal opposition. MacDonald had negotiated an electoral pact with Herbert Gladstone, the Liberal chief whip, in 1903.[21] Furthermore, the historian of the 1906 general election has noted the way in which both the LRC manifesto and its candidates' election addresses 'followed Liberal policies', and that the candidates' language was reminiscent of Liberalism.[22] In the election of 1906, this meant that 79 per cent of the LRC candidates mentioned free trade, Home Rule and reform of the Education Act, and 75 per cent mentioned licensing reform. These were the four most popular issues in the Liberal pantheon. Ahead of them in Labour election addresses came increased working-class representation, Taff Vale, unemployment and old age pensions. Of these 'labour' issues, only the issue of increased labour representation did not find a place in Liberal election addresses.[23]

As a minority party, Labour certainly could not set the agenda for the election, but the fact remained that most Labour candidates were happy to follow the Liberals. In a survey of the successful Labour MPs' reading, it was revealed that the books cited as most influential were the Bible and those by Ruskin and Carlyle. Only two cited Marx, three Blatchford, three William Morris and five Sidney Webb. In all, only eight Labour MPs cited socialist books as being influential to them (and two of these, W. C. Steadman and James Haslam, were Lib-Lab MPs), despite eighteen probably considering themselves to be socialists.[24] The members of the Parliamentary Labour Party of 1906 were therefore not revolutionaries; they believed social change could come through the existing institutions of society.

How, then, would they act within the House of Commons? Keir Hardie had, in 1898, laid out a strategy for Labour MPs: 'I admit freely that agitation from the floor of the House of Commons is the most effective, and from this it follows we ought to aim at getting men in. But they must go there as agitators – rude, wild, unkempt agitators, if you will. Of smooth, smug, respectable politicians there are already enough and to spare.'[25] Faced with the existence of a sizeable Labour Party in parliament, the *Labour Leader* rejected such an approach, on the grounds that the British public would not take kindly to

---

[20] Labour Party, *Conference report*, 1906, 3.

[21] See Bealey and Pelling, *Labour and politics 1900–1906*, chs vi, ix.

[22] Russell, *Liberal landslide*, 78.

[23] Ibid. 65, 79.

[24] Stead, 'The Labour Party and the books that helped to make it'.

[25] *Labour Leader*, 8 Oct. 1898, in *Keir Hardie's speeches and writings*, 96.

'sheerly destructive parliamentary tactics', though it also warned against 'simple endorsement of the Government's policy'.[26] Given the view of the state and parliament held by most Labour MPs and leaders it was already determined how the PLP would act. Its behaviour would reflect acceptance of traditional political behaviour in the Commons. Stephen Yeo has argued that Labour held this view because in England the state is very old and that its development has been that of 'the great arch', that there has been no sudden break in its development.[27] Henry (later Lord) Snell, in trying to empathise with MacDonald's feelings upon entering the Commons, described his own, and provided evidence for Yeo's arguments:

> I have elsewhere endeavoured to describe the emotions of a thoughtful man on the day when, for the first time, he becomes a member of the British Parliament, and the thrill that he feels when he makes his first appearance at its doors. . . . If the new member is a normally healthy human being, possessing some knowledge of the history of his country and the place of Parliament in its wonderful story, he will probably regard this as the greatest day of his life. . . . If our new member is not moved to emotion as he enters upon his great heritage, or if he remains unaware of his partnership in the great fellowship of service which the House of Commons represents, his life there may be useful but it can scarcely be happy.[28]

Feelings of this sort had more in common with Bagehot's description of the parts of the constitution 'which excite and preserve the reverence of the population – the *dignified* parts', than with Hardie's view that Labour MPs 'were not in Parliament as gentlemen of easy means, using the House of Commons as the first club in Europe'.[29]

Thus Labour parliamentarians drew together the state, parliament and English history into one indivisible unit. For MacDonald, 'religion, national experience, economic and industrial evolution, have given the State a personality which impinges on the individual will and modified its direction and motives'.[30] The Labour Party was therefore ruled by a perception of English history which it could not betray. Hardie's strategy of Labour MPs becoming 'rude, wild, unkempt agitators' had to be rejected.[31] *Justice* warned of the effect of entry into parliament

> upon newcomers [which] is very insidious and very curious to watch. . . . The working class members who enter the House of Commons [it referred to

---

[26] *Labour Leader*, 9 Feb. 1906.
[27] Yeo, 'Socialism, the state, and some oppositional Englishness', 314.
[28] Zygmunt Bauman, *Between class and elite: the evolution of the British Labour movement: a sociological study*, Manchester 1972, 208n.
[29] Walter Bagehot, *The English constitution*, Glasgow 1963, 61; *Times*, 14 Feb. 1906.
[30] MacDonald, *Socialism and government*, i. 5.
[31] See MacDonald's warning to Labour MPs to act in a parliamentary manner: *Labour Leader*, 10 Aug. 1906.

Lib-Lab MPs] become highly respectable, prosperous, and somewhat self-conscious bourgeois. Their dress, their appearance, their manners, and, unfortunately, their politics accommodate themselves to their new surroundings very rapidly. They would not think of outraging the most obsolete and ridiculous of the 'forms of the House' for any consideration whatever.

*Justice* asked whether the new Labour MPs would be able to resist this effect, concluding that some would, but some would not.[32] *Justice* had seen the pressures as wholly external, whereas many of the new MPs carried with them the internal pressures of their own beliefs. Criticisms of the moderating effect of parliament were not merely made by the left outside the Labour Party. Philip Snowden, elected in 1906, also commented upon his fellow MPs:

> The Labour members quickly adapted themselves to the customs of the House of Commons. There was a practice in those days that when a member left the Chamber he stooped at the Bar and made a profound obeisance to the Speaker. It was rather amusing to see the Labour members, whose advent to Parliament was expected to outrage all the conventionalities, performing this custom with more correctness than the Tory members.[33]

It was in such a context that the parliamentary behaviour of Victor Grayson, the Socialist and Labour MP for Colne Valley, caused such resentment within the PLP. Interrupting debate on a licensing bill on 15 October 1908, Grayson demanded that the House deal with the problem of unemployment. He was asked to leave the House, and received no support from the Labour MPs. As he left, it was to them he turned, declaring, 'I leave the House with pleasure. You are traitors to your class. You will not stand up for your class. You traitors.' Two days later, he again interrupted proceedings, this time calling the Commons 'a House of Murderers'.[34] One of Grayson's biographers states that the ILP and trade union MPs of the PLP then formed a common front against him, with Snowden even alleging that he had spent his quarterly payment from the ILP on a single sumptuous dinner that had been the talk of Westminster. He presented no proof. It was simple character assassination, the effects of which could be expected to be profound in a Nonconformist and puritan organisation like the Labour Party.[35]

The PLP soon came to see its role as foremost defender of the 'democratic'

---

[32] *Justice*, 17 Feb. 1906. W. L. Guttsman argued that before 1914 the politics, class and income of Labour MPs largely kept them out of 'Society', but after 1918 there was 'a growing integration of the Labour benches into the life of the House of Commons and eventually in the wider "Society" ': *The British political elite*, London 1968, 247. Nevertheless even before 1914 the left had already become concerned. For Hyndman's observations on the effects of parliamentary life on Labour MPs see his *Further reminiscences*, 275.

[33] Snowden, *Autobiography*, i. 124–5, 133.

[34] *Hansard*, 4th ser. cxci. 495–7, 631–4.

[35] David Clark, *Victor Grayson: Labour's lost leader*, London 1985, 57, 60. The more political responses to Grayson and the sentiment of the left that he expressed are dealt with later in this chapter.

House of Commons. MacDonald argued that while the House of Commons needed reform, 'to degrade in the imagination of the people even a bad House of Commons is a crime – a most heinous crime for Socialists. . . . The Socialist more than any other citizen should preserve that respect for the political institutions of Democracy which alone makes the decrees of these institutions acceptable to the people.' He further argued that the Labour Party could not act as obstructionists as the Irish Party had previously done, for whereas parliament was an alien power for the Irish, it was Labour's 'own heritage'.[36]

Therefore, for MacDonald, the House of Commons stood supreme above all other considerations, to be defended from its attackers, whether the aristocratic House of Lords or the left wing of the labour movement. While the latter attack was ongoing and would increase in intensity during the industrial unrest of 1910 to 1914, the rejection of Lloyd George's budget in November 1909 represented to the Labour Party an attack on the progressive history of Britain. 'For three hundred and fifty years', explained *Labour Leader*, 'the House of Commons had been encroaching steadily upon the prerogatives of the Peers . . . with one swoop, all this progress has been swept back.'[37] British socialists had always seen one of their main tasks as the defeat of the landlords, and the Labour Party, seeing the House of Lords as the strongest bastion of landlordism, entered the fray against them. 'The battle against the Lords', Hardie told the 1910 Labour conference, 'is peculiarly ours.'[38] W. C. Anderson explained the importance of the issue arguing that the question was one of 'English liberties' and that 'The democracy of these islands have an account, long overdue, against the peers. . . . Their lordships were ill-advised to tamper with the Constitution . . . a rash and revolutionary act which is contemptuous of the House of Commons and of democracy.' This call to arms to Labour supporters was despite Anderson's confession that 'the constitution is only venerable and valuable so long as it keeps the poor in subjection', but it was worth defending, he argued, because others had done so; 'Pym had pleaded for it, Hampden had laid down his life for it, Cromwell had drawn sword for it on many a hard-fought field.'[39] Thus the general election of January 1910 was seen as a re-run of the English Civil War, with the Labour Party playing a major role in defence of popular English liberties.

Labour did not play an independent role in the election. Neal Blewett has argued that, 'in so far as Labour conducted a national campaign it was as part of the Radical wing of the Liberal Party. Labour speeches differed little in tone from Radical ones; the majority of Labour candidates were little more than surrogates for Radicals.'[40] But while the Labour Party appeared radical

---

36 MacDonald, *Socialism and government*, i, pp. xxv, xxvi–xxvii.
37 *Labour Leader*, 3 Dec. 1909.
38 Neal Blewett, *The peers, the parties and the people: the general elections of 1910*, London–Basingstoke 1972, 236.
39 W. C. Anderson, *Hang out our banners*, Manchester 1909 (election leaflet).
40 Blewett, *Peers, parties and people*, 109.

in regard to its call for the abolition of the House of Lords, its appeal was also conservative. Anderson had called the Lords 'rash and revolutionary', while Labour fought in defence of its own Whiggish interpretation of history and the British constitution.

Such ideas were held, not because of the particular leadership of the Labour Party, but because of the very nature of the ideas and strategy accepted by the party. Through the rejection of class as the major division within society, Labour accepted the unitary nature of the nation, seeing one national history of which they were part, with the House of Commons forming the core of this national history. Within these ideas, they concluded that their role included an essential element of defending English liberty and democracy. Since Labour accepted this history, and since Labour, as Hardie explained, 'aimed at becoming a great political power in the land . . . it must conform as nearly as possible to the political institutions already in existence with which the public mind is familiar'.[41]

### Those without respect: critics of the Parliamentary Labour Party

The Labour Party in parliament achieved some initial successes, such as the reversal of the Taff Vale decision and some government action on school meals, workmen's compensation and unemployment; even the SDF was not at first highly critical. But disappointment among some Labour supporters soon set in, because of Labour's inability to pressurise the Liberal government with its huge majority, and because of poor by-election results. Between 1906 and 1908, Labour fought ten by-elections, winning only Jarrow and coming bottom of the poll on five occasions. In 1909 Labour won Sheffield Attercliffe, and in the 1910 elections, increased its representation to forty in January and forty-two in December. But this rise was due to the affiliation of the Miners' Federation of Great Britain to Labour rather than an increase in popularity. In all the fourteen by-elections Labour fought between 1911 and 1914, as a result of pressure from the left rather than as a strategy of the leadership, it found itself bottom of the poll.[42]

There were two phases of opposition to the Labour Party's political strategy. The first phase (1907–10) was dominated by the left of the ILP, with the SDF and Clarion groups offering support. The second phase (1910–14) was centred upon the industrial unrest and syndicalist theory of social change. The opposition of the first phase continued after 1910, but it too found itself

---

[41] Labour Leader, 23 Mar. 1901, in Yeo, 'Socialism, the state, and some oppositional Englishness', 324.
[42] Roger Moore, The emergence of the Labour Party 1880–1924, London 1978, 108–9; Blewett, Peers, parties and people, 381, 387, 389. See also Roy Douglas, 'Labour in decline 1910–14', in Kenneth D. Brown (ed.), Essays in anti-labour history: responses to the rise of Labour in Britain, London–Basingstoke 1974, 105–25.

the target of syndicalist criticism, and in response found itself aligning with the Labour Party, and even joining the counter-attack against syndicalism. This second phase represented great dangers for the Labour Party, for not only did the syndicalists offer a completely alternative strategy, but the Liberal government relied upon the support of the Labour and Irish parties for survival. Far from placing Labour in a position of strength, this led to weakness, for the Labour leadership did not want to bring down the government and hence had their sphere of movement severely restricted. Therefore, Labour's ideologues conducted a sustained propaganda attack upon extra-parliamentary activity.

## Let us reform the Labour Party

In his 1907 New Year's greeting to the ILP, Hardie announced that 'the party in the House of Commons has more than come up to expectations'. The simple proof was that it had thirty elected MPs, hence 'the ILP has succeeded where its critics have failed'.[43] This was a reference to the SDF whose only MP, Will Thorne, had been elected under the auspices of the LRC. But, within months, criticism was coming from inside the ILP. T. D. Benson and others protested against the idea that the ILP existed solely for putting men into parliament. 'A Hardie, or MacDonald, or Snowden, agitating and speaking in the country regularly is, in my opinion', he wrote, 'worth a dozen Labour members in the House.'[44] MacDonald rejected such notions; he particularly saw himself as a skilled parliamentarian. 'Governments are not afraid of Socialist speeches', he confidently asserted; 'they are very much afraid of successful criticisms in detail.' With an air of superiority brought by his position he added that his critics could not know what went on in parliament.[45] H. Russell Smart replied that if he could not know what was going on in the Commons, then how much more ignorant were the public.[46] This feeling of superiority was not confined to MacDonald alone, nor the British Labour Party, for, as Robert Michels observed of the European socialist parties, 'in view of their greater competence in various questions, the socialist parliamentary groups consider themselves superior even to the congresses, which are the supreme courts of the party, and they claim effective

---

[43] *Labour Leader*, 4 Jan. 1907.
[44] Ibid. 19 Apr. 1907. See also H. Russell Smart, ibid. 17 May 1907.
[45] Ibid. 10 May 1907. See also 24 May 1907. Radical MPs in the nineteenth century had criticised the shortage of public seats in the Commons which 'excluded those whom it professed to represent': Quinault, 'Westminster and the Victorian constitution', 96. MacDonald felt that if critics sat in the Strangers' Gallery they would appreciate the work of the parliamentary socialist better. He did not mention the difficulties of this, but suggested a daily labour newspaper would serve the same purpose: *Labour Leader*, 10 May 1907.
[46] Ibid. 31 May 1907

autonomy'.[47] At the 1907 Labour conference, the leadership had secured a resolution on the relationship of conference to parliamentary party that declared that, 'Resolutions instructing the Parliamentary Party as to their action in the House of Commons be taken as the opinion of the Conference, on the understanding that the time and method of giving effect to those instructions be left to the Party in the House, in conjunction with the National Executive.'[48] This attitude on the part of the parliamentary leadership partly resulted from the belief that, since parliament was sovereign over the nation, so the parliamentary party should be sovereign over the party.

Despite *Labour Leader*'s announcement in June 1907 that the controversy had blown over,[49] the election of Grayson in July was to provide a focus for the left's frustration. At the celebration meeting for himself and Pete Curran (elected for Jarrow), Grayson argued that 'what was needed was that people should go to the House realising that in its stupendous mountain of tradition there was something so alien to real reform that it would take revolutionary and unconstitutional means to break it'.[50] It was in this light that he saw his outburst over the plight of the unemployed, because while he wanted the House of Commons, 'a worn out and antiquated machine . . . scrapped and replaced by something more in consonance with the desires of a new era', his strategy for achieving this was 'a strong Socialist party in the House of Commons'.[51] Grayson saw the role of this party as much like that of the Irish party, a role MacDonald had rejected. The conflict came to a head at the 1909 ILP conference.[52] The National Administrative Council (NAC) won the main votes. It was decided that an MP who refused to sign the Labour Party constitution, as Grayson had refused, could not receive a salary from the ILP. But the conference referred back a section of the NAC report censuring Grayson for refusing to share a platform with Hardie at Holborn. The 'Big Four' of the NAC, MacDonald, Hardie, Snowden and Glasier, then resigned. This move strengthened the dominance of the 'Big Four', for, as Michels observed

> resignation of office, in so far as it is not a mere expression of discouragement or protest . . . is in most cases a means for the retention and fortification of leadership. . . . [T]he opponent is forced to exhibit in return an even greater deference, and this above all when the leader who makes use of the method is really indispensable, or is considered indispensable by the mass.[53]

[47] Robert Michels, *Political parties: a sociological study of the oligarchical tendencies of modern democracy*, trans. Eden Paul and Cedar Paul, New York 1962, 157.
[48] Moore, *Emergence of Labour*, 104. For later views on the sovereignty of the conference see Snowden, *Autobiography*, i. 87–8, and R. H. S. Crossman's introduction to Bagehot, *English constitution*, 42–3.
[49] *Labour Leader*, 14 June 1907.
[50] Ibid. 9 Aug. 1907.
[51] Victor Grayson, *The appeal for socialism*, Stockport n.d. [1908], 13, 9.
[52] Many of Grayson's supporters had expected the battle sooner, but Grayson failed to speak at the Labour Party conference held in January: Clark, *Victor Grayson*, 61.
[53] Michels, *Political parties*, 81.

The strength of the Labour Party meant that the 'Big Four' could retreat into positions of strength. They also maintained full access to the ILP and other publishing facilities. Their counter-offensive took two forms. First, they defended constitutionalism. Hardie argued that the earlier anti-parliamentarism of the movement had meant that 'Socialism, in those days, was treated as a plant of continental growth which could never find lodgement in Great Britain.' To circumvent this, the ILP had been formed; its parliamentarism meant that 'a Labour party is accepted as part of our political system equally with the Liberal and Tory parties. That of itself is a gain of no mean order.' Even the continental parties had left their revolutionary 'childhood' and entered a stage of 'responsible manhood'. He implied that 'British Socialism' had led the way.[54] Another supporter of the leadership, T. Gavan Duffy, continued the argument along these lines, defending as peculiarly British the fact that 'the Labour Party is not a Socialist Party'. The alliance of trade unionists and socialists, he argued, was an acceptance of British political institutions and 'the traditional conservatism of the British temperament. . . . The British Labour Party . . . is the product of a quarter of a century's strenuous unparalleled propaganda; it marks the dawn of a new era; it is not an acorn, it is the oak; its roots are deep down in the nurtured soil of the British character.'[55]

The supporters of the Labour Party had extended the charge of un-Englishness to include not only those who advocated revolutionary change, but also those reformists who disagreed with the labour alliance strategy. But this was only one side of the counter-offensive. Supporters of the labour alliance also sought to out-manoeuvre opponents to their left. They argued that they were the true followers of Karl Marx. Basing themselves upon a passage in the *Communist manifesto* that declared that 'the Communists do not form a separate party opposed to the working-class parties', the 'Big Four' argued that 'the ILP was formed by Socialists, who desired to follow the Marxian policy of uniting the working class into an independent party'.[56] Hardie became the most enthusiastic user of this line. He declared that 'the Labour Party is the only expression of orthodox Marxian Socialism in Great Britain', and that 'the founders of the ILP, and even more so, of the Labour Party were . . . in the direct line of apostolic succession from Marx'.[57] But he was not alone; even MacDonald wrote that the policy of the ILP had been to 'unite for political purposes with industrial organisations of the workers. . . . This policy

---

[54] J. Keir Hardie, *My confession of faith in the labour alliance*, London n.d. [1909], 1, 2, 11. MacDonald's *Socialism and government* was ammunition in the same battle.
[55] T. Gavan Duffy, *The Labour Party in parliament – what it is: what it does: what it wants*, London n.d. [1910?], 2–4.
[56] See the open letter explaining their resignations: *Labour Leader*, 16 Apr. 1909.
[57] Hardie, *Labour alliance*, 13, 14. See also his series of articles on Marx: *Labour Leader*, 12, 19, 26 Aug. 1910.

is, indeed, but the carrying out of what Marx advised.'[58] This twin attack, that the Labour Party was not only Marxist but 'the only political form which evolutionary socialism can take in a country with the political traditions and methods of Great Britain',[59] may have contained contradictions, but it gave the left little room to move, particularly since their actual strategy differed little from that of the Labour Party.

Logie Barrow has argued that the breakaway of left ILP branches to join with the SDF and *Clarion* groups in the formation of the British Socialist Party (BSP) was a split between those who favoured the 'educationalistic' method against the 'legislativistic'.[60] However, whether these socialists were awaiting the inevitable breakdown of capitalism, like the SDP,[61] or wished to 'make socialists', like the Clarionettes, they wished to rely on parliamentary methods as their main propaganda weapon. The SDP rejected the economic struggle to concentrate on the political struggle, and this meant that its activity was confined to municipal councils and parliament (the latter unsuccessfully). A manifesto of the executive council of the SDP on 'The paralysis of parliament' claimed that 'capitalist parliamentarism, like landlord parliamentarism before it, has been tried and found wanting in the land of its birth', but saw direct action, 'by general strike or otherwise' as impossible. It concluded that 'as matters stand in Great Britain . . . political methods are still indispensable if any peaceful revolution is to be brought about'.[62] Since its proposed alternative of a constituent assembly was stillborn, it found itself fighting another general election in December 1910. Blatchford, who rejected violence as un-English and favoured education of the people in socialism, admitted that he did not 'mean that no advance towards Socialism can be made until the masses are intellectually and morally elevated to the due pitch for it. Let social legislation go on apace. Let us get all the Socialism we can by instalments. The best social educator is Socialism.'[63] Thus he too had to accept parliamentary socialism. The left ILP, who found expression in a pamphlet written by four members of the NAC, warned that the impotence of the PLP presented 'the danger . . . that many have not only lost confidence in their politicians but are fast losing *all* faith or interest in Parliamentary politics'.[64]

58 MacDonald, *The socialist movement*, 234.
59 Ibid. 235.
60 'Determinism and environmentalism in socialist thought', in Raphael Samuel and Gareth Stedman Jones (eds), *Culture, ideology and politics*, London 1982, 194–214.
61 The Social-Democratic Federation renamed itself the Social-Democratic Party in 1907.
62 *Justice*, 19 Mar. 1910.
63 Thompson, *Robert Blatchford*, 133–4.
64 Leonard Hall and others, *Let us reform the Labour Party*, Manchester n.d., 1.

## The industrial unrest and syndicalism

The years after 1910 saw an explosion of industrial unrest. In 1907, 2.15 million working days were lost due to industrial action; in 1910, 9.87 million; in 1911, 10.16 million; in 1912, due to the national miners' strike, 40.89 million; in 1913, 9.8 million; and in 1914, 9.88 million.[65] The years between 1900 and 1912 saw a 10 per cent fall in average real wages,[66] a fall that the presence of the Labour Party in the Commons had been unable to prevent. The rejection of ideas of class politics by the Labour leaders had its corollary in the actions of the trade union officials. In 1896 an act of parliament had offered conciliation facilities to employers and union negotiators. After 1900, when George Askwith became the Board of Trade's 'trouble-shooter', these facilities were expanded, and union officials were appointed as 'labour correspondents', sending information to a central statistical office.[67] The unrest of 1910-14 was very much due to pressure from below in reaction against the union leaderships.

The existing political organisations claiming to represent the working class, through acceptance of parliament as the proper forum for politics, were not well-placed to benefit from the industrial action. Glasier had called strikes 'irrational and futile'.[68] MacDonald, while admitting that 'the fundamental cause of labour unrest is low wages', argued that the Labour Party would not necessarily take the workers' side. Instead Labour would take the side of the 'general community' where this was necessary.[69] Arthur Henderson, Will Crooks, George Barnes and a Lib-Lab MP, Charles Fenwick, actually tabled a bill to make strikes illegal without thirty-days' notice, and including a clause making anyone who 'incites, encourages or aids' a strike liable to a fine of between £10 and £200.[70]

There were no other sizeable left-wing groups ideologically equipped to deal with strikes. The Fabian executive had written to the press before the threatened rail strike of 1907 that 'in the case of the nation's principal means of land transport, resort to the characteristic trade-union weapon of the strike is . . . a national calamity . . .'.[71] The *Clarion* said that 'Socialistic teaching has consistently pointed out the futility of the strike, and advocated the better way of arbitration.'[72] The attitude of the revolutionary SDP was strikingly

65 Donald Read, 'Crisis or golden age?', in Read, *Edwardian England*, 16.
66 Bob Holton, *British syndicalism 1900–1914: myths and realities*, London 1976, 28.
67 Ibid. 33.
68 Glasier, *On strikes*, 1.
69 *Hansard*, 5th ser. lxxxiv. 15 Feb. 1912, 46, 53.
70 Chris Wrigley, *Arthur Henderson*, Cardiff 1990, 45.
71 Niles Carpenter, *Guild socialism: an historical and critical analysis*, New York–London 1922, 63–4.
72 *Clarion*, 16 Sept. 1910.

similar to that of the mainstream left. Hyndman wrote that 'we of the Social Democratic Party and *Justice* are opposed to strikes on principle'.[73]

Syndicalists positively encouraged strike action, seeing it as not only a method for improving workers' living standards but also as the vehicle for social transformation. While the syndicalists may not have initiated strikes themselves in most instances, they certainly fitted the mood of the time, and increased their influence in the working class at the expense of both the ILP/Labour Party and BSP, as the fused ILP left, *Clarion* groups and SDP became in 1912.[74] These groups played down the influence of syndicalism, while at the same time conducting a campaign declaring it to be un-English. MacDonald judged that 'Syndicalism in England is negligible', and *Justice* that 'as a matter of fact, there is practically no Syndicalism in this country'.[75] The SDP 'old guard' were concerned about the influence of syndicalist ideas within the BSP. The executive announced in 1912 that 'political action is the principle function of the party. . . . Syndicalism is avowedly opposed to Socialism. There is no probability that Syndicalist methods will find favour in Great Britain.'[76] The threat to the BSP's political strategy had to be taken seriously. Organisers of the new BSP in Birmingham were promoting a strategy of 'general and combined strikes of the exploited, developing towards the final Lock-out by the nation of its exploiters', and only secondly of placing 'militant Socialists in parliament'.[77]

Labour and social-democrats, supposedly disparate groups, agreed upon another point, that syndicalism was foreign and could not take root in the political soil of Britain. They seemed little concerned that they had once had to argue against such accusations about their own socialism.[78] The first point of attack was that the word syndicalism was 'a word imported from France'.[79] MacDonald expanded this point: 'It is in vain that one searches English dictionaries for the word Syndicalism. It is a French stranger in our language, with no registered abode as yet. Had it not been an ugly word it would probably never have been brought over, for it has achieved fame by reason of its capacity to frighten.' A. S. Headingley offered some advice in *Justice*: 'I do not see what Syndicalism has to do on these shores, and think that the English

[73] *Justice*, 10 Aug. 1907, in Walter Kendall, *The revolutionary movement in Britain 1900–21: the origins of British Communism*, London 1969, 28.
[74] For the relationship between the syndicalists and the industrial unrest see Holton, *British syndicalism*, 76–7, and Joseph White, *Tom Mann*, Manchester 1991, 156–8.
[75] J. Ramsay MacDonald, *Syndicalism: a critical examination*, London 1912, 39; *Justice*, 23 Mar. 1912.
[76] Ibid. 2 Nov. 1912.
[77] *Manifesto of the Birmingham section of the British Socialist Party*, 1911, British Library of Political and Economic Science, BSP collection, archives collection miscellaneous 155, fo. 59.
[78] Even in 1912 *Justice* was advertising a forthcoming series of articles, 'Pioneers of the class struggle', by Theodore Rothstein, which would show 'the British origins of the class war idea, which some of our "evolutionary" friends imagine to have been imported from Germany by Karl Marx' (17 Aug. 1912).
[79] *Labour Leader*, 5 Apr. 1912.

language is rich enough to give an English word to represent an English movement.'[80]

Political socialists also knew that they could rely on a further line of defence against syndicalism, for as the miners' MP William Brace told the Commons, 'If any hon. Member . . . is under the impression that Syndicalism is likely to gain a foothold amongst the miners in particular and the workers in general, he is not paying much of a compliment to the innate common sense of the British working man.'[81] MacDonald was inclined to agree with this point generally; he argued that, 'there is . . . a real unity called a nation, which endows the individual with traditions, with habits, with a system of social conduct. The Syndicalist . . . – being one who lays down that this national inheritance is unreal, is nothing – can build up no policy upon it'. However, the evidence of the Unofficial Reform Committee, the election of two well-known syndicalists to the South Wales Miners' Federation executive, and the influence of the syndicalist pamphlet *The miners' next step*, in south Wales, led MacDonald to explain that there, 'racial temperament and economic hardship offered special promise for the Syndicalist propaganda'.[82] Clearly, the real national unity did not extend to all Britons. When it suited, the force of Englishness could be proved only against its exceptions.

The response of syndicalists to accusations of un-Englishness was largely indifference. They were proud of their international connections and influences. Tom Mann noted with admiration that French syndicalists 'are, for the most part, anti-patriotic and anti-militarist, e.g., they declare that the workers have no country'.[83] On returning to Britain from Australia in 1910 he went with Guy Bowman to France to learn from French syndicalist experience. Upon returning he advised on 'a policy to adopt':

> Now, without urging a close imitation of the French, or any other method I strongly believe that, on the average, the French policy is the one that will suit us best; for whilst the temperament of the French is undoubtedly different from that of the British, their interests are exactly as ours, and their enemy is also ours – the Capitalist system.[84]

E. J. B. Allen, who had formed the Industrial League in 1908 to promote industrial unionism and was later a member of Mann's Industrial Syndicalist Education League, answered the question, 'Is syndicalism un-English?' 'Syndicalism is a natural product, peculiar to no nationality. . . . Even the British worker can understand the meaning of the phrase: "The product to the

---

[80] MacDonald, *Syndicalism*, p .v; *Justice*, 16 Mar. 1912.

[81] *Hansard*, 5th ser. viii. 21 Mar. 1912, 2121.

[82] MacDonald, *Syndicalism*, 55, 43. For syndicalism in south Wales see Holton, *British syndicalism*, chs v, vii. Morgan argues that the new militancy and syndicalism in south Wales was in part the result of English migrants to the coal fields, but that there was indeed an element of Welshness about it: *Rebirth of a nation*, 71, 79, 153–4.

[83] *Industrial Syndicalist*, July 1910, 16–17.

[84] Ibid. 17.

producer, the tools to those who use them".'[85] Syndicalists saw class as the fundamental division within society, hence unity between workers in different countries was more important than worrying about the use of un-English words. As Mann told a conference on industrial syndicalism in Manchester in November 1910, 'we must remember we are Europeans. . . . We want a universal term – Syndicalism.'[86]

This concentration on class by syndicalists was one reason why many socialists declared their methods un-English. The same argument had been used against the SDF. But the syndicalists also rejected the traditional British institutions of the state and parliament, which were presented as being at the core of 'British socialism'. Mann saw parliament not as 'the people's House' but as an instrument of class rule; it 'was not brought into existence to enable the working class to obtain ownership and mastery over the means of production. . . . Parliament was brought into existence by the ruling class . . . to enable that ruling class to have more effective means to subjugate the working class.'[87] Syndicalists also rejected nationalisation, which was the Labour Party's strategy for achieving socialism. The *Syndicalist Railwayman* declared that the workers 'have little reason for placing any great confidence in the State as an employer. As the conflict 'twixt capital and labour becomes keener, the workers are having impressed upon them the real character and functions of the existing State. . . . The State is essentially a ruling class organisation and its functions are chiefly coercive.'[88] This meant a fundamental rejection of the belief in the unity of the nation and its expression in the state and parliament. This rejection made syndicalist ideas incompatible with Labourism, and the fear of its increasing influence made syndicalism the target of much Labour criticism.

There were however some expressions of Englishness/Britishness from within the syndicalist movement. One of the most famous syndicalist documents, the 'Don't shoot' leaflet, which called on soldiers not to fire on strikers, resulted in the prosecution and imprisonment of Tom Mann, Fred Bower and the two Buck brothers. It stated that 'England with its fertile valleys and dells, its mineral resources, its sea harvests, is the heritage of ages to us', and ended, 'Help US to win back Britain for the British, and the World for the Workers.'[89] The *Transport Worker* reported an incident in the resistance to a police baton charge on a demonstration in support of the Liverpool general strike of August 1911 thus:

85 *Syndicalist*, July 1912, in Holton, *British syndicalism*, 27.
86 *Industrial Syndicalist*, Dec. 1910, 18. Mann maintained an attraction to European unity, writing later that 'many things could be far better managed if Europe as a whole were responsible under one administrative department; but pettifogging nationalism asserts itself': *Memoirs*, London 1967, first publ. 1923, 120.
87 *Industrial Syndicalist*, Jan. 1911, 15. Mann arrived at this position gradually: Holton, *British syndicalism*, 64–5.
88 Raymond Challinor, *The origins of British Bolshevism*, London 1977, 70.
89 Mann, *Memoirs*, 236–8.

To the credit of one man who showed his British pluck, and did not display absolutely disgraceful cowardice as did the police with their batons, this pedestrian threw off his coat, and putting up his fists knocked down two constables to the ground, and took their truncheons off them, but met his fate by half a dozen constables surrounding him, knocking him to the ground, and kicking him. This was too much for the crowd, and well it might be. No man if he had the sense of liberty or the feeling of a Britisher could stand such treatment.[90]

The first example shows that many syndicalists had passed through the socialist movement, as it echoes Morris and Blatchford. The second example shows a continuing tradition of opposition to state authority couched in terms of radical patriotism.

## The battle of the ballot

The two major socialist organisations in Britain declined in the five years preceding the Great War. The ILP declined from 887 branches in 1909 to 672 in 1914. Between 1909 and 1911 its pamphlet sales dropped by half. The BSP claimed 40,000 members at its foundation in 1912, yet two years later its membership had halved.[91] Neither Leonard Hall nor H. Russell Smart, leading ILP dissidents who had helped to form the new party, were present at the 1913 conference. They had both gone over to syndicalism. Hall had scrawled on the back of an envelope before the founding conference of the BSP, 'the SDP resolution for Conference is too parliamentarian & non-industrial & will need amending'.[92] These falling memberships were despite union membership rising from 2.5 million to 4.1 million between 1910 and 1914.[93] Neither the ILP nor BSP could relate to the massive wave of industrial unrest. Both parties lost members to the syndicalists; Mann and Bowman were prominent examples of those leaving the SDP. The official historians of the BSP recorded 'a subdued mood' in 1913, because unity had not brought the expected results and syndicalist influence in the party was considerable.[94] South Wales ILP branches were learning centres for syndicalism.[95] The Labour Party failed to win a single by-election after the 1910 elections. Geoffrey Foote has agreed that syndicalism presented the greatest challenge to labourism since Marx, for 'while syndicalism never won over the majority of trade unionists, it fitted the realities of Edwardian Britain in which the violence of industrial strife increased distrust of a respectable Labour leader-

---

90 Ibid. 221.
91 Morgan, 'Edwardian socialism', 101; Kendall, *Revolutionary movement*, 28, 36–7, 43–4.
92 Hall to H. B. Williams, 1912, BLPES, BSP collection, archive collection, miscellaneous 155, fo. 39.
93 Read, 'Introduction', in his *Edwardian England*, 16.
94 H. W. Lee and E. Archbold, *Social-democracy in Britain*, London 1935, 210.
95 Holton, *British syndicalism*, 80.

ship'.[96] Clifford Sharpe wrote that 'Socialist thought, (as well as outside public opinion) is in a condition of flux',[97] and socialists sought to respond by reformulating their socialism. The Webbs saw syndicalism as 'a very natural, and . . . very pardonable reaction from the intolerable social condition of today', but leading to 'a serious deterioration of moral character'.[98] With the failure of their 'crusade' of Poor Law reform, they moved towards working within the Labour Party. Likewise, G. D. H. Cole was rethinking his socialism. In 1910 he had seen the Labour Party as an 'admirable' body, but soon decided that 'the present Labour Party can never become a majority and would be sadly at a loss to know what to do if it did become one'. In developing guild socialism, he sought a transformation of society through trade unionism.[99]

The leaders of the ILP tried to rebuild their influence and restore confidence in parliamentary socialism. Labour leaders warned of a loss of faith in both the Labour Party and parliamentarism. Hardie, closer to the mood of the rank-and-file of the party than most leaders, warned against MacDonald's elevation to chairman of the Labour Party. He wrote to Glasier:

> You know I fear JRM coming into the chair. . . . His mental make-up, his love of being in the know of everything, and his quite justifiable ambition, all make for a certain course which makes it easy for the party, but which appears to me to head straight for destruction. Sooner or later the revolutionary spirit of the working class will assert itself, and if it finds no response in the party in Parliament, nay finds itself regarded with scarcely concealed aversion, then the results are going to be serious. All the tricks which impose so easily upon the elected person inside will increase the fury and disgust of the men outside.[100]

Hardie's answer was to make the ILP appear more radical; hence he told the 1912 conference that the ILP 'is not a reform organisation; it is revolutionary in the fullest sense of the word. . . . Comrades of the working class, we do not want Parliament to give us reforms. We are not asking Parliament to do things for us. We are going to Parliament ourselves to master Parliament.'[101] MacDonald addressed the criticism of the Labour Party's parliamentary record at the 1911 ILP conference:

> We have been told that we do not raise Socialism in the House of Commons . . . and that if our members in the country could only open their newspapers one morning and read of a full-dress debate on Socialism they would be

96 Foote, *Labour Party's political thought*, 85, 89.
97 J. M. Winter, *Socialism and the challenge of war: ideas and politics in Britain 1912–18*, London–Boston 1974, 30.
98 Ibid. 39.
99 Ibid. 100, 102.
100 Stephen R. Ward, *James Ramsay MacDonald: low born among the high brows*, New York 1990, 65–6.
101 *Labour Leader*, 31 May 1912.

pleased. I do not know if I am differently constituted from other people, but if I found that our representatives in the House of Commons tried to appeal to me as an outsider by making propaganda speeches in the House of Commons I should be far more disgusted than pleased.[102]

Not for the first time, Hardie declared MacDonald 'the greatest intellectual asset in the movement'.[103] But two years later he made a speech at conference in direct contradiction to MacDonald's. He said that he intended 'to put down a Socialist motion calling for the overthrow of the existing order of society, and the creation of a Socialist State'. His acceptance of parliamentary procedure rather dented the impact of this, for he continued 'but unless he was fortunate at the ballot he would not have the opportunity of bringing this forward'.[104] MacDonald was temperamentally less inclined to indulge in left-wing rhetoric. Instead he sought to appeal to the common sense of the government to strengthen the Labour Party, to keep dissent within peaceful, moderate, constitutional channels. In an article at the end of 1910 he explained that the ILP had grown out of dissatisfaction with the SDF 'on the ground that it was "foreign" to British evolution and experience'. He argued that Labour was being weakened by such measures as the Osborne judgement, which prevented trade unions from financing the Labour Party. The working class, feeling itself weakened, had to resort to other methods, and could be forced into 'the paths of revolution and anarchy'. This would 'undo those feelings of general security and confidence which have kept our political history progressive but unbroken, whilst that of other peoples has been full of gaps and sudden changes'. 'A fully armed Labour', he declared, 'is a reasonable and peaceful Labour.'[105]

Snowden, who liked to show people from the village where he had been born and brought up around parliament, was asked by one of these whether there would be a revolution. He replied, 'I hope not, I think not. We have too many traditions, too many good things inherited from the past.' But by 1913 he warned the Commons that 'if the people lose faith in Parliament, they will turn to other methods to try to remedy their grievances and to improve their conditions, and if Parliament fails, then the country will be given over to a condition of anarchy'.[106] *Labour Leader* was keen to show that parliamentary methods worked. A week after a special edition on the industrial unrest, it devoted two full pages to a report of parliamentary proceedings under the headline 'The government and the strikes – Labour members fight men's

[102] ILP, *Conference report*, 1911, 68. A gap of twenty-three years separated the first two debates on socialism. Snowden in 1923 used the same motion as Hardie in 1900.
[103] Ibid. 82.
[104] Ibid. 1913, 73.
[105] J. Ramsay MacDonald, 'The trade union unrest', *English Review*, Nov. 1910, 728, 731, 739, 736.
[106] Colin Cross, *Philip Snowden*, London 1966, 105, 119–20.

battles in the House of Commons.'[107] After a further year of strikes, and in the wake of the 'Don't shoot' prosecutions which had brought syndicalism immense publicity, the ILP launched a campaign with the aims:

1. To restate the position and policy of the ILP.
2. To proclaim Socialism as the remedy for the oppression of Labour.
3. To drive home the lessons of the strikes, and to show the need for united political action.

A fourth aim, which remained unfulfilled before the war, was to double the membership of the ILP.[108] It was made clear that the major thrust of the campaign was to restore faith in parliamentary methods. A model resolution was provided for meetings:

That this meeting, whilst recognising the value of strikes mainly as a driving power on Parliament and as a method of securing small measures of reform and wide publicity for working-class wrongs, insists strongly that the conquest of political power and the social ownership of the means of life hold out the only hope of escape from Landlordism and Capitalism.[109]

The ILP also issued a series of four leaflets, of which 750,000 were distributed.[110] One asked readers to 'Stop a minute!': 'What do you think of Parliament? You think that Parliament is very far away. You think that what is said and done there does not closely touch you. You think that in any case you cannot move Parliament one way or the other. You are wrong on all these points. . . .' It then corrected the misapprehending reader, claiming that parliament had the power to give all children equal chances, to feed all children, to stamp out sweating and to fix the hours of labour.[111] Another leaflet told how voting could win liberty, strike a blow against poverty and break the power of the landlord and the capitalist. 'The vote is the symbol of your citizenship', it declared.[112]

The ILP's perception was that its methods for achieving socialism were adapted to suit British conditions and the national character. Thus in its battle against syndicalist ideas it found itself defending British political institutions as much as its conception of socialism. MacDonald declared that 'Socialism must be Parliamentary, or nothing.'[113] But the fact that this battle had to be undertaken, and with such vigour, suggests that for all the ILP's belief that permanent national characteristics favoured parliamentary change alone, British workers did not always concur.

---

107 *Labour Leader*, 25 Aug. 1911.
108 Ibid. 20 Jun. 1912.
109 Ibid. 27 Jun. 1912.
110 ILP, *Conference report*, 1913, 15.
111 ILP, *The power of parliament*, London n.d.
112 ILP, *The battle of the ballot*, London n.d.
113 MacDonald, *Syndicalism*, 6.

## More radical patriotism

Labour was a radical party of the opposition, and while it may have supported the Liberal governments of 1905 onwards more than many of its supporters would have liked, it still found itself in bitter opposition to many aspects of government policy. In three areas its opposition was expressed explicitly in terms of a radical patriotic discourse, above any other terms used at the time. These were relations between the governments of Britain and Russia; the treatment of South African strikers in early 1914; and the use of violence and repression by the state against opposition, whether industrial or political.

Russia under tsarist rule was the regime most hated by the British left (including Radical Liberals), particularly after the bloody suppression of the 1905 revolution. Thus, when the Liberal government negotiated an *entente* with the government of Tsar Nicholas II in August 1907, the British left was outraged.[114] But the language with which this outrage was expressed was largely that of patriotism and an innate belief in the superiority of British forms of rule. The *New Age* under the editorship of A. R. Orage, a socialist under the influence of Morris-like aesthetics, declared immediately against any agreement. During the negotiations, the *New Age* asked, 'Is it too late to save our national honour from a gross betrayal?' Two weeks later it described a demonstration in Trafalgar Square against the negotiations as 'a number of English patriots, incensed at the foul alliance of their country with a set of brutal butchers calling themselves the Russian Empire'.[115] The following year the friendship between the British and Russian governments developed further, and an official visit by Edward VII to the tsar was planned. MacDonald called this 'an insult to our country'.[116] But there were problems for Labour. In 1902, when Edward VII was crowned, the Labour Party in Parliament had not existed. The ILP at that time could afford a measure of republicanism. Hence it had issued two leaflets against the monarchy, though neither called for abolition.[117] But by 1908 the Labour Party was searching for respectability, so while the leaders were still theoretically republicans, in practice republicanism had been dropped. As Snowden explained, when asked directly about the issue, 'In theory I am a republican, but I attach so little importance to this as a practical question that I would not lift my little finger to interfere

114 A. J. A. Morris points out that Radicals were less united than Labour in their opposition to the government's Russian policy. Some Radicals believed Anglo-Russian friendship would, according to the *Manchester Guardian*, 'diminish very sensibly the risks of a European war', while Radicals interested in the Balkans also saw advantages in the friendship. But despite this Labour could offer no policy distinctive from the Radicals: *Radicalism against war, 1906–1914*, London 1972, 181–2, 204, 206–7.
115 *New Age*, 4, 18 July 1907.
116 *Labour Leader*, 29 May 1908.
117 *Mock loyalty*, ILP platform no. 48, London 1902, and *On royalty*, ILP platform no. 59, London 1902.

with the monarchy.'[118] MacDonald wanted to provide theory to this position. Since, he argued, the power of the monarchy was held only in potential, but not used,

> the political reformer may pass it by without notice, even though on political grounds he may be a republican. . . . Indeed, he may see in it some utilitarian value. When, like ours, it is an old and well-established part of the constitution . . . it preserves for the execution of . . . ceremonies that dignified formality which is essential to their being done well.[119]

Therefore, when it came to attacking the king's visit to Russia, James O'Grady explained to the Commons that

> whatever strong criticisms the Labour Party might have to offer . . . they wanted in no sense to say anything that would reflect upon the honour of His Majesty the King. No one could object to an ordinary English gentleman visiting his relatives. It was only when they heard that this visit was to be of a representative character that they raised their protest. He desired to say that Gentleman in his side of the House had nothing but the highest admiration for the splendid and noble work His Majesty had done in the cause of the amity of nations and of international peace.[120]

Hardie, who had a reputation as an extreme republican,[121] now sought to offer advice on upholding the position of the monarchy. 'If the initiative did not come from the King, but from the Government', he urged, 'it would do much to enhance the King's position and reputation among the bulk of the people of this country.' Happily, the foreign secretary was able to assure him that the government took all responsibility.[122]

It was only after making clear that their later comments were not meant to cause offence to the king that O'Grady and Hardie made their main points. O'Grady spoke of 'this country [that] loved free institutions, the right of free speech and a free press . . . things [that] could not be said to exist in Russia', and warned that 'if we mixed in evil company the result was bound to be that we should to a certain extent be contaminated'. Hardie said it was not too late to cancel the visit, for 'better far would it be to offend the Czar than the best blood and conscience of the British Empire'.[123]

When in 1909 the Tsar made a visit to the Cowes regatta, all the previous year's sentiments returned. The Labour Party issued a manifesto saying, 'It is an insult to our national good fame and to our self-respect that our Sovereign

---

118 Socialism – yes or no, London n.d.
119 MacDonald, Socialism and government, ii. 40–2.
120 Hansard, 4th ser. cxc. 4 June 1908, 211–12.
121 See, for example, Labour Leader, 30 June 1894, in Morgan, Keir Hardie, 71–2. See also Benn, Keir Hardie, 122–3.
122 Hansard, 4th ser. cxc. 4 June 1908, 259.
123 Ibid. 212, 261.

should receive *in our name* the head of such a state.'[124] Hardie, in the Commons, contrasted the political situations of the two nations: 'The Czar is the head of a practically autocratic state. King Edward is the head of a more or less popular and democratic government.'[125] The Labour opposition was based on a belief in the superiority of British over Russian rule, and made no mention of the British empire. Victor Grayson, while condemning the tsar's visit, had to declare that 'I do not associate myself with the idea that we have so much right to assume an attitude of superiority.'[126]

A second example of radical patriotism in Edwardian Britain is provided by the response of the British labour movement to the state's suppression of the South African general strike of early 1914, when among other measures martial law was declared and nine trade union leaders were deported. The majority of the labour leaders in Britain presented this as an attack upon popular English liberties.[127] The protests in Britain were massive. *Justice* estimated that 250,000 took part in the demonstration of 1 March, and the *Clarion* reported a procession seven miles long.[128] This demonstration had been called by the South African Constitutional Rights Committee, with a resolution condemning 'the action of the South African Government in declaring martial law and deporting nine trade union leaders, whom we heartily welcome to this country, . . . [as] a denial of the fundamental rights of British citizenship'.[129] Glasier urged as many as possible to respond to the call of the organisers, in language drawing together themes of class and nation, in which the latter dominated:

> Now may our old England of the main from her freedom's height blow her thunder across the seas! Now may the workers of Great Britain run up the Red Flag and the Union Jack side by side! Now may the beacon fires of public opinion be lighted from town to town and the old Magna Charta and Habeas Corpus which our fathers won for us with their blood be unrolled once more in the sun and borne as an oriflamme by a ten-millioned host to the Houses of Parliament! For now surely, the hour has come when this old England – this Britannia – of ours, should send forth her Grand Remonstrance.[130]

This was flying the banner of radical patriotism with a vengeance. In the Commons, MacDonald led the Labour protest. He drew on ideas of his own 'Imperial Standard', that was meant to carry English liberty to all corners of

---

[124] ILP, *By order of the czar: death and imprisonment*, Common sense politics no. 11, London 1909. Original emphasis.

[125] *Hansard*, 5th ser. vi. 22 July 1909, 678.

[126] Ibid. 728.

[127] See Barrow, who argues that the response stressed the events were an attack upon white labour within the empire: 'White solidarity in 1914', in Samuel, *Patriotism*, i. 275–87. This is compatible with the argument presented here.

[128] *Justice*, 5 Mar. 1914; *Clarion*, 6 Mar. 1914.

[129] *Justice*, 26 Feb. 1914.

[130] *Labour Leader*, 26 Feb. 1914.

the empire. He began by saying that 'the South African Government . . . is destroying the constitutional liberties of the British people, and that is doing a great dis-service to the Empire of which it is part'.[131]

The Labour Party did not base its response on the international interests of the working class, but on the threat to the empire and the liberties of its citizens. It propelled a democratic and libertarian view of English history across the seas to the greater Britain.

The third example is the response of the British labour movement to the use of violence and repression by the state. It has already been shown that a connection had been made between the state/parliament and a view of Britain, progressing through its history towards democracy and increasing popular liberties. The use of state violence told against this view. The leaders of the labour movement therefore opposed state violence as something foreign and aberrant to this development. Examples of this approach are found in socialist newspaper headlines above the accounts of domestic state violence, and it was usually with Russia that comparisons were made. Thus when on 14 July 1907 police attacked the demonstration in Trafalgar Square against the Anglo-Russian *entente*, the *New Age* wrote of 'Russia in Trafalgar Square' and 'The Whitehall Cossacks', and *Justice* asked: 'Are Scotland Yard and the Foreign Office controlled from St Petersburg?'[132] Other examples include *Labour Leader* describing 'Tsar Haldane and Territorial serfs' in relation to the new Territorial Army, and describing the 'Don't shoot!' prosecutions as 'Russian Methods'. Birmingham BSP, referring to the jailing of Tom Mann, asked, 'Do you know that a determined attempt is being made to Russianise England and that the first steps are the suppression of free speech, and the incarceration of all agitators and reformers?'[133] The use of repression was portrayed as un-English and alien, and was opposed as a conspiracy. While this allowed the left to portray itself as the upholder of a more true Englishness and a real patriotism, it also meant subscribing to a belief in the superiority of English governance.

In the Edwardian period, the long hoped-for labour alliance became a reality. Trade unions were convinced by hostile legal decisions that their interests needed to be represented at Westminster, and to achieve this they combined with the socialist societies, often despite their socialism. The supporters of this alliance in the ILP found in it no conflict with their perception of politics. Their view of national history made parliament the legitimate arena for social change. The House of Commons stood at the centre of the advance to liberty. This conception was only strengthened by the constitutional struggle

---

131 *Hansard*, 5th ser. lviii. 12 Feb. 1914, 367–8.
132 *New Age*, 18 July, 1 Aug. 1907; *Justice*, 20 July 1907
133 *Labour Leader*, 26 Feb. 1909, 29 Mar. 1912; *Special supplement and programme of the third BSP concert at the Colonnade Hotel*, 30 Mar. 1912, BLPES, BSP collection, archives collection miscellaneous 155, fo. 96.

against the House of Lords. The left deployed a radical patriotic vocabulary against infringements of English liberty.

But the supporters of the labour alliance found their beliefs threatened by the left of the labour movement, indeed by the working class itself. Syndicalism and industrial action menaced the parliamentary socialists' version of British national identity. Tortuous arguments were often necessary to explain why British workers, with their innate common sense, were taking to strike action which appeared to be inspired by the foreign doctrine of syndicalism. Englishness alone was not felt entirely adequate to prevent workers from turning away from parliamentary methods. The political socialists thought it necessary to embark upon campaigns to convince their audience of the efficacy of parliament. These campaigns, as a side effect, reinforced more traditional views of what constituted legitimate politics in Britain.

# 6

# Socialism and the German Menace in Edwardian Britain

Edwardian society witnessed a marked growth in the expression of militarist sentiment. Pressure groups claiming large memberships were formed to promote conscription and a bigger Royal Navy. Invasion and spy scares flared up.[1] This was a result of an increasing awareness of the commercial and military threat to Britain's established position posed by an ascendant Germany,[2] combined with the 'lesson' of the Boer War, revealing British military inefficiency and the poor physical condition of potential army recruits.[3] Internally this led to reorganisation of imperial and home defences, driven forward by the creed of national efficiency, while externally British governments sought to end the nation's diplomatic isolation through understandings with Japan, France and Russia.

The British left responded with an unbalanced two-pronged approach. The first element of this was an indifference to foreign policy at state level, remaining largely willing simply to blame 'capitalism' for all events. C. H. Norman, in an article in the New Age censuring this neglect of foreign policy, argued that it was due to a belief that socialism was only economic, that it was difficult to obtain accurate information, that there was a sparseness of democrats in the diplomatic service, that the principles of foreign policy were obscure and tedious to study, and that this resulted in a general lack of interest and a willingness to leave it to experts.[4] William P. Maddox has calculated that between 1906 and 1914 only 3½ per cent of Labour MPs' speeches and questions in the House of Commons were related to foreign policy.[5] The second element was an enjoyment in campaigning against the most visible foreign policy events, and involvement in the Second International since it gave an impression of internationalism.

The response of the left was not united. This also showed an imbalance, for while the majority of the left could be termed anti-militarist, opposing

---

1   See Anne Summers, 'Edwardian militarism', in Samuel, Patriotism, i. 236–56; A. J. A. Morris, The scaremongers: the advocacy of war and rearmament 1896–1914, London 1984.
2   See Paul M. Kennedy, The rise of the Anglo-German antagonism 1860–1914, London–New York, 1987
3   G. R. Searle, The quest for national efficiency: a study in British politics and political thought, 1899–1914, Oxford 1971, chs i–iii.
4   C. H. Norman, 'Social democracy and foreign policy', New Age, 9 Sept. 1909.
5   Cross, Philip Snowden, 123.

increased armaments, two of the largest circulation socialist newspapers, *Clarion* and *Justice*, regularly gave much space to the minority who argued that there was a 'German menace' which had to be countered by increased arms spending. The fact that two vocal minorities, one within general political society, the other within the socialist movement, were questioning whether the British nation could continue its existence without a drastic reorganisation of national life meant that ideas of what constituted the nation, its character and interests were widely discussed on the left.

## Socialists and national defence

The policy of the Second International was complete opposition to any increase in armaments. But since its foundation in 1889 it had also supported the right of national defence.[6] A historian of the collapse of the Second International has described this policy as anti-militarism reconciled with a 'Jacobinical patriotism'.[7] Many French socialists were deeply attached to the French revolutionary tradition, from which they arrived at a position of the defence of the republic. Jean Jaurès pointed out that the French revolutionaries had been internationalists, but also patriots. Hence he argued

> if we, French Socialists, were indifferent to the honor, to the security, to the prosperity of France, it would not only be a crime against *la patrie* . . . it would be a crime against humanity. A free, great, strong France is necessary to humanity. It is in France that democracy has obtained its most logical form – the Republic; and if France falls reaction will rise in the world.

A historian of French socialist patriotism has pointed out that Jaurès was a sincere advocate of peace, but 'he taught the Socialists to defend France, to view Germany with suspicion, to respect Russia as France's necessary ally, to regard the severance of Alsace-Lorraine as an unpunished crime, to favor French imperialism, and in general to approach the international situation from "the national point of view" '.[8] Hence in August 1914, despite Jaurès's assassination, French socialists put memories of the French Revolution at the service of the *Union Sacrée*.[9]

German socialist leaders had given little attention to foreign affairs until their parliamentary representation was halved in the election of 1907, which

6  James Joll, *The Second International 1889–1914*, London 1955, 45–6.
7  Georges Haupt, *Socialism and the Great War: the collapse of the Second International*, Oxford 1973, 131.
8  Harold R. Weinstein, *Jean Jaurès: a study in patriotism in the French socialist movement*, New York 1936, 64–5, 133.
9  John Schwarzmantel, 'Nationalism and the French working-class movement 1905–14', in Eric Cahm and V. C. Fisera (eds), *Socialism and nationalism in contemporary Europe (1848–1945)*, ii, Nottingham 1979, 78.

the government had fought as 'a test of whether Germany is capable of developing from a European into a world power or not'.[10] While the left of the German Social Democratic Party (SPD) wanted increased agitation against militarism, leaders such as August Bebel wanted to refute the 'slanderous' charges that the SPD was anti-national. He maintained that social changes were necessary, and explained that 'what we oppose is not so much the idea of a fatherland as such, that anyway belongs to the proletariat rather than the ruling classes, but the conditions . . . prevailing in this fatherland of ours'.[11] Gustav Noske told the *Reichstag* after the elections that the SPD's stand on militarism was 'conditioned by our acceptance of the principle of nationality'. Social Democrats, he said, would defend the nation 'with as much determination as any gentleman on the right side of this House'.[12] With the two major socialist parties in Europe both believing in national defence, the action of the Second International could only result in what one historian has called 'a dialogue of the deaf'.[13]

The alternative to this belief in national defence was known in the decade before the First World War as 'Hervéism', after the French socialist Gustave Hervé, who argued that workers had no country and should turn their guns on their own ruling classes. But this was a minority position across Europe.[14] All sections of the British delegation to the 1907 Stuttgart International Congress supported the anti-war resolution which also reaffirmed the policy of national defence.[15]

This position of national defence shows the limited differences between those in Britain who were anti-militarists and those who were anti-Germans. The commitment to national defence led to a conflict with the idea of a single international working-class interest, since it logically led to the conclusion that all classes within a given territory had at least a single common interest opposed to the interests of those of all classes within other territories, and which over-rode class interests. Harry Quelch, an anti-German in the SDF/BSP, thus presented an argument with which few anti-militarists would have disagreed:

> Convinced internationalists as we are, recognizing that, theoretically, there is no cause of quarrel between the workers of the world; that the proletarian has no country to fight for, and therefore no occasion to fight – we must recognize that as a matter of fact humanity is at present divided into different

10 Carl E. Schorske, *German social democracy 1905–1912*, New York 1972, 59.
11 Ibid. 75–6; Dieter Groh, 'The "unpatriotic socialists" and the state', *JCH* i (1966), 157.
12 Schorske, *German social democracy*, 77.
13 Jolyon Howorth, 'The left in France and Germany, internationalism and war: a dialogue of the deaf 1900–1914', in Cahm and Fisera, *Socialism and nationalism*, ii. 81–100.
14 Hervé's books, *Anti-patriotism* and *My country, right or wrong* (1910) were translated into English, and circulated by the Socialist Labour Party and some syndicalists such as Guy Bowman, the translator of one: Kendall, *Revolutionary movement*, 49, 75.
15 Douglas J. Newton, *British Labour, European socialism and the struggle for peace 1889–1914*, Oxford 1985, 167.

nationalities with conflicting interests. . . . I submit here that, in the main, we have, for practical purposes, to take the present groupings of peoples in Europe as a working basis, and to recognize that willy-nilly there is, as a rule, in each national group, in spite of all differences, certain principles which bind together as a nation those within that group, and that notwithstanding personal, class, and other antagonisms, are bound together by a common interest to defend the national autonomy and the right of each nationality to work out its own salvation.[16]

Quelch argued for a citizen army and a strong navy, but acceptance of this position meant that even anti-militarists would not deny Britain adequate defence. Thus *Labour Leader* declared in 1910 that 'no sane politician would dream of opposing expenditure necessary for National Defence',[17] and MacDonald told the Commons in 1911 that the Labour Party 'stood for adequate national security'.[18] The anti-militarists' opposition to armaments was therefore conditional. They argued simply that even with reductions the adequate defence of the nation could be maintained.[19] In response to taunts from Conservative MPs, George Barnes defended Labour's stance; beginning with internationalism he showed how this was both a British and a patriotic tradition:

The right hon. Gentleman the Leader of the Opposition rather chided my hon. Friend the Member for Merthyr Tydvil (Mr Keir Hardie) last week because he said he was always arguing in favour of other countries and against his own. Why should he not? Why should I not? After all, we have great examples to follow in this respect. If one goes back over the history of our own country, we find men like John Bright and others who have stood up on many occasions, as we are endeavouring to stand up now. It is no dishonour surely to tell one's own country when he thinks it is in the wrong. That is the position we take up. We yield to nobody in love for our country; we yield to nobody in our desire to see it adequately protected . . . but . . . we on these benches are going to take upon ourselves the responsibility of saying we think this country is being badly advised.[20]

Since it was not principle at stake but a different interpretation of the requirements of the nation it meant that some Labour MPs refused to vote against armaments increases, or even supported them. Douglas J. Newton has shown how the Labour Party in parliament was divided over voting for or

---

16 Harry Quelch, *Socialism and foreign affairs*, 1912, in *The challenge of socialism*, ed. Henry Pelling, London 1954, 141–2.

17 *Labour Leader*, 18 Mar. 1910.

18 *Hansard*, 5th ser. xxii. 16 Mar. 1911, 2480.

19 See, for example, ibid. 4th ser. clxx. 5 Mar. 1907, 700–2.

20 Ibid. 5th ser. xxiii. 20 Mar. 1911, 114. This was of course also a Liberal tradition. During the naval scare of 1909 Arthur Henderson reproached the Government for 'the abandonment of the position for which Liberalism has been forced to stand as the stout defender in this country': ibid. 5th ser. ii. 17 Mar. 1909, 1133.

against armaments increases. In March 1906 seven Labour MPs voted with the government on increased naval estimates; in 1907 three refused to support a reduction motion; in March 1909 two supported the government; in July 1909 five voted against reductions. The affiliation of the Miners' Federation MPs increased the rebel faction. Thus, in March 1910, eight Labour MPs voted with the government. In March 1911, six voted against a Radical motion to cut the Royal Navy by 1,000 men. On this occasion only seventeen Labour MPs voted for the motion, another eighteen being absent. Newton comments that this 'vote was final proof that less than half the Labour Party's MPs could be relied upon in the House to support proposals to reduce armaments, in spite of all the efforts [of] the ILP, in spite of the influence exerted by the leadership, and in defiance of the Labour Party Conference'. In July 1912, eight rebelled against the Labour Party, voting against another Radical motion for the reduction of the Navy. The rebels on this occasion included Labour's chief whip, G. H. Roberts.[21] Some of these rebellions could be explained by the fact that Labour MPs represented arsenal or dockyard seats, for example, Woolwich, Chatham and Barrow. J. H. Jenkins, Alex Wilkie, Charles Duncan and Will Crooks all represented such seats and were regular rebels. But others such as Bowerman and Wilson had no such direct interest. These rebels shared the majority of the left's belief in national defence, and believed that the international situation allowed no reductions in spending. J. A. Seddon, an ILP member, supported Haldane's Territorial and Reserve Forces Bill, saying, 'I am not one of those who say there should be no defence of the nation. Notwithstanding what may be said against the old country, I think it is still the best country, and I am prepared under proper conditions to see that it is defended.'[22] To show just how close the position of the anti-militarists could be to those who voted for arms increases, it is worth quoting MacDonald in 1912. He said, 'I am not going to do anything or say anything which would deliberately at any given moment, in 1912 say, so diminish our power of self-defence that it would be unequal to any struggle which might be put upon us. I am not going to say that; I have never said it and I never will say it.'[23]

A further way in which socialists and Labour MPs justified support for military expenditure increases was to argue that the matter lay outside the sphere of party politics. This was the line that Blatchford had taken in the Boer War. After the war, when he had come to believe that Germany posed a military threat to Britain, he continued to argue this, though he added an anti-democratic tinge to it. He said party politics wasted time in discussion on armaments expenditure, calling this 'the unpatriotic squabbling of our political parties'.[24] By the next year he called for 'a determined public and – a

21 Newton, *British Labour*, 158, 182–3, 204, 205, 235–6, 237, 244, 302.
22 *Hansard*, 5th ser. i. 4 Mar. 1909, 1652.
23 Ibid. 5th ser. xli. 22 July 1912, 877.
24 *Clarion*, 17 June 1904.

MAN' to avert the danger.[25] After a series of articles written by Blatchford appeared in the *Daily Mail* during the election campaign at the end of 1909, he explained to *Clarion* readers that 'the appeal I made was a national appeal; it has been misread as a Party stratagem'. He continued: 'I am a Socialist, not a Liberal nor a Tory. But I made my appeal to the Empire, not as a Socialist, but as a British citizen. . . . Imperial defence is not a party question: it is an Imperial question. We who believe that national security should come before all party questions, make our appeal to all Britons as Britons.'[26] The *New Age*, another socialist newspaper which supported the demand for a big navy, also argued that questions of national defence should be 'raised out of the sphere of party politics. There is no conceivable reason why the differences which separate Liberals, Conservatives, and Socialists in regard to internal affairs should also separate them in regard to the question of National Defence.'[27] In the Commons, Labour MPs voting against their party often did so with the explanation that 'it was not a political question'.[28] Those on the left were not alone in seeking to raise the question of defence above party politics; indeed National Efficiency, which was more usually associated with the right, disparaged party politics in favour of the expert.[29]

Even anti-militarists drew an eventual line between defence of their nation and their opposition to increased armaments. Philip Snowden was one of the principal speakers on the ILP anti-militarist campaign of 1913–14. He argued:

> It is not in the courts of kings nor in the chambers of diplomacy that the war problem is going to be solved. The workers of all lands are increasingly recognising that militarism and capitalism are the common enemies of the workers of all lands. Thirteen millions of men in Europe are enrolled under the red flag of Socialism, and in that fact you have a stronger safeguard of peace than in all your battleships and all your armed camps.

Yet he qualified such statements, continuing that 'much as we who sit on these benches oppose war, I am sure we should not hesitate for a moment to vote any sum, however large, if we were convinced that it was absolutely necessary for the defence of our own shores'.[30] It was statements such as this that led Blatchford to comment that 'The Labour Party seem to have fallen between . . . two stools. They object to expenditure on the Navy and the Army; but they have never spoken out boldly for the abolition of the Navy and the Army.'[31] Effectively, therefore, the division on the left over the

---

25  Ibid. 17 Feb. 1905.
26  Ibid. 31 Dec. 1909.
27  *New Age*, 14 Mar. 1908.
28  *Hansard*, 4th ser. clxx. 1052 (J. H. Jenkins).
29  Searle, *Quest for national efficiency*, ch. iii.
30  Cross, *Snowden*, 129.
31  *Clarion*, 16 Apr. 1909.

question of national defence was over the nature of the threat faced by Britain, with the anti-militarists arguing that no real threat existed. F. W. Jowett replied to Blatchford that only a small but efficient army and navy were needed, and 'the bulk of those who find themselves unable to agree with you [over the size of the armed forces] . . . would never think of making use of such an argument [as abolition of all defence].They are men and women who love their country, as you do.'[32] Jowett was correct; apart from the small Socialist Labour Party and the Socialist Party of Great Britain there were very few socialists who rejected the idea of national defence.[33]

### Socialists and patriotism in Edwardian Britain

One socialist who did reject national defence was Bax. In 1911 he wrote an article entitled 'Patriotism *v.* socialism', in which he declared that he was 'an internationalist to the point of absolute indifference to the national interests of any particular country, my own included'. He was, he said, an 'anti-patriot' wishing to see the British 'punished and humiliated in their national vanity'.[34] The response was an article by F. Victor Fisher called 'Patriotism *and* socialism'.[35] Fisher refused to debate publicly with Bax since 'the very worst thing the Socialist movement could do is convince the great mass of the people, who must be converted to Socialism if Socialism is to be realised, that Socialism entails anti-patriotism'. As a mirror image to the anti-patriots there was in Edwardian Britain a small group of socialists who saw patriotism as essential to the advancement of socialism. This was a continuation of the Merrie England theme but with the patriotic element pushed to the fore in a period when international tensions gave it added significance. This group of socialists, led by Fisher, went on to form the core of the labour 'super-patriots' during the First World War. Hence their super-patriotism was not a sudden aberration caused by war, but a logical outcome of their pre-war political thought, a point to which neither of their historians draws attention.[36]

These socialists accepted the nation and patriotism as real and permanent forces. Hedley V. Storey believed that 'Love of native land is not mere sentiment: It is a great fact. It is inevitable. It grows out of the nature of things.'[37] Likewise, Fisher wrote that 'the ties of blood are a real and natural factor of

---

[32] Ibid. 23 Apr. 1909.
[33] Both groups had seceded from the SDF: Kendall, *Revolutionary movement*, ch. iv; Challinor, *Origins of British Bolshevism*.
[34] *Justice*, 22 July 1911. Bax in fact went on to support the British war effort in 1914, though he continued to deny that he was patriotic: *Reminiscences and reflexions*, 254–5.
[35] *Justice*, 29 July 1911. Original emphasis.
[36] See Roy Douglas, 'The National Democratic Party and the British Workers' League', *HJ* xv (1972), 533–52, and J. O. Stubbs, 'Lord Milner and patriotic labour, 1914–1918', *EHR* lxxxvii (1972), 717–54.
[37] *Clarion*, 16 June 1911.

deep potency. The ties of common tradition are the steel links of nationhood.
. . . And just as a son loves and protects his mother with the most tender love,
so the citizen should love and defend the motherland'.[38] Fisher's version of
England contained little of which even the most conservative patriot could
disapprove, for besides its land, sea, rivers, hills and woods, it also included
physical prowess and military achievement.[39] Harry Roberts, another
patriot-socialist, wrote a series of seven articles hoping to appeal 'to public-
spirited men of all Parties and all schools of political thought to lay aside their
labels for a moment and consider (as patriotic Englishmen) the problem of
England and the English people'. Blatchford was indignant. He wrote to A.
M. Thompson:

> Every paragraph of the articles by Roberts ought to begin: 'As R[obert]
> B[latchford] says in Merrie E[ngland]'; or 'as RB says in the Dispatch', or 'as RB
> said in the Mail, in B[ritain] for the B[ritish], in the Clarion', or 'as A. M.
> T[hompson] says in the Clarion', or 'as A. M. T. said in his book on Japan'. But
> he never even mentions us.[40]

These socialists urged the rest of the left to take the national and patriotic
way to socialism. Lack of patriotism by socialists was seen as an obstacle to
socialism. Roberts argued that 'for a Socialist to refer to the defence of England otherwise than with a sneer is to mark himself down as a renegade and a
traitor to all the principles of the "wee free kirk" of Socialism. . . . This is one
of the many reasons why Socialists are not more popular with the average
Englishman.'[41]

These patriot-socialists therefore combined demands for 'an invincible
Navy' and compulsory military training with 'a patriotism which cares for
England, and its order and its character, and its honour as a good housewife
cares for her home'.[42] Storey urged that 'therefore every Socialist should be a
patriot and preach patriotism as part of his gospel'.[43] A practical proposal
along these lines was presented in a pamphlet by A. P. Hazell and W. Cook,
with a preface by Jack Williams. All three were members of the SDF. Called
*Work for the unemployed!: a national highway for military and motor traffic*, it was
published by the Twentieth Century Press, the SDF's publishing company,
but was not an official publication. It proposed an extensive network of roads
around Britain, since 'it is plain enough that, if some solution is not found for
the social evil arising out of competition, that the majority of the people must
continue to physically degenerate and become unable to defend themselves

---

38 *Justice*, 29 July 1911.
39 Ibid.; *Clarion*, 10 Jan. 1913.
40 Blatchford papers, Manchester Central Library, MS F 920 5 B27, vol. 2, fo. 16.
41 *Clarion*, 7 Apr. 1911.
42 Ibid. and 5 May 1911.
43 Ibid. 16 June 1911.

against their national enemies'.[44] This national highway was to consist of a 40 ft-wide zone including a light railway and a track for cycles and general traffic, a mono-railway allowing travel between London and Edinburgh in three hours, a 60 ft-wide 'motor track and military road'.[45] This Bonapartist fantasy was seen both as a socialist palliative and a patriotic endeavour. Patriot-socialists in Edwardian Britain had constructed a combination of inward and outward-facing patriotism.

## The German menace

The significance of national defence rose considerably when the nation was perceived to be in danger, and in Edwardian society there was a national anxiety about invasion by Germany. A minority of socialists shared this anxiety; foremost among them were Hyndman and Blatchford, two of Britain's most prominent socialists. This is partly the explanation for the imbalance between the anti-Germans' numbers and their impact. Since the *Clarion* was privately owned and edited by it proprietors, Blatchford and Thompson, it had no requirement to be representative, except to the extent that circulation had to be maintained. The election of twenty-nine Labour MPs led to a massive rise in circulation of all socialist newspapers, including the *Clarion*, despite its Germanophobia. In January 1906, the *Clarion* claimed a circulation of 56,000; two and a half years later it claimed 82,100.[46] *Justice*, since its foundation in 1884 had borne the subtitle 'The organ of social democracy', and it was the official organ of the SDF and subsequently the BSP. However it was not owned by the party but by the Twentieth Century Press Ltd, since the party, having no existence in law, could not own property. This made conference control over *Justice* difficult. The editors, Quelch until his death in 1913, and H. W. Lee afterwards, were anti-Germans. With Hyndman as the founding father of the SDF, Blatchford as the most popular socialist journalist in Britain, and the control of two papers, the anti-Germans were assured of a platform. The *New Age*, another privately-owned socialist journal, also gave support to demands for a big navy and a citizen army.[47]

In mid 1904 Blatchford began to write articles in the *Clarion* with titles such as 'Can England be invaded?: forewarned is forearmed', 'The German menace', and 'England's foolhardy neglect in the North Sea'.[48] In these he warned that invasion was not only possible, but probable, and that 'if we want to keep our Empire, our wealth, our liberty, *our* honour, we have got to pay for

44 A. P. Hazell and W. Cook, *Work for the unemployed!: a national highway for military and motor traffic*, London n.d., 5.
45 Ibid. diagram on pp. 8–9.
46 *Clarion*, 12 Jan. 1906, 12 June 1908.
47 See, for example, *New Age*, 6 June 1907, 15 Feb. 1908.
48 *Clarion*, 10, 17, 24 June 1906.

them and to fight for them. That which is won by the sword must be kept by the sword.'[49] In 1905 Hyndman followed Blatchford and put forward his case for the defence of England. 'The bourgeois French Republic is progressive, undoubtedly', he wrote. 'The bourgeois English Monarchy (Ltd) is less progressive. . . . But to permit the people of either France or England to come under the Kaiser's mailed fist would appear to me un-Socialistic as well as unpatriotic.'[50] He was contemptuous of the German socialists and people (and he was to become increasingly so). 'Our forefathers', he wrote, 'to whom we English owe our enfranchisement, from tyranny like that which they [the German people] submit to meekly, risked their liberty, their lives, and all that men hold dear, rather than exist under the conditions Germans are content with to-day.'[51]

It was Blatchford rather than Hyndman who suggested reasons for the perceived German expansionism. He argued that Germany, with its growing population and inability to grow its own food, with the desire for a proper seaboard, and the German ruling class's belief in German superiority, was forced to look outwards.[52] Hyndman usually simply referred to Prussian aggression as shown by its wars with Denmark, Austria and France in the decade of unification.[53] The core of Blatchford and Hyndman's arguments as to why socialists should defend Britain, the biggest imperial power in the world, was that Britain allowed more political liberty than Germany. Blatchford's 'case for efficient national defence' was that, 'There is no nation in the world so free as Britain. There is no nation where the subject has an equal liberty of speech and action. I believe and feel very strongly that with all Britain's faults there is no country so good to live in as our own.'[54] Hyndman cited the right of asylum as evidence of Britain's liberty, though the tone of the article was such that it showed his anti-foreigner feeling, since he wrote that it 'astound[ed]' him that foreigners in the SDF should oppose an adequate navy in the land that had granted them asylum.[55] Thompson also argued, 'My sober conviction is that our forefathers and our living champions of democracy have won for us, the inhabitants of Great Britain, certain rights and liberties which it would be worth the lives of all the Socialists in the kingdom to defend.'[56]

It was through the idea of a citizen army that the anti-Germans added a radical edge to their demands for the defence of Britain. Again this was in line with the policy of the Second International since 1889 and reaffirmed at Stuttgart in 1907, as supporters of the citizen army pointed out to their

[49] Ibid. 3, 10 June 1904.
[50] Justice, 27 May 1905, in Tsuzuki, Hyndman and British socialism, 200.
[51] Justice, 12 Aug. 1905.
[52] Clarion, 17 Feb. 1905, 21 Aug. 1908.
[53] Justice, 14 Mar. 1908; Hyndman, Further reminiscences, 396.
[54] Clarion, 16 Apr. 1909.
[55] Justice, 29 May 1909.
[56] Clarion, 8 Mar 1907.

opponents.[57] The official history of the SDF recorded, three decades later, that 'It was doubtful if any aspect of [the SDF's] work in this country was ever so misunderstood and consistently misinterpreted and misrepresented.'[58] In 1908, in response to Haldane's Territorial Army Bill, Will Thorne, the SDF's sole MP, introduced a citizen army bill to the Commons. It proposed that 'every male subject domiciled in the United Kingdom shall be liable to military training', except those 'following the sea as a profession or occupation', 'persons unfit physically', and 'those who have a fixed conscientious objection to using arms'. The latter would be trained for 'ambulance work, or other non-combatant duties'. No provision was made for absolutist objection, except up to twelve month's imprisonment with hard labour, with no relief from liability to service.[59] The SDF attempted to reinforce their arguments for a citizen army by linking it to an English revolutionary democratic tradition.[60] Thus W. H. Humphreys quoted Thomas Paine, who, he argued, had shown that 'a nation which desired its liberty must be prepared to defend it by armed force'.[61] Quelch had argued that 'an unarmed nation cannot be free. . . . An armed nation, on the contrary is a guarantee of individual liberty, of social freedom, and of national independence.' These were English ideals cherished by socialists, and could be promoted through a citizen army 'by the inculcation of true patriotism and of international co-operation and interdependence'.[62] Alongside this, the SDF played on the traditional English dislike of standing armies, using the slogan 'No standing army; no military caste; no military law; but every man a citizen and every citizen trained and capable of bearing arms at need.'[63] As a historian of patriotism has remarked, 'Arms thus became the badge of liberty in the old, archaic way.'[64]

The citizen army proposal could tenuously be presented as a socialist measure in defence of liberty. However, Blatchford and Hyndman became increasingly vocal in their extended demands for national defence, moving out from the socialist movement into the capitalist press. In September 1909, Blatchford went to Germany to report on German army manoeuvres for the *Daily Mail*, returning an advocate of conscription. During the the general election

57 See, for example, *Justice*, 10 Nov. 1906, 29 Oct. 1901.
58 Lee and Archbold, *Social-democracy in Britain*, 194.
59 Ibid. 280–1, 282.
60 In France, Jaurès's proposal for *L'Armée nouvelle* could more easily be linked with a native revolutionary tradition: Weinstein, *Jaurès*, 135–7.
61 W. H. Humphreys, *The case for universal military training as established in Australia*, London 1912, 1. Humphreys subtitled his name 'ex-private, Royal Scots' and the SDF's foremost advocate of the citizen army, Robert Edmondson, used his rank of sergeant-major. See his *An exposition and exposure of Haldane's Territorial Forces Act 1907*, London 1908, and *Justice*, 8 Feb. 1908.
62 Harry Quelch, *Social democracy and the armed nation*, London 1900, 4, 11.
63 Lee and Archbold, *Social-democracy*, 198. Edmondson argued that a citizen army, unlike a standing army or the Territorial Army, could not be used to aid the civil power: *Exposition and exposure*, 1–3.
64 Grainger, *Patriotisms 1900–1939*, 300–1.

campaign of January 1910 he wrote a series of ten articles for the *Daily Mail* which called for two years compulsory military service and an additional £50m. to be spent on the Royal Navy.[65] While the vast majority of the left, including *Justice*, dissociated themselves from Blatchford, Hyndman invited him to chair an election meeting in Burnley.[66] In July 1910, Hyndman, in a letter to the Conservative *Morning Post*, announced his support for increased expenditure to maintain British naval superiority. To pay for this he demanded the government borrow £100m.[67] It was this turning outside the socialist movement for a platform that brought down a storm of condemnation on Blatchford and Hyndman. Hyndman was unperturbed. He replied that if to call for a bigger navy 'is to be a jingo, then I am a jingo; if this is to be a bourgeois, then I am a bourgeois; if this is to be an opponent of organised Socialist opinion, then I an opponent of organised Socialist opinion'.[68] On 8 September of that year, a further letter from him appeared in the *Morning Post*. Blatchford responded to criticism with an article entitled 'An outburst of rabid jingoism' in which he wrote that 'strange as it may seem to busy people fed on Labour speeches and radical newspapers, England has good points. . . . We hear too much of her faults and of her merits not enough.'[69] Even before the First World War, therefore, some socialists had moved to a position where patriotism had become their foremost concern.

### The anti-militarists

The vast majority of the left opposed increased armaments and Germanophobia. The ILP passed anti-militarist resolutions annually at its conferences, with very few, if any, dissenters. Only five delegates voted against the anti-militarist resolution at the 1910 conference, after G. Moore Bell, a delegate from Woolwich, had declared that 'it was their business to say that they would not allow a reactionary nation to lead the other nations of the world captive'. Another delegate asked whether Bell was not inspired by the vested interests of Woolwich. Yet Bell did not receive the support of all seven Woolwich delegates.[70] In 1911 only three delegates voted against the anti-militarist resolution, in 1912 and 1913 it was passed unanimously, and in 1914 there were again three dissenters.[71] There is evidence that *Clarion* readers did not support Blatchford's position. Few anti-militarist letters were

---

[65] R. J. Q. Adams and Philip P. Poirier, *The conscription controversy in Great Britain, 1900–1918*, Basingstoke–London, 1987, 20. Blatchford turned against conscription after soldiers were used to break strikes: *Clarion*, 1, 22 Nov. 1912.

[66] Newton, *British Labour*, 213.

[67] For the letter see *Justice*, 20 Aug. 1910.

[68] Ibid. 3 Sept. 1910.

[69] *Clarion*, 30 Sept. 1910.

[70] ILP, *Conference report*, 1910, 66–8.

[71] Ibid. 1911, 95; 1912, 96; 1913, 103; 1914, 120–1.

published in the *Clarion*, but it would appear that this was a result of editorial decisions, for Thompson remarked after one of his articles that 'all who have written so far are opposed to my views'.[72] Blatchford wrote that 'my article on the German danger, has, as I expected, brought me a good many letters from well-meaning Socialists who do not understand'.[73] When such letters were published, the editor had a tendency to dissect them, answering point by point.[74] In a *Clarion* referendum, readers voted 2,485 to 1,786 against compulsory military service.[75] It was in the SDF/BSP that the issue had most repercussions, because while the ILP was united in hostility to militarism and the *Clarion* had no organisational framework, *Clarion* groups being largely recreational, the SDF/BSP witnessed real differences between fairly evenly balanced forces. *Justice* had to report that 'rain interfered . . . to mar the success' of a Trafalgar Square demonstration in favour of a citizen army in April 1907. A month later it admitted that there was a 'very considerable apathy' around the citizen army agitation.[76]

The ILP prided itself on its expressions of internationalism. From its foundation in 1893 it had welcomed fraternal delegates from Europe. At the founding conference, the German socialist Eduard Bernstein had addressed the delegates in response to Tillett's attack on continental socialists.[77] In 1896 the congress of the International was held in London, and delegates from the ILP attended all subsequent congresses. Hardie, for example, attended London in 1896, Amsterdam in 1904, Copenhagen in 1910, and Basle in 1912.[78] Larger ILP branches organised continental trips. The fifth trip organised by Bradford ILP unfortunately had to be cancelled, since it was planned for Saturday 15 August 1914.[79] But the ILP saw internationalism as a plurality of patriotisms. Hence, while May Day was a celebration of international working-class solidarity, it was held firmly within the national tradition, using much that was symbolic of England. Glasier explained that 'internationalism does not involve the extinction of nations, but the brotherhood of nations. Nations are forms of social organisation, and national or patriotic sentiment is an expression of social emotion.'[80]

This was a rejection of the idea that workers have no country, and it meant that workers within a territory did have a national interest in common with their ruling class. Thus the ILP believed in national defence, and did not argue for the abolition of the army or navy. They argued instead that Britain's defences were adequate without increases. In the Commons, William Brace

72 *Clarion* 8 Mar. 1907.
73 Ibid. 7 Aug. 1908.
74 See, for example, ibid. 1 July 1904.
75 Ibid. 28 Jan. 1910. The *Clarion* claimed 70,000 readers at the time.
76 *Justice*, 27 Apr., 25 May 1907.
77 ILP, *Conference report*, 1893, 5.
78 Morgan, *Keir Hardie*, 180.
79 Bradford ILP, *Yearbook 1914*, Bradford 1914, 9.
80 *Labour Leader*, 26 Oct. 1910.

argued for a reduction in the navy 'as more in consonance with the best interests of the nation'.[81]

The ILP attempted to claim a true patriotism for themselves. The corollary
to this was that the militarists were not real patriots. This could be argued in
one of two ways. First, it could be shown that the most vocal 'patriots' were
shareholders in armaments companies. This had been done to a small extent
during the Boer War, and Hardie had written a series of five articles called
'Patriotism and profit'.[82] In 1913 Fenner Brockway, editor of *Labour Leader*,
and J. T. Walton Newbold, a Quaker, set to work uncovering the existence of
what they claimed was an armaments ring. They published lists of shareholders in arms companies who were also leaders of the conscription and navy
pressure groups, MPs and high-ranking officers in the army and navy.[83] Philip
Snowden's longest Commons' speech ever was based on Newbold's
research,[84] but the national press ignored this 'Dynamite!' and Churchill
refused to answer questions on it.[85]

Second, it could be claimed that the militarists were 'bastard patriots'
since their claims to be British were doubtful. *Labour Leader* had used this
approach during the Boer War, claiming it was a war for Jews. The theme
reappeared during the naval scares of the Edwardian period. C. H. Norman
wrote an article in the *New Age* 'exposing' this 'bastard patriotism'.[86] 'The
time has come', he wrote 'for all lovers of the honour of their country to stand
fast against the dangerous militarist agitation now engineered by a reptile
Press, out-of-work generals, non-combatant Whig lawyers, and a corrupt
Court. The object of these men, few of whom are Englishmen, is to deprive
the citizens of this country of their liberties.' He then 'exposed' Lord
Rothschild as 'a Jew financier', Ralph Blumenfeld, editor of the *Daily Express*
as an 'American gentleman with a German name', the *Daily Mail* as Irish-
owned and edited, and Leo Maxse as 'another Jingo with an "all-British"
name'. The author of the popular play *An Englishman's home* he revealed as
having 'the truly English name of Du Maurier'.[87] 'The British workman', he
concluded, 'is being deluded by this unholy alliance of Jew financiers, American and Irish journalists and peers, into the belief that Conscription is a worthy ideal.'[88] The combined effect of these two approaches was to show that

---

81  *Hansard*, 4th ser. clxx. 5 Mar. 1907, 700–2.
82  See *Labour Leader*, 18 July, 1, 8, 29 Aug., 5 Sept. 1903.
83  Ibid. 22 May, 5, 12 June 1913; J. T. Walton-Newbold, *The war trust exposed*, Manchester–
London n.d. [1913].
84  It filled twenty-two columns of *Hansard*: Cross, *Snowden*, 131.
85  *Labour Leader*, 5 June 1913.
86  *New Age*, 4 Mar. 1909.
87  It was of course a Cornish name.
88  The article provoked two pieces of correspondence. Ethel M. Harter, who wrote the
song 'A call to arms', and whom Norman had 'exposed' as having the maiden name of de
Fonblanque, wrote that her family had come to Britain before 1750 as Huguenot refugees.
'X' urged that the article be reprinted as a leaflet: *New Age*, 11 Mar. 1909.

militarism was the result of both sectional and foreign interests, that had little to do with true patriotism.

The ILP also made use of the widespread feeling that compulsory military service, whether it be conscription or a citizen army, was alien to the traditions of England. In 1904 the Royal Commission on Army Reform recommended the introduction of compulsory military service; this, *Labour Leader* declared, 'has a sound as hateful to British tradition as slavery'.[89] A month later Harry Snell replied to advocates who argued that since every European country had conscription then so should Britain. 'Britain is different from every other country in Europe . . .', he wrote. 'Britain is an island and seems to have been meant by nature for the home of free institutions.'[90] It was in these terms that ILP conferences declared their opposition to conscription. MacDonald's resolution as chairman in 1909 argued that 'the immunity from compulsory military service which our nation enjoys, is one of the greatest heritages of freedom'.[91] In the autumn of 1913 the ILP ran a 'No Conscription Campaign' in which more than two hundred demonstrations and meetings were held.[92] The climax was a demonstration at Kingsway Hall at which Jaurès spoke for French socialists, Molkenbuhr for German social democrats, and Vandervelde for Belgian socialists. The French author Anatole France also spoke.[93] This internationalism was combined with radical patriotism, since an anti-conscription leaflet was entitled 'Resist the foreign yoke of conscription!' It urged 'let us preserve the civic character of the British nation' and declared, 'the spirit of militarism is alien to the traditions of the British race. The British nation is the freest of all European nations; it has spread its language, its trade, its political institutions afar over the world as no other nation has done – *and the British nation has no conscription or compulsory military training!'*[94] To argue that imperialism had been more successful the British voluntarist way was an unusual argument for socialists to use.

The SDF/BSP was most divided over the issue of anti-militarism and anti-Germanism. It did not split however until a year and a half into the First World War. This was largely because the anti-militarist opposition was also foremost in the left unity campaign that led to the formation of the BSP in 1911.[95] In the years up to Hyndman's approach to the capitalist press there had been opposition to his Germanophobia. Letters responded to every anti-German utterance in *Justice*. Zelda Kahan, a leader of the anti-militarist opposition, responded to Hyndman's outbursts during the naval scare of 1909

89 *Labour Leader*, 3 June 1904.
90 Ibid. 8 July 1904.
91 ILP, *Conference report*, 1909, 84. The Labour Party conference passed the same resolution.
92 Ibid. 1914, 21–2.
93 Newton, *British Labour*, 310–11.
94 ILP Coming-of-age campaign leaflet no. 7, Manchester–London n.d. [1914]. Original emphasis.
95 Kendall, *Revolutionary movement*, 55.

by accusing him of allying himself with the 'jingo naval scaremongers', and Hackney Central branch condemned 'the anti-German attitude of Hynd-man, Blatchford and *Justice*'.[96] But it was after Hyndman's letter to the *Morning Post* in July 1910 that the opposition became more organised and the debate more bitter. At the 1911 SDF conference, Kahan moved a resolution calling for the party to 'combat with the utmost energy, the demands for increased armaments'. Quelch responded with an amendment calling for an adequate navy and a citizen army. The conference delegates were evenly divided, twenty-eight to twenty-eight. A branch vote was subsequently taken, with Quelch's amendment winning forty-seven to thirty-three.[97] The following year, at the first conference of the BSP, Quelch presented a paper on 'Socialism and patriotism' in which he said the BSP 'were Internationalists, not Anti-Nationalists'. He argued that 'International Socialism claimed the fullest possible liberty for every individual nationality.' Therefore the nation had to be defended, even in the present under capitalism. W. Gallacher of Paisley responded that 'it was no use juggling with the word patriotism; they had to take it in its generally accepted meaning . . . . They should condemn all idea of patriotism and all idea of militarism, unless it took the form of shooting down those who exploited them.' Again Quelch won the vote, this time by eighty-three to sixty-five.[98] Quelch came top of the poll in the subsequent election for the executive, though Kahan and E. C. Fairchild were also elected as internationalists. The conflict now took place on the executive committee. On 14 December 1912, Kahan moved a resolution which was passed by one vote declaring that 'so far as the workers are concerned there is nothing to choose between German and British Imperialism and aggression. The Executive Committee . . . dissociates itself from propaganda for increased naval expenditure.' The resolution bound all members of the executive to this decision.[99] Fisher then resigned from the executive. In a letter to *Justice* explaining his action, he complained of 'a violent and bitter anti-nationalism' and indulged in racism aimed at his opponents:

> I am persuaded that if we as a Party – self-named the BRITISH Socialist Party – permit it to be believed among the general public that Socialism stands for treason against the national security, and that, moreover, such a policy is largely inspired by comrades alien in blood and race, we may bid a long farewell to any hope of influencing national opinion in the direction of that social regeneration of which Socialism is the only possible expression.[100]

On 15 February 1913 the executive suspended Kahan's resolution when two of the anti-militarist members were absent. Fisher, therefore, rescinded his

96  *Justice*, 17 Apr., 1 May 1909.
97  Kendall, *Revolutionary movement*, 54.
98  BSP, *Conference report*, 1912, 20–2.
99  Ibid. 1913, 37.
100  *Justice*, 4 Jan. 1913.

resignation and Kahan resigned.[101] At the conference that year a compromise was reached when Hyndman agreed not to prejudice the BSP by public expression of his views; the anti-militarists were beaten or did not stand for re-election to the executive. No clear position had been reached and the party remained divided.

On the eve of the Great War the vast majority of the British left supported the idea of national defence. Most did so because they believed that Britain, almost naturally, enjoyed greater political liberty than any other country, and was more democratic. This involved a national self-deception, since no women had the vote, and neither did 40 per cent of adult males.[102] But the democratic delusion was very strong; it did not matter that Germany had universal manhood suffrage. National myths can be stronger than facts. The larger part of this group believed, however, that there was no threat of invasion by Germany, that Britain's defences were adequate, and that any increase in armaments would threaten peace and thus reduce the safety of the nation. They sometimes argued this in terms of radical patriotism, and they argued that should Britain be in danger they would not oppose increased armaments. Those who believed there was a danger from Germany argued for more efficient home defence (which could include imperial defence), usually a citizen army and a bigger navy. Part of this group believed that patriotism was an essential part of socialism, which should be put to the forefront of their propaganda. This group was liable to use anti-foreigner statements against their critics. This meant that the attitude of the left to a future war would largely depend on their belief in the existence of a threat dangerous to the continued survival of Britain as a nation marked out by its inherent freedom, rather than on socialist principles.

101 Ibid. 15 Feb. 1913.
102 Neal Blewett, 'The franchise in the United Kingdom, 1885–1918', P&P xxxii (1965), 27–56.

# 7

# The Left, Patriotism and the First World War, 1914–1917

## July and August 1914

Arthur Marwick has commented that 'prior to August 1914 . . . war was widely expected as an eventual probability, but it was scarcely visualised at all as an immediate contingency. This explains why the breaking of war brought both a sense of long-sought release and an atmosphere of panic and untempered emergency.'[1] This was the experience of most European socialists. Only on 24 July did Huysman, permanent secretary of the Second International, telegraph members of the International Socialist Bureau to inquire whether a meeting should be organised. The ISB met on 29-30 July; it decided to discuss 'The proletariat and the war' at the forthcoming congress in Paris on 9 August.[2] On 27 July, the German Social-Democrat leader, Ebert, said to a friend, 'They look too much on the black side. . . . I'm sure it's nonsense. There will be no war.'[3] About the same date, W. C. Anderson wrote his editorial for that week's *Labour Leader*. Published on 30 July it declared: 'The first shots have been fired between Austria and Servia, but I am not certain even now, that the Big Powers of Europe and the financial interests behind them will allow the struggle to be carried very far. . . . Despite all the signs to the contrary, there will, I believe, be no war.' This optimism meant that there was very little time for member parties to carry out the agreed resolutions of the International. At Stuttgart in 1907 the International had left the form of action in each country to be taken against war to each country's parliamentary representatives.[4] British socialists had been foremost advocates of a general strike against war; it had been Hardie who was joint sponsor of such a resolution at the 1910 Copenhagen Congress. The Labour Party in 1912 approved an investigation into the practicalities of a general strike, though the ILP had been forced to drop the idea due to trade union indifference.[5]

The British left therefore lacked plans for what to do in the event of war,

---

[1] *The deluge: British society and the First World War*, 2nd edn, Basingstoke–London 1991, 69.
[2] Haupt, *Socialism and the Great War*, 187, 199. It had been intended to hold the congress in Vienna.
[3] Joll, *The Second International*, 162.
[4] Ibid. 198.
[5] Newton, *British Labour*, ch. x.

but the vast majority of the left were united in the last days of July and first days of August in their desire to demonstrate to preserve peace.[6] Francis Johnson, ILP secretary, telegraphed the fifty largest ILP branches instructing them to organise demonstrations, and forty-three ILP anti-war demonstrations were held.[7] The British section of the ISB called a national demonstration against war on 2 August in Trafalgar Square. According to the *Daily Herald*, 20,000 people listened to Hardie, Henderson, Lansbury, Hyndman, Thorne, Marion Phillips, Cunninghame Graham, Margaret Bondfield and Robert Williams, and passed the following resolution:

> We protest against any step being taken by the Government of this country to support Russia, either directly or in consequence of an undertaking with France, as being not only offensive to the political traditions of the country but disastrous to Europe, and declare that as we have no interest, direct or indirect, in the threatened quarrels which may result from the action of Servia, the Government of Great Britain should rigidly decline to engage in war, but should confine itself to efforts to bring about peace as speedily as possible.[8]

As Mary Hamilton wrote later, 'Russia was the focal point; it was against being dragged into war to support Russia that they thundered. . . . Serbia was the arch-villain of the piece. Behind her stood Russia, and Czarist Russia was a far more fearsome apparition than Germany as we knew it.'[9] The next day, MacDonald replied to the foreign secretary's speech in the Commons. MacDonald was probably representative of the majority of the British left on 3 August. 'I want to say this to the House, and say it without equivocation', he said:

> If the right hon. Gentleman had come here today and told us that our country is in danger, I do not care what party he appealed to, we would be with him and behind him. If this is so, we will vote him what money he wants. Yes, and we will go further. We will offer him ourselves if the country is in danger. But he has not persuaded my hon. Friends who co-operate with me that it is, and I am perfectly certain, when his speech gets into cold print tomorrow, he will not persuade a large section of the country. If the nation's honour were in danger we would be with him. . . . If the right hon. Gentleman could come and tell us that a small European nationality like Belgium is in danger, and assure us he is going to confine the conflict to that question, then we would support him. What is the use of talking about coming to the aid of Belgium, when, as a

---

6  Though Blatchford wrote to Thompson that, 'I shall write today a cautious article counselling peace . . . but I do not think really that European peace is possible until Germany has been defeated and humiliated. Also I realize the great possibility that we shall be at war with Germany before the *Clarion* comes out. And I hope we are, Yours Bob': Blatchford letters, Manchester Central Library, MS F 920 5 B27, vol. 2, fo. 25, [4?] Aug. 1914.

7  Newton, *British Labour*, 327; *Labour Leader*, 6 Aug. 1914.

8  *Daily Herald*, 3 Aug. 1914; *The left and war: the British Labour Party and World War I*, ed. Peter Stansky, New York–London 1969, 84.

9  M. A. Hamilton, *Remembering my good friends*, London 1944, 66–7.

matter of fact, you are engaging in a whole European war which is not going to leave the map of Europe in the position it is in now. The right hon. Gentleman said nothing about Russia. We want to know about that. We want to try to find out what is going to happen, when it is all over, to the power of Russia in Europe, and we are not going to go blindly into this conflict without having some sort of a rough idea as to what is going to happen.[10]

These objections to the coming war involved judgements about the situation based on the idea of the nation rather than on socialism. Within the next thirty-six hours the situation had changed in such a way that most of the left were satisfied that all MacDonald's objections had been answered. Germany had violated Belgian neutrality to which Britain had treaty obligations. It was felt that not to respond would damage the honour of Britain, and place the nation in danger. This was combined with massive support for the war. On 1 August 1914, the principal recruiting station in London recruited eight men. On 4 August, it took twenty policemen twenty minutes to help the officer in charge through the gathered crowds.[11]

Most of the British left gave way to this massive popular pressure and their own basically patriotic feelings and supported the war. On 5 August the Labour Party executive met and backed MacDonald's sentiments of 3 August by eight to four but a meeting of the Parliamentary Labour Party the same evening rejected MacDonald's suggestion of abstention in the war credits vote. The Labour Party had committed itself to supporting the war effort and MacDonald resigned as chairman.[12] Later that month the Labour Party and TUC agreed to an industrial truce and Labour agreed to an electoral truce and to aid in raising an army through the Parliamentary Recruiting Committee. The BSP executive, including its anti-militarist members, signed a manifesto declaring that 'the Party naturally desires to see the prosecution of the war to a speedy and successful issue'.[13] Of the larger socialist parties only the ILP stood out against the war.

There are major difficulties in attempting to classify the attitudes of both parties and individuals to the First World War. As Marwick has pointed out, 'it is scarcely possible to draw a rigid line between pro-war and anti-war elements'.[14] Arthur Henderson was a supporter of the war but also a member of the General Council of the Union of Democratic Control until he joined Asquith's coalition government.[15] MacDonald was a founder of the UDC, prominent in the ILP, the most bitterly-hated opponent of the war, yet in a

---

10 *The left and war*, 58.
11 Adams and Poirier, *The conscription controversy in Great Britain*, 59.
12 Newton, *British Labour*, 332–3.
13 *Justice*, 17 Sept. 1914.
14 Arthur Marwick, 'Working-class attitudes to the First World War', BSSLH xiii (1966), 9.
15 Marvin Swartz, *The Union of Democratic Control in British politics during the First World War*, Oxford 1971, 147–8.

letter to the mayor of Leicester *declining* to appear on recruiting platforms, he wrote:

> Victory . . . must be ours. England is not played out. Her mission is to be accomplished. . . . History will in due time apportion the praise and the blame, but the young men of the country, must, for the moment settle the immediate issue. . . . Whoever may be in the wrong men so inspired will be in the right. . . . To such men it is enough to say 'England has need of you'. . . . They will gather to her aid.[16]

MacDonald's biographer has commented that 'politically, his position was only a hair's breadth away from Henderson'.[17] It was this sort of complication that could lead Robert Williams, a leader of the Transport Workers' Union and a socialist, to write a pamphlet in which he declared, 'I am well-nigh unable to determine my own attitude.'[18] In effect opponents of the war were largely defined by their enemies. MacDonald's resignation of the chairmanship of the Labour Party marked him off as an opponent of the war in the eyes of the supporters of the war. John Hodge, at the evening meeting of the PLP on 5 August, bluntly stated the choices before socialists: 'either we were for our country or we were against it'.[19] The war, being an extreme event, presented moderates with difficulties they were unwilling to face.

### The pro-war left

Historians of the British left agree that it was loyalist patriotism that determined the majority of the left's support for the First World War.[20] Contemporary socialist opinion saw this as unexpected. Fenner Brockway, editor of *Labour Leader*, felt himself 'facing the shock of betrayal', and David Kirkwood, a young shop steward on the Clyde, saw that 'within a week, the so-called "international solidarity of labour" was exploded by the force of national patriotism'.[21] However, the left in the decades up to 1914 had constructed a radical version of patriotism which accepted the idea of national defence, particularly for Britain, since they saw it as the natural home of democracy, liberty and free institutions. It was in the same terms as these that the pro-war left argued for support for the government and nation in August 1914.

---

16  Snowden, *Autobiography*, i. 364.
17  Marquand, *Ramsay MacDonald*, 180.
18  *Un-common sense about the war*, Herald pamphlet no. 4, London n.d., 2.
19  Wrigley, *Arthur Henderson*, 77.
20  See, for example, Ralph Miliband, *Parliamentary socialism: a history of the British Labour Movement 1867–1974*, 2nd edn, London 1972, 43; James Hinton, *Labour and socialism*, Brighton 1983, 98; F. M. Leventhal, *Arthur Henderson*, Manchester–New York 1989, 50.
21  Fenner Brockway, *Inside the left: thirty years of platform, press, prison and parliament*, London 1947, title of ch. vi; David Kirkwood, *My life of revolt*, London 1935, 81.

Radical patriotism was still love of country and an acceptance of the notion of national identity. Thus Mary Hamilton wrote of the Labour MPs, 'They were British citizens, first: only in second line members of a party.'[22] The *New Age* also agreed with such sentiments: 'While our special concern is with the proletariat of our own country, it cannot be a matter of indifference to us what the fate of our own country itself may be', it commented. 'We think it no shame to Socialists and Democrats to put patriotism today before their own particular propaganda.'[23]

This acceptance of 'my country, right or wrong' was however combined with a deeply-held belief that, according to the orthodoxies of radical patriotism, Britain and its allies were indeed in the right. Most importantly, from this point of view, Germany was clearly the aggressor. The violation of Belgium, 'that plucky little nation', as Hyndman echoed the official view, was both the occasion of Britain's declaration of war and for the left's declaration of support.[24] And if this was the cause of war, it followed that Britain and its allies had 'clean hands'.[25] Second to this was a belief that Britain's independence would be threatened if Germany was not faced in battle. The whole executive of the BSP, anti-German and anti-militarist alike, had 'always maintained the right of nations to defend their national existence by force of arms. . . . The national freedom and independence of this country are threatened by Prussian militarism.'[26] Third was a belief that, in fighting for Britain, the pro-war left was fighting for liberty and democracy. Blatchford called the war a war of 'the democracies of a continent against the tyranny of the sceptre and the sword'.[27] J. H. Thomas, Railwaymen's leader and Labour MP, implored young men, from recruiting platforms, 'If you love liberty as I love liberty and if you respect freedom as I respect freedom, then it is your duty immediately to come to your country's aid.'[28] Jessie Cockerline, a Bradford socialist, decided that, 'The sword is drawn and it is drawn in the cause of democracy, in the cause of liberty and honour and we must, each one of us, realise that it can never be sheathed whilst the terror of the Kaiser's dreams of universal domination have the remote possibility of being realised.'[29] If other socialists felt the same, they could reply to an advertisement in the *Clarion*:

---

[22] M. A. Hamilton, *Arthur Henderson: a biography*, London 1938, 96.
[23] *New Age*, 6 Aug. 1914.
[24] *Justice*, 13 Aug. 1914.
[25] *New Statesman*, 8 Aug. 1914.
[26] *Justice*, 17 Sept. 1914. See also Clynes, *Memoirs 1869–1924*, 179.
[27] *Clarion*, 14 Aug. 1914. The question of tsarist Russia was largely ignored by the pro-war left.
[28] Gregory Blaxland, *J. H. Thomas: a life for unity*, London 1964, 87.
[29] *Yorkshire Factory Times*, 27 Aug. 1914, in Keith Laybourn and Jack Reynolds, *Liberalism and the rise of Labour 1890–1918*, London 1984, 183.

DEMOCRATIC INSTITUTIONS
versus
GERMAN 'KULTUR'
Which side are You on?
. . .
JOIN THE FELLOWSHIP COMPANY
of the Cheshires, and fight side by side
With SOCIALIST COMRADES[30]

This was a 'Pals' company for socialists, organised by J. Hunter Watts, a member of Manchester Clarion Club and the BSP. Thus support for the war could be accommodated with relative ease within the radical patriotism to which the majority of the left subscribed in 1914.

Some socialists were not satisfied with individual support for the war, and wished to see an organisation to consolidate this support and also to atone for the anti-war stance of the ILP and parts of the BSP. In April 1915 the Socialist National Defence Committee was formed, largely by those socialists who, before the war, had argued for patriotism to be placed in the forefront of propaganda for socialism. The war gave them their opportunity. The leading figure in the SNDC was Victor Fisher, who in early 1915 resigned from the BSP because of the anti-war attitude of its left-wing. Also involved were Blatchford and Thompson, the Labour MPs G. H. Roberts, Stephen Walsh, George Barnes and George Wardle, the socialist author H. G. Wells, and Bert Killip from the BSP executive.[31] The preoccupations of the SNDC are best shown in its own words, through the manifesto issued on 1 September 1915. 'In this hour of peril', it explained

> when the independence of peoples is brutally menaced and the established public law and liberties of Europe are ruthlessly violated, a handful of pseudo-Socialists in this country are breaking the national solidarity and weakening the national effort in the face of the enemy. It has become a duty for true British Socialists to expose and repudiate the errors of these dreamers. Some of them are extreme pacifists; some are aliens by birth, blood or sentiment; all of them are *consciously or unconsciously* the agents of German Kaiserdom, and traitors to the imperishable ideals of liberty and democracy which have united free Britain, independent Belgium and Republican France in an indissoluble and glorious alliance.

It went on to explain that 'Socialism expresses itself internationally, but it cannot develop anti-nationally. It must evolve according to national temperament and national rights.'[32] Thus the SNDC, like much of the left, believed that theirs was a true British socialism, and combined this with an

---

30 *Clarion*, 23 July 1915.
31 Much of this section draws on Douglas, 'The National Democratic Party and the British Workers' League', and Stubbs, 'Milner and patriotic labour'.
32 *Socialists and the war: manifesto of the Socialist National Defence Committee*, London 1915.

intolerance towards aliens (mainly Russian Jews) who refused to support the war. To the SNDC to be anti-war was to be not only anti-British but also un-British. One could think one's self into alienness.

The SNDC was formed out of sentiments that included anti-German racism and general xenophobia. Its patriotism was pluralist only in so far as Britain's allies were concerned. While many pro-war socialists differentiated between the German people and their ruling class, the super-patriots condemned the German people as a whole. An early example was a verse of thirty-six lines in *Clarion*, written by 'Bezique', entitled 'Kultur: a definition'. The first six lines, which set the tone of the verse, were as follows:

> It is homicide and thieving;
> It is lying and deceiving;
> It is slaughter – pity spurning,
> And it means cathedral burning.
> It is devilry applied;
> It is damned infanticide . . .[33]

As the war progressed, this racism became more virulent. In July 1915, Blatchford was arguing that the Germans were an 'insatiable race of savages', 'organised race of spies', and 'race of treacherous homicidal robbers', and decided that 'something very near to extermination of the German people' would be needed to keep the peace permanently.[34] George Barnes explained that 'we now know that we are not only fighting Prussian militarism, we are fighting a people with a "kink" in their mental and moral make-up'.[35] The SNDC played a full part in the campaign for internment of aliens that followed the sinking of the *Lusitania*. The language of these socialist super-patriots was little different from that of right-wing patriots such as Horatio Bottomley, who called the German people 'an unnatural abortion, a hellish freak'.[36]

The super-patriots soon made contact with the radical right. Lord Milner, who was chairman of the National Service League, made contact with Fisher, and was pleased by what he heard. He wrote to Lord Willoughby de Broke in October 1915 that 'the impression made upon my mind certainly was encouraging. I found these men intelligent, patriotic, and not at all narrow minded. They represent . . . the essential patriotism of the working class.' Within a few months, Fisher was being paid £1,660 per year by Milner's contacts.[37] In March 1916, the SNDC was re-formed as the British Workers' League, now with an imperial rather than national outlook.

[33] *Clarion*, 1 Jan. 1915.
[34] Ibid. 16 July 1915.
[35] *Herald*, 2 Dec. 1916.
[36] Cate Haste, *Keep the home fires burning: propaganda in the First World War*, London 1977, 126, and ch. vi for the anti-alien agitation.
[37] Stubbs, 'Milner and patriotic labour', 723, 726–7.

It is difficult to judge the strength of the super-patriotic group on the British left during the First World War. The *Clarion's* circulation dropped to 10,000 a week, because of its patriotism, Thompson believed.[38] Hyndman took only a small minority of the BSP into his new National Socialist Party. The *British Citizen and Empire Worker*, paper of the BWL, claimed a circulation of 30,000, and by the summer of 1917 the BWL claimed 154 branches.[39] It could also rely on some support from many prominent Labour politicians and financial support from the radical right. However, as war dragged on, casualty lists grew longer and conscription was imposed, the bulk of the labour movement edged closer to the ILP rather than to the BWL.[40]

## The anti-war left

The anti-war left was a small proportion of the left, and only a tiny minority when compared to the population as a whole. It must be remembered that the extent of anti-war feeling was not static. ILP branches witnessed some growth as they gathered around themselves Liberals who opposed the war and particularly conscription, and thus their own party. The City of London branch of the ILP grew from sixty-five members in August 1914 to 175 members in November 1916. The branch's annual report for the year ending February 1915 recorded that

> A new type of member has been attracted to us. . . . But the attractive force of the one party which has remained loyal to the principles of internationalism and pacifism, which are also the principles of the only true civilization, of ideal Christianity, and of any Socialism which is more than a catch-word for street corners, has overcome all lesser doubts and hesitations.[41]

The ILP was the only political party of any size that, as a whole, opposed the First World War.[42] Only two ILP MPs, Clynes and James Parker, supported the war effort. Only a handful of branches repudiated the executive's anti-war manifesto of August 1914. However, there is evidence that a sizeable minority felt 'some surge of fatherland in their hearts', as a delegate from Ilford explained to the 1915 conference in Norwich. The NAC declared at the same conference that 'such matters as enlistment and the urging of recruitment are matters for the individual conscience', despite having recommended that branches take no part in the recruiting campaign.[43] The ILP

---

38 Blatchford, *My eighty years*, p. ix.
39 Douglas, 'The National Democratic Party and British Workers' League', 536.
40 See below for the later history of the BWL.
41 Swartz, *The UDC in British politics*, 99–102.
42 The Socialist Labour Party also opposed the war, but in 1914 had only 200 members. Among its leaders it lost only Johnny Muir, editor of its paper *The Socialist*, to patriotism: Challinor, *Origins of British Bolshevism*, 123–49.
43 ILP, *Conference report*, 1915, 86–7, 11, 10.

always had much respect for the individual's liberty, but there was another reason for this freedom of action. Fenner Brockway estimated that one-fifth of the party had succumbed to pro-war patriotism, and figures given for Bradford ILP in the *Bradford Pioneer* in February 1916 tend to support this claim. Of a total membership of 1,473, there were 461 'young men' in the branch. Of these, 113 were in the trenches, five were killed or missing, twelve were wounded or prisoners of war, and six were in the Royal Navy.[44] In a strong branch of the ILP, therefore, before conscription, just under 30 per cent of those eligible had opted to join the armed forces. The NAC made concessions to loyalist patriotism to maintain the unity of the party, despite its official anti-war stance.

The entire executive of the BSP had, in September 1914, issued a manifesto calling for victory for the allies. The same manifesto also accepted conditional participation in recruiting campaigns.[45] However, fifteen out of the eighteen London branches demanded that the statement be withdrawn. In order to keep the anti-war opposition divided, the pro-war leaders refused to sanction a national conference for 1915, instead a series of divisional conferences were held. These revealed a party almost evenly divided between support for and opposition to the war, and the anti-war group won a one-seat majority on the executive.[46] Despite this, *Justice* remained outside their control, its editor, H. W. Lee, having declared in January 1915 that he 'wish[ed] it to be distinctly understood that in no case will I advocate a policy on the war in opposition to' victory for the allies.[47] This forced the anti-war group to publish its own paper, *The Call*, which first appeared in February 1916. The final battle came at the BSP conference in April 1916. In a test vote on holding the conference in private, to protect anti-war speakers from prosecution, the pro-war section led by Hyndman lost the vote seventy-six to twenty-eight. Hyndman then led his section out of the conference, while the anti-war delegates stood on chairs singing 'The Red Flag'.[48] The pro-war section seceded from the party to establish the National Socialist Party, putting patriotism ahead of their socialism.

Contemporary socialists and various historians have attempted to classify the various groups opposed to the war. Generally they can be divided into four groups, though it is perhaps best to bear in mind the equivocal and shifting nature of anti-war thought.[49] First there were those who opposed the war on political grounds, opposing the diplomacy that had led to the war. This

---

[44] Brockway, *Inside the left*, 47; Tony Jowitt, 'Philip Snowden and the First World War', in Keith Laybourn and David James (eds), *Philip Snowden: the first Labour chancellor of the exchequer*, Bradford 1987, 52–3.

[45] *Justice*, 17 Sept. 1914.

[46] Kendall, *Revolutionary movement*, 91–2.

[47] *Justice*, 21 Jan. 1915.

[48] BSP, *Conference report*, 1916, 3.

[49] This classification is based on Fenner Brockway, *Socialism over sixty years*, 131, and *Inside the left*, 52; Cross, *Philip Snowden*, 135; Robert E. Dowse, *Left in the centre: the Independent*

group included the non-socialist Union of Democratic Control. It was perhaps the most influential group among opponents of the war, simply because it offered ideas about how the war came, and how future wars could be prevented through the House of Commons. The main thrust of the UDC and its socialist supporters' argument was that secret diplomacy had enabled the formation of alliances that had resulted in two armed camps facing each other, which meant that war could not be localised but spread across to western Europe. The solution was, therefore, the democratic (parliamentary) control of foreign policy.[50]

The second group comprised pacifists and socialists influenced by Christianity. Among this group were individuals such as George Lansbury and organisations such as the No-Conscription Fellowship. They shared a moral opposition to the war; as Clifford Allen, chairman of the NCF, explained at its first national convention in 1915, this diverse group shared 'one objection to conscription . . . with intense fervour, and that was a belief in the sanctity of human life'.[51]

The third and fourth groups saw the causes of the war in socialist terms: capitalist rivalries had resulted in war. As John Maclean explained,

> even supposing Germany is to blame, the motive force is not the ambitions of the Kaiser . . . but the profit of the plundering class in Germany. . . . Every interested person knows that Germany's easiest road of entry into France was by Belgium. Sir Edward Grey only had to wait till neutrality had been broken to seize a 'moral' excuse for Britain taking up arms. The real reason was, and is, that he and his class knew that war between British and German capitalism had to come sooner or later.[52]

This was the line taken by the anti-war group in the BSP, the SLP and part of the ILP. However, the difference between the third and fourth groups was that only a tiny minority around Maclean believed the imperialist war should be turned into a civil war against the British ruling class, and thus supported the idea of revolutionary defeatism. Apart from this group and some absolutist pacifists, the rest of the anti-war left believed in national defence and therefore that an Allied victory was necessary.

The UDC were absolutely clear on this. Its first pamphlet, written by E. D.

*Labour Party 1893–1940*, London 1966, 21; Jowitt, 'Snowden and the First World War', 45–6.
[50] See, for example, ILP, *How the war came*, Labour and war pamphlet no. 1, 2nd edn, London 1915; A. Fenner Brockway, *Is Britain blameless?*, Manchester–London n.d. [1915]; J. Ramsay MacDonald, *War and the workers: a plea for democratic control*, UDC pamphlet no. 8, London n.d.
[51] Arthur Marwick, *Clifford Allen: the open conspirator*, Edinburgh–London 1964, 24–5. For sympathetic responses to such Christian pacifism see letters to Lansbury from Geraldine Cammell and J. H. Dadswell, 11 Aug. 1918, and A. L. Pennell, 13 Aug. 1918, BLPES, Lansbury papers, vol. 8.
[52] Kendall, *Revolutionary movement*, 88–9.

Morel, declared, 'This country is at war, and has for the moment one over-whelming preoccupation: to render safe our national inheritance.' This was stressed again: '*It is imperative that the war, once begun, should be prosecuted to a victory for our country.*'[53] The ILP, too, wanted to see an allied victory. 'Obviously the war must be finished now', its first pamphlet began, 'and whatever may be the rights and wrongs of its origin, a victory for German arms and the worst elements in German society which the war has put into authority, would bring political results to Europe which no one who loves peace and liberty could welcome.'[54] MacDonald, as an ILP delegate at the 1916 Labour conference, the first held in wartime, replied to a critic:

> Mr Sexton had said he did not want the Germans to win. Who did? Was there any man present who was so unutterably unfair as to believe that any of them wanted the Germans to win? Not at all. . . . If they had gone astray it was not because they wanted any mishap to befall our nation either as a political entity or as a spiritual expression of human needs and human endeavours.[55]

Likewise, E. C. Fairchild, a member of the anti-war group in the BSP, said the war 'imperils the future of socialism', but 'all action should be rigorously avoided, calculated to endanger national defence'.[56]

This reinforces the argument that the anti-war left was defined by its opponents. And their opponents were certainly willing to define them as pro-Germans.[57] G. H. Roberts MP pointed out the contradiction in the anti-war movement: 'Mr MacDonald had said: Who of us want Germany to win? Mr Wallhead [of the ILP] had said: We are opposed to the War. If they were opposed to the War they were not anxious that their country should win.'[58] This was the starting point of those who attacked the anti-war left as anti-British. Hardie was one of the first to feel the wrath of pro-war emotion. He had organised a meeting in Aberdare on 6 August 1914; the proposed chairman, C. B. Stanton, withdrew, explaining that 'although I am a Socialist, I am a Britisher'. The meeting was disrupted, and later, as Hardie found refuge in the house of a sympathiser, a crowd shouted 'Turn the German out!'[59]

---

[53] E. D. Morel, *The morrow of war*, 1914, in Stansky, *The left and the war*, 88, 94–5, 101. See also *The Union of Democratic Control: what it is and what it is not*, UDC leaflet no. 14, London n.d. Original emphasis.

[54] ILP, *How the war came*, 1.

[55] Labour Party, *Conference report*, 1916, 101.

[56] *Justice*, 28 Oct. 1915, in Kendall, *Revolutionary movement*, 97. See also BSP, *Conference report*, 1916, 8, 10.

[57] This section is confined to attacks by the left. For examples of attacks by those outside the labour movement see Marquand, *Ramsay MacDonald*, 186–90; Swartz, *The UDC and British politics*, ch. vi; Holroyd, *Bernard Shaw*, ii. 348, 354–8.

[58] Labour Party, *Conference report*, 1916, 105.

[59] McLean, *Keir Hardie*, 156–7. After Hardie's death, Stanton won the seat as a pro-war labour candidate against the official Labour candidate. Stanton was secretly funded by Unionists: Barry M. Doyle, 'Who paid the price of patriotism?: the funding of Charles Stanton during the Merthyr Boroughs by-election of 1915', EHR cix (1994), 1215–22.

When anti-war pamphlets appeared, the pro-war left poured vitriol on their authors. Robert Blatchford called Bernard Shaw's *Common-sense about the war* 'the meanest act of treachery ever perpetrated by an alien enemy residing in generous and long-suffering England'; he regarded the pamphlet as 'an outrage' that would be 'joyfully received and largely quoted in Germany'.[60] Pro-war socialists were quite prepared to make unfounded allegations about opponents of the war. Hyndman condemned the 'revolting lies' which filled 'pro-German pamphlets . . . published at great expense' by the ILP, and explained that 'we are curious to know where it is getting money for all its publications in favour of the Germans against the Allies'.[61] When challenged by the BSP executive, Hyndman explained that he had meant the UDC, whom the *Clarion* called the 'Union of Fools and Traitors'.[62] Aberdeen BSP asked who was behind the anti-war group in the party enabling them to set up *The Call*. The editor ridiculed the questioners: 'The Crown Prince is acting sub-editor, and Treitschke has returned from the grave to contribute, with von Bernhardi to our columns. Our financial resources are unimpeachable. We hold the Kaiser's draft on the Bank of England to cover all expenses.'[63] But the hostility could have a more serious side, for H. Alexander believed that pro-war elements in the BSP actually gave information to the police about anti-war members. Certainly *Justice*, on 23 December 1915, incited the arrest of a Russian member, asking 'Who or what is Peter Petroff?' Pro-war socialists also had a less liberal attitude to the freedom of the press in wartime. When the *Labour Leader* and ILP offices were raided by police in August 1915, the *New Statesman* said the ILP 'has issued pernicious literature', had a 'policy of anti-nationalism', and hence concluded that the raid was 'a little belated'.[64]

A second line of attack on anti-war groups was that they were unrepresentative of the labour movement, and that they were not genuinely working-class. A. M. Thompson wrote that the 'Britain-for-the-Prussian Party' was but a 'small gang of Labour misleaders'.[65] Will Crooks decided that these 'doctrinaire intellectuals' carried 'little weight' with their 'frankly pro-German propaganda'.[66] At the 1916 Labour conference, G. J. Wardle MP, speaking for the executive, asked who spoke for Labour, 'the small coterie of the Independent Labour Party or the great Trade Unions of the country?'[67]

Pro-war socialists used xenophobia and anti semitism against Russian Jews and socialists who refused to fight alongside tsarist Russia, the country that

60  Holroyd, *Bernard Shaw*, ii. 354; *Clarion*, 20 Nov. 1914.
61  *Le Canard Enchaîné*, 17 Mar. 1915, in Kendall, *Revolutionary movement*, 94.
62  *Clarion*, 24 Sept. 1915.
63  *The Call*, 9 Mar. 1916.
64  *New Statesman*, 21 Aug. 1915. Most of the seized material was returned, and *Labour Leader* claimed (2 Sept. 1915) a boost in circulation as a result of the raid.
65  *Clarion*, 2 Apr. 1915.
66  Will Crooks, *The truth about the war makers*, London n.d., introduction, 4–5.
67  Labour Party, *Conference report*, 1916, 103.

had forced them to flee religious or political persecution.[68] Since East London Jewish members played a major part in the anti-war section of the BSP, pro-war members used anti semitism against them. In October 1914, J. F. Green, who in 1905 had declared that 'for the international Social-Democrat there is no such word as "alien"', ventured 'to crave a little of your space in order the deplore the pro-German attitude of several Russo-Jewish refugees in this country'. 'It is hardly decent', he complained, 'when we are fighting for our national existence, that men who are allowed to live here in a fuller enjoyment of liberty than in any other country should be denouncing the Government for going to the war with Germany.'[69] When criticised in letter after letter, one of which asked mockingly whether Green's letter had been written by a socialist or a member of the tsar's Black Hundreds, Green repented.[70] He was not anti-Jewish, he wrote, but Jews could not be 'real Russians' or 'real Englishmen'.[71] In mid 1915, *Justice* attacked East London Jews for not contributing sufficiently to the war effort. Their hostility to Russia was misleading them about the nature of the war, 'with all the acuteness of their race'. *Justice* even regretted Marx's 'characteristic Hebrew detachment from national feeling'.[72] In April 1916, E. C. Fairchild, editor of *The Call*, condemned A. S. Headingley who had attacked 'anti-English cosmopolitan intriguers and Russian Jews of pro-German sympathies', who, Headingley said, had an easy task in the BSP as the 'truly British element' were all at the front.[73] The *Daily Herald* condemned attacks on foreigners, appealing to their perception of people's Englishness:

> It is unworthy of the dignity of the British people, who are supposed to be members of a powerful and civilised nation, to indulge in demonstrations against those who may be living in our midst, and who have been declared our enemies.... Shall we then in this hour of crisis disgrace the name of England by reducing ourselves to the level of untutored savages?[74]

Anti-foreigner attacks by supporters of the war did not lead the left to reject patriotism. On the contrary, as during the Boer War, they claimed that their opposition was based on a true patriotism, unsullied by militarism or base materialism. Upon the outbreak of war, Clement J. Bundock, assistant editor of *Labour Leader* wrote that, 'A patriot in truth is not he who will declare his country right when he knows it is wrong, but he who is jealous of his country's honour and dignity and will protest against the defamation of his country's

---

68 For official moves against Eastern European Jews in Britain see Julia Bush, *Behind the lines: East London Labour 1914–1919*, London 1984, ch. vi.
69 *Justice*, 6 May 1905; 22 Oct. 1914.
70 Ibid. 5 Nov. 1914.
71 Ibid. 3 Dec. 1914.
72 *Justice*, 3, 10 June 1915, in Bush, *Behind the lines*, 177.
73 *The Call*, 20 Apr. 1916.
74 *Daily Herald*, 7 Aug. 1914.

name and bow his head in shame when he sees that name dishonoured. British patriots today are bowed in shame.'[75] George Lansbury, showing some hesitation about taking action to oppose the war, would have no questioning of the *Daily Herald*'s patriotism:

> If we regard our own country, its people and its valued institutions to be the test of real patriotism then we yield second place to none. But we are husbanding our resources, and waiting our opportunities to smash once and for all that spurious patriotism which has exploited the nation's energies and capacities, for reasons no higher than the impulse of the hog.[76]

The fight for peace was a patriotic duty, the *Daily Herald* claimed: 'Let no man who loves his country cease working for peace', a headline implored. The desire for peace, it claimed, was patriotic since 'love of country truly expressed would preserve the lives of men'.[77] Ramsay MacDonald claimed that diplomats had too narrow a view of patriotism, whereas

> The ordinary intelligent workman citizen has a conception of his country, her traditions, her honour, and the way to maintain them all, different from that of the average diplomatist; the view of the citizen is higher and embraces a wider field of thoughtfulness than that of the diplomatist; in the crowd of citizens there is always an able and influential section which stands for conciliation, and would successfully work for it if it knew in time that danger threatened.[78]

Hence, were secret diplomacy to be brought to an end, this conciliationist section of citizens would bring their wider patriotism to bear to preserve peace and solve diplomatic problems. It was clearly this section, around the ILP and UDC, that opposed the war. There was a defensiveness over the question of patriotism, but the anti-war left's response to accusations that they were unpatriotic was to argue that, indeed, they were the true patriots. They would not accept the patriotism of 'my country, right or wrong', for this was too narrow a definition. They argued from an oppositional stance that the government at war was not the nation, and misrepresented its true interests.

During the Boer War, anti-war groups had happily accepted the label 'pro-Boer', since they had seen in the government's enemies, who were, anyway, small agrarian societies facing an industrialised, imperial power, virtues admired by the left. In the First World War, largely accepting that Britain represented liberty against German despotism, the anti-war left refused to accept the 'pro-German' taunts thrown at them. From early in the war the left was forced to respond to this accusation. *Labour Leader* tried to distin-

---

75 *Labour Leader*, 13 Aug. 1914.
76 *Daily Herald*, 19 Aug. 1914.
77 Ibid. 14, 26 Aug. 1914.
78 MacDonald, *War and the workers*, 14.

guish its position. 'We are not pro-German. We are not anti-British. We are pro-Peace. We are anti-War', it explained.[79] C. H. Norman explained his position as 'simply that I am on the side of the British people, *not* on the side of the British ruling classes. . . . I am not pro-German, pro-Russian, pro-French, pro-Belgian; but I am pro-English in the sense that *I know no reason why the British workers should be slaughtered in the interests of Russia and France.*'[80]

The anti-war left supported its oppositional patriotic position in two main ways. First it condemned profiteering and high prices, pointing out that those responsible were claiming the mantle of patriotism. Second they condemned what they called 'British Prussianism', the suppression of English liberties through the restriction of anti-war activities and even more through the introduction of conscription. As well as the national defence position of the majority of the anti-war left, these two areas of agitation helped to maintain the unity of the labour movement despite differences of opinion on the war. The pro-war left, with few exceptions, still made radical social demands in wartime and opposed the introduction of conscription.

In the early part of the war, the anti-war left saw little point in anti-war agitation. Such agitation was met with much hostility. The BSP was in any case too divided to be very effective, and could not act officially as an anti-war party. The ILP believed anti-war activity to be futile. The NAC instructed branches to continue 'educational Socialist propaganda, with its note of fraternity and internationalism [which], though not dealing specifically with the war, may help to prevent panics, wild jubilations, and excitements, and to repress outbursts of loud and boastful jingoism'.[81] This did not mean that the left dropped out of activity altogether. Rather than agitate against the war, it concentrated on the social effects of the war. And in this, both pro- and anti-war socialists and trade unionists could be involved. Upon the outbreak of war, most of the left became concerned about its effects on wages and particularly employment. On 4 August 1914, Henderson, secretary of the Labour Party, had called a meeting for the next day to form a national Peace Emergency Committee. Before it could meet, the government's declaration of war and the Labour executive's approval of this made such a committee redundant. The meeting went ahead with more than 100 delegates, and the War Emergency Workers' National Committee was formed to watch out for workers' social and economic interests in wartime. Both pro-war and anti-war socialists and trade unionists sat on the committee, from Hyndman

---

[79] *Labour Leader*, 29 Oct. 1914. See also ibid. 7 Jan. 1915.
[80] C. H. Norman, *British militarism: a reply to Robert Blatchford*, Manchester–London 1915, 4. Original emphases.
[81] *Labour Leader*, 13 Aug. 1914, in Haste, *Keep the home fires burning*, 143; William Gallacher, *Revolt on the Clyde*, London 1978, 24.

to MacDonald.[82] Locally, pro- and anti-war labour activists co-operated in relief committees.[83]

The needs of a modern war soon removed worries about mass unemployment as more and more people were drawn into the army or industry, and, to aid this, labour leaders were drawn into the organisation of the war effort. At a national level this resulted in the Treasury Agreement with the trade unions, the invitation to the Labour Party to join the government, which they accepted in May 1915, and a host of lesser appointments, for example Hyndman's appointment to the Consumer Council. This co-option of labour could extend to the personal interview of Kirkwood, deported Clyde shop steward, with Winston Churchill, Minister of Munitions. Kirkwood was seen as a leading anti-war figure; he was a hero of the January 1917 Labour conference for promising to return to Glasgow rather than go back to deportation. According to him his interview with Churchill went as follows:

'How do you do, Mr Kirkwood? I have heard a good deal about you', [Churchill] said.
'I dare say you have', I replied.
'Yes, and I want you to know that, whatever happens, nothing is to be allowed to stand in the way of the production of the munitions of war.'
'Quite right', I said.
Then he rang a bell, saying: 'Let's have a cup of tea and a bit of cake together.'
What a difference so small a thing can make!

On the next page of his autobiography, Kirkwood boasted that production 'records were made only to be broken. . . . In six weeks we [the Mile-End shell factory] held the record for output in Great Britain.'[84] Keith Middlemas has described this as 'patriotism blend[ing] nicely with self-interest'.[85] James Sexton of the Dock Labourers explained at the 1916 Labour conference how 'when the boys came home again they would have the same old employer to fight as they had before, but after what they had done in defence of the Country their claim would be so irresistible that no one could refuse their fair share

[82] Royden Harrison, 'The War Emergency Workers' National Committee, 1914–1920', in Asa Briggs and John Saville (eds), *Essays in labour history 1886–1923*, London 1971, 211–59. The ILP joined as a party in early 1915, though its members had already taken part in other capacities.
[83] For examples see Bush, *Behind the lines*, ch. ii (East London), and Laybourn and Reynolds, *Liberalism and the rise of Labour*, 188 (Bradford).
[84] Kirkwood, *My life of revolt*, 165, 166. Unfortunately an account of this meeting by Churchill does not seem to be extant. Most historians follow Martin Gilbert in using Kirkwood's autobiography as the authoritative account: *Winston S. Churchill*, IV: *1916–1922*, London 1975, 35–7. Churchill wrote a foreword for Kirkwood's autobiography in which he praised the combination of 'sturdy independence', 'mood of political revolt' and 'his lively realisation of all that British liberty means to the mass of our island folk': Kirkwood, *My life of revolt*, p. vi.
[85] Keith Middlemas, *Politics in industrial society: the experience of the British system since 1911*, London 1979, 73.

in the products of the country'.[86] W. N. Ewer mocked the subjects of this co-option of labour in 'A new national anthem' in the *Herald* of 19 June 1915:

> Long may our great King live,
> Long may he reign to give
> Garters and gauds.
> Till Lib. and Lab. MPs
> Have all become KGs
> GC or KCBs
> Possibly Lords.
>
> Every wise democrat
> Who has the sense to rat
> Honoured shall be.
> Knighted he's sure to get
> Or made a baronet,
> Shoved in the Cabinet
> Or the PC.
>
> All title-hunting snobs,
> All who are out for jobs,
> Loudly should sing:
> 'To be a titled swell
> Gladly my soul I'll sell;
> Democracy to Hell!
> God save the King!'

This did not mean that the pro-war left did not criticise employers and share-holders. Even the rabidly patriotic *Clarion* urged 'Hang the exploiters ... *pour encourager les autres*.'[87] But it fell more naturally to the anti-war left, for whom questioning the patriotism of the capitalist class was a major source of satis-faction; it was radical, but not necessarily anti-war. J. W. Kneeshaw shared a joke made by W. C. Anderson, an ILP MP. He referred to the familiar recruit-ing poster of a child asking the question, 'Father, what did you do during the great war?' 'When the shipowner's child asks him that question his reply will be simple and comprehensive, said Mr Anderson, he will reply, "I did every-body". Such is his patriotism.'[88] The 'conscription of riches' campaign, which was led by the WEWNC, appealed to both pro- and anti-war groups, as Harri-son has argued as a rallying point rather than as a coherent ideology, and was

---

86 Labour Party, *Conference report*, 1916, 101.
87 *Clarion*, 15 Oct. 1915. See also leader entitled 'Hang the traitors', about profiteering ship owners: 22 Jan. 1915.
88 J. W. Kneeshaw, *Profits and patriotism*, Manchester n.d., 5; Robert Williams, 'Shipowners as patriots', and leader 'The real enemies of Britain', *Herald*, 23 Jan. 1915; George Lansbury, 'Patriots of the purse', ibid. 14 Aug. 1915; W. C. Anderson, 'Patriotism of the pocket', *Labour Leader*, 11 Feb. 1915; Hardie, 'Patriotism measured in millions', ibid. 25 Mar. 1915.

posed in terms of 'fair play' and 'equality of sacrifice'. Hence it did not directly challenge the war.[89]

For all their criticism of the government and profiteers, the co-option of their pro-war colleagues and even some of their anti-war colleagues (Snowden, a leading anti-war ILP MP, through his work on the all-party committee on liquor and the Central Control Board [Liquor Traffic], directly played a part in the war effort), the anti-war left were forced to look to the state to ameliorate conditions for the working class. Since they rejected industrial action[90] they had no choice but to work through government-sponsored committees. There was also a widespread approval of the collectivism that the state was forced by circumstances to adopt.[91]

And the labour leaders were drawn into many of these experiments. As Miliband has noted, it was a 'dual role'. Not only were they representatives of the working class to the state, they were also representatives of the state in its relations with the working class. In this way, labour leaders began to step across the threshold between oppositional and state patriotism, for 'A host of Labour representatives became deeply involved in the business of the State and, with their service in the new bureaucracy that was born of the war, acquired a stake, if not in the country, at least in the country's official business.'[92]

## 'They who fight for freedom, must themselves be free':[93] the left and individual liberty

A second area where the left, pro- and anti-war, was able to maintain its essential unity was in opposition to infringements of individual liberty, particularly with regard to conscription. While the potential dangers of industrial conscription played a major role in the trade unions' opposition, it was mainly in terms of language about traditional English liberties that the opposition was framed. While the vast majority of the left accepted ideas of national defence, they also had radical ideas about the nation that was to be defended. As C. H. Norman explained, there were two aspects to patriotism: 'Patriotism is a passion impelling a person to serve his country (1) either in defending it from invasion; (2) or, in upholding the rights and liberties of the people, and maintaining the national laws and institutions against tyrannical infringements.' The governing classes, he argued, wanted to restrict patriotism to the former meaning, while its true importance was in the latter.[94]

---

89 Harrison, 'The War Emergency Workers' National Committee', 247, 259, 255.
90 For example, see Morgan, *J. Ramsay MacDonald*, 68.
91 For example, see Marwick, *The deluge*, 201–2.
92 Miliband, *Parliamentary socialism*, 47.
93 J. W. Kneeshaw, *How conscription works*, Manchester n.d., 11.
94 C. H. Norman, *Nationality and patriotism*, Manchester–London 1915, 6.

MacDonald in a speech in Glasgow explained his own philosophy of patriotism, and the need to defend his idea of the nation against domestic enemies:

> When I like to think of my country at its best I think of it as the great liberal land where exiles came to dwell; the land where men and women thought honestly, spoke truly, none daring to make them afraid; the land which believed the best national service that could be rendered was the service of thinking men and thinking women, each contributing to the national intelligence his or her portion of that intelligence; the land where freedom of speech was a corner-stone and freedom of thought a keystone to the arch.(Applause.) That is the land I love and I like to think Great Britain was and still may be. The ILP for the last two years and eight months has been standing by the soul of Great Britain, whilst others have been deserting and selling it in every market place. (Loud applause.) Therefore, I say to you, we must fight for liberty; we must not allow Prussian militarism to come into this land under the pretence that it alone can defend the nation.[95]

Thus MacDonald counterpoised a version of a free Britain in peacetime with wartime Britain where alien ideas of the suppression of free speech and thought intruded. Before the war, any movement against political liberty was condemned as 'Russian methods'. Now in wartime, with the propaganda effort of the government and its supporters portraying the war as one of British liberty against Prussian tyranny, with Russia an ally of Britain, the left called any movement against political liberty 'Prussianism'.[96] This could in fact only strengthen the desire for victory over Germany. The Defence of the Realm Act under which much of the suppression of anti-war opinion took place was therefore seen not as the expression of the vast majority of British MPs, but as a piece of interloping Prussianism. This language entered into all opposition to suppression of opponents of the war. When the offices of *Labour Leader* and the National Labour Press in Manchester and London were raided, Bingley ILP passed a resolution calling 'upon the Government to cease their attempts to Prussianise the country', and the executive of the Textiles Union condemned 'such German methods'.[97] When much of the seized material was returned, *Labour Leader* pointed out the 'futility of Prussianism' and declared that 'British liberty triumphs over British Prussianism'.[98] After Lloyd George and Arthur Henderson were shouted down by the Clyde Workers' Committee on Christmas Day, 1915, and this was reported in the Glasgow ILP paper, *Forward*, the paper was suppressed. The *Herald* called this 'still more Prussianism'.[99] *The Call* described the jailing of John Maclean and the

---

95  J. Ramsay MacDonald, *Patriots and politics*, Manchester–London n.d. [1915], 5–6.
96  Though the term had been in use since 1870: Daniel Pick, *War machine: the rationalisation of slaughter in the modern age*, New Haven–London 1993, ch. ix.
97  *Labour Leader*, 26 Aug. 1915.
98  Ibid. 2 Sept. 1915.
99  *Herald*, 15 Jan. 1916.

deportations as 'Prussianising Britain'.[100] The 1917 Labour conference unanimously condemned the Clyde deportations as 'savour[ing] of that Prussianism we seek to destroy'.[101]

In retrospect however some of the anti-war left were much more disposed to praise wartime British 'tolerance'. Kirkwood wrote in his autobiography:

> What a country! Imagine such a series of incidents and such a scene in any other country! It is incredible. Had I been anywhere but in Britain, I should have been quietly dispatched as a nuisance or a traitor! Nuisance I may have been. Traitor I never was. Sometimes some of my colleagues wonder when I speak of this land in the way I do. I have most reason to know that it is in very truth the land of the brave and the free, for these soldiers were brave men, but they respected freedom. . . . [T]hey never forgot that we were all British, they played the game in the British way and I hope they think the same of me.[102]

During the war, with the threat of and subsequent introduction of conscription, the anti-war left did not praise British tolerance and liberty. The majority of the left, anti- and pro-war, opposed the introduction of conscription. The super-patriots who called for conscription formed a minority, and thought in terms of a citizen army. Hence Blatchford could only bring himself to support 'conscription on "British lines" '.[103] Many on the left saw maintaining voluntary recruiting levels as a patriotic way of avoiding the need for compulsion in a war that used up millions of men. In August 1914, the Parliamentary Recruiting Committee had been established, enabling the political parties' organisations to be used for recruiting. Henderson was joint president with Asquith and Bonar Law. The TUC, General Federation of Trade Unions and the Labour Party set up the Labour Recruiting Committee in September 1915 in an effort to encourage voluntary recruiting to head of conscription.[104] It was perfectly compatible to support the war and oppose conscription. J. H. Thomas, opposing the second military service bill, which extended conscription to married men, emphasised that his 'protest against disuniting the people' did not weaken his determination to aid the war effort. He told the Commons that he 'repudiate[d] that we are enemies of the country. I challenge any man to say that we could have done more than we have done,

---

100 *The Call*, 20 Apr. 1916.
101 Labour Party, *Conference report*, 1917, 111. When faced with the executions after the Easter Rising in Dublin, the British left did not use such language. The *Herald* used its pacifism to avoid comment: 'No lover of peace can do anything but deplore the outbreak in Dublin.' Labour's *Memorandum on war aims* of Dec. 1917 did not mention Ireland. Fifteen Labour MPs did vote for the Irish Nationalists' censure motion on martial law, but three voted against. James O'Grady spoke for Labour because he was Irish: see Geoffrey Bell, *Troublesome business: the Labour Party and the Irish question*, London 1982, 33–7.
102 Kirkwood, *My life of revolt*, 140–1. See also Snowden, *Autobiography*, i. 414.
103 *Clarion*, 22 Jan. 1915.
104 See Roy Douglas, 'Voluntary enlistment in the First World War and the work of the Parliamentary Recruiting Committee', *JMH* xlii (1970), 564–85; Labour Party, *Conference report*, 1916, 5–6.

more than we shall continue to do, to obtain recruits, to maintain industrial peace, to do everything possible to win the war.'[105] It was in the same sentiment that the Labour Party special delegate conference of 6 January 1916 rejected an amendment for compulsion by 2,121,000 to 541,000 votes. A joint NUR/ASE resolution reaffirmed the TUC's protest against compulsory military service. The resolution 'rejoice[d]' at the success of voluntarism. It was passed by 1,998,000 to 783,000 votes.[106] As 1915 had progressed, monthly recruiting figures had fallen. The National Registration Act had been passed to calculate the availability of potential recruits, and a last attempt at voluntarism was made through the Derby Scheme. In January 1916 the coalition government introduced a military service bill for single men. Throughout these months the left voiced its opposition to conscription. It did so mainly in language about ideas of British liberty and traditions of freedom from compulsion, arguing that conscription was an adoption of the Prussianism with which Britain was supposed to be at war.

Labour Leader argued that the imposition of conscription could be worse than defeat by Germany, for it would 'crush our spirit' and 'degrade the soul of our nation'.[107] Many on the left, therefore, saw compulsory military service as an attack on the very basis of British national identity. Opposition to conscription voiced this concern. The ILP NAC issued a model resolution to trades councils, trade unions, Labour and socialist organisations. 'It will be a strange recompense for all the sacrifice our country is making to crush Prussian military despotism in Germany', it appealed, 'if advantage is taken of that sacrifice to thrust a system of Prussian militarism on the British nation.' It therefore urged these bodies to pass the resolution: 'That this meeting . . . declares its strongest opposition to compulsory military service, believing conscription in any form to be a violation of the principles of civic freedom hitherto prized as one of the chief heritages of British liberty, and that its adoption would constitute a grave menace to the progress of the nation.'[108] Within a few weeks, eighty-five ILP branches, eighteen trades councils, LRCs and Labour Parties and ten trade union branches had passed the ILP resolution.[109] That the response was not better was largely because labour bodies were passing their own resolutions, couched in the same terms. For example, Shoreditch Trades Council declared conscription to be 'contrary to the sentiments and principles of the British people, subversive of the free and democratic character of their institutions; and involves a serious menace to the liberty and freedom of the labour movement'. Bradford Trades Council opposed conscription 'in any form, military or industrial, and urged Parliament to offer their utmost opposition to any proposal to impose upon the

---

105 Blaxland, J. H. Thomas, 94–5.
106 Labour Party, Conference report, 1917, 7.
107 Labour Leader, 30 Dec. 1915.
108 Ibid. 10 June 1915.
109 Ibid. 1 July 1915.

British people a yoke which is one of the chief concerns of Prussian milita-rism'.[110] The Labour Party conference in 1916 passed a resolution by 1,796,000 to 219,000 votes protesting 'emphatically against the adoption of conscription in any form, as it is against the spirit of British democracy and full of dangers to the liberties of the people'.[111]

It was Glasier for the ILP who expanded all this language into the fullest objection to conscription in two pamphlets in 1915.[112] In these he claimed that to see soldiers in uniform everywhere was 'as though some foreign rule had suddenly fallen on us – as though the nation had become continental-ised, in fact', and this meant that 'the birthrights of British citizenship embodied in the Magna Charta, Habeas Corpus and Bill of Rights are no longer inviolable'.[113] He went on to say that 'British Civicism' was 'the very secret of Britain's greatness', and that it was not militarism but 'that boyish spirit of freedom and adventure which has spread the English race and speech across every sea'.[114] He argued that militarism was a result of British capital-ists' fears of losing their foremost place in the world and their desire to regain control over the people who were beginning to learn how to use democ-racy.[115] Conscription was their latest attempt, done under the cover of war, and he urged resistance: 'In the face of this affronting challenge to all that is consecrate in the life and freedom and hopes of the democracy does it not behove us to unfurl our banners and boldly defend our heritage? The peril of Junkerdom and military tyranny is not less if it comes from within instead of without our gates.'[116] As in so much of the anti-war left's discourse on con-scription, it was taken for granted that the war had to be fought, but that vol-untary recruiting was superior to compulsion. 'That is the British principle: it applies all round. And it is the right principle. It is the voluntary principle. It is the true Socialist principle', Glasier wrote.[117]

The outcome of all this was that a special conference of the Labour Party voted three to one against conscription. The executive and Parliamentary Labour Party then instructed the Labour ministers to resign from the govern-ment. Henderson declared that he would vote for conscription whatever the Labour movement decided. Asquith made minor assurances (some of which he subsequently broke), and the Labour ministers withdrew their resigna-

110 *Herald*, 19 June 1915; Laybourn and Reynolds, *Liberalism and the rise of Labour*, 189. See also the No-Conscription Fellowship manifesto, 'Shall Britons be conscripts?', *Herald*, 8 Jan. 1916.
111 Labour Party, *Conference report*, 1916, 116–17.
112 J. Bruce Glasier, *Militarism*, Labour and war pamphlet no. 2, Manchester, 1915, and *The peril of conscription*, Labour and war pamphlet no. 3, London 1915.
113 *Militarism*, 1, 2.
114 Ibid. 4.
115 Ibid. 14.
116 *Peril of conscription*, 8.
117 Ibid. 21. See also George Lansbury, 'Labour can yet kill conscription', *Herald*, 1 Jan. 1916.

tions. Labour reaffirmed its opposition to the military service bill by 1,716,000 to 360,000 votes, but decided by 649,000 to 614,000 votes not to fight for its repeal should it become law. The government view of what was in the national interest therefore prevailed over the labour movement's view even within the movement itself.[118] However, a significant outcome was that in the campaign against conscription moderate pro-war and anti-war socialists and trade unionists had worked together.

In the last days of peace, the British left, like most of their European comrades, were unprepared for war. As the realisation dawned on them that war was probable, they united in a desire to preserve peace. But once war broke out and the British government declared war on Germany, the majority of the left supported the war effort out of simple and loyal patriotism. As Clynes later wrote, 'it seemed to me that we could no longer declare for peace when the country was at war'.[119] Some on the left had no hesitation in supporting the war. J. H. Thomas, who arrived in New York on 4 August, rushed back to support his country. Snowden, on the other hand, did not return from his world tour until February 1915. When he arrived he immediately declared his opposition to the war, but his decision to stay away for six months was likely to have been due to the 'intolerable conflicts' in his mind.[120] His opposition, like that of most of the anti-war left, was ambivalent. As one historian has explained, 'the ILP opposed the War but at the same time was unwilling to build a mass movement in opposition. It opposed the War and yet wanted Britain to win it. It opposed the advocacy of military solutions and yet had nothing but praise for the men who volunteered to fight.'[121] Using Kirkwood's terms, it seems fair to say that the anti-war left were nuisances rather than traitors.[122] This conditional opposition was largely the result of belief in the British nation as something real, defined by democracy and liberty, and that patriotism was a valid and real emotion. With the defence of the working class's social conditions and the fight against conscription, it was a reason for the maintenance of the unity of the British labour movement. The pro-war left found itself, to its pleasure, drawn into the running of the state, and this reinforced its belief in the possibilities of state-introduced socialism. And if the state was a progressive institution, then loyalist patriotism too could be seen as progressive.

118 Labour Party, *Conference report*, 1916, 7, 8, 117–24; Leventhal, *Arthur Henderson*, 58–9.
119 Clynes, *Memoirs 1869–1924*, 173.
120 Blaxland, *J. H. Thomas*, 86–7; Cross, *Snowden*, 133.
121 Jowitt, 'Snowden and the First World War', 40.
122 Kirkwood, *My life of revolt*, 140–1.

# 8

# *The Battle for British Socialism, 1917–1921*

Samuel Hynes has described a turning point in the psychological attitudes of
the British towards the First World War after 1916: 'The war spirit was running down; only the momentum of the war itself continued undiminished.'
He comments that this is not just a historical view, but was also a contemporary perception.[1] The anti-war left expected such a turning-point, believing
that reason would win through against what they saw as the hysteria of jingoism.[2] The left, therefore, repeatedly announced the arrival of turning points.
These announcements continued to be made from 1916 to 1918.[3] Despite its
lack of certainty, the anti-war left felt that circumstances were beginning to
favour their stance. Conscription, lengthening casualty lists, food shortages,
higher prices and industrial unrest gave the anti-war left hopes of a political
reaction against the war. Yet it was an event outside Britain that had most
impact on the British left, whether pro- or anti-war. The repercussions of the
Russian Revolution on the British left form the substance of the following
chapters. This chapter deals largely with the impact within the left, while
chapter 9 deals with the left's relationships with outside political forces and
the electorate.

### The turning of the tide?

First reactions to the March revolution in Russia were determined by attitudes to the war. The pro-war left had been embarrassed by fighting a war for
democracy in alliance with a despotic power they had consistently opposed
before the war. Blatchford had written that two powers were not guilty in the
outbreak of war, Britain and France. 'And they were both democracies', he
claimed. He made no mention of Russia.[4] Hyndman, who had a history of
Russophobia going back to 1878, remained worried that 'the success of Russia' would be 'a misfortune to the civilised world'.[5] However, by January 1915,
he had put his name to a letter in *Justice* which absolved Russia of blame for

---

1 Samuel Hynes, *A war imagined: the First World War and English culture*, London 1990,
101, 99.
2 Cf. Taylor, 'Patriotism, history and the left'.
3 See, for example, ILP, *Conference report*, 1916, 7; *Socialist Review*, Jan.–Mar. 1917, 1; *The
Call*, 'A call for action', 3 May 1917; *Labour Leader*, 3 Jan. 1918.
4 *Clarion*, 7 Aug. 1914.
5 See Tsuzuki, *Hyndman and British socialism*, 19, 21; *Justice*, 13 Aug. 1914.

the war, and declared that since Germany's intention was to annex Belgium, crush France and cripple Russia, the war had to be won by the Allies.[6] The pro-war left largely tried to ignore the alliance with Russia in wartime, though the *New Statesman* noted that, in the past, 'the sympathies of the ordinary Englishman, without distinction of party or class, have always been enlisted against the Russian government'. The situation had now changed, it said. After all, 'You cannot in common decency accept a man's help and abuse him at the same time.' To reinforce this, it asked, 'After all, might not even Russian tyranny be less black than it had been painted?'[7]

The news of an anti-tsarist revolution in Russia was greeted with relief by the pro-war left. It made their claim of a war between democracy and autocracy more solid, and it relieved fears about Russia's capacity for continuing the war. G. J. Wardle, a pro-war Labour MP, responding to Bonar Law's 'friendly greeting' from the 'Mother of Parliaments . . . to the Parliament of an Allied country', declared that 'Two facts stand out with regard to this revolution – it is parliamentary and it is constitutional. It betokens no weakening of Russia's will in regard to the War.'[8] The alliance was no longer contrary to British traditions, which largely meant parliamentarianism and political liberty. The reaction of the pro-war left was less conditioned by internationalism than by the wartime alliance, and therefore their own patriotism. A telegram signed by twenty leading Labour and trade union figures headed by Henderson illustrated this. The Russian people were congratulated for 'deliver[ing] themselves from the power of reactionary elements which are impeding their advances to victory'.[9]

The anti-war left, on the other hand, were confident that the revolution gave a tremendous boost to the peace movement internationally. As opponents of the war, they had maintained their unequivocal hostility to tsarism, which, in itself, had been a major reason for opposing the war, and celebrated its fall with enthusiasm. MacDonald at the Leeds Convention summed up these varied motives:

> It is fashionable in some quarters in this country to say 'We congratulate the Russians upon the revolution, but in some respects we regret it.' But today we congratulate the Russians on the Revolution without any reservations whatsoever. We do it not because the Revolution has happened, but because for years we wanted it to happen. We are glad not because we are compelled to be glad – but because it is in accordance with our democratic principles to be glad. . . . When this war broke out organised Labour in this country lost the initiative. It became a mere echo of the old governing classes' opinions. Now

6 Ibid. 28 Jan. 1915. Among those signing the letter were Bax, Fisher, Lee, Thorne and Tillett.
7 'Our alliance with Russia', *New Statesman*, 9 Jan. 1915.
8 *Hansard*, 5th ser. xci. 22 Mar. 1917, 2085, 2090.
9 R. Page Arnot, *The impact of the Russian Revolution in Britain*, London 1967, 21.

the Russian Revolution has given you the chance to take the initiative your-
selves.[10]

The Leeds Convention, held on 3 June 1917, was organised to welcome the
revolution, and it represented the medley of reasons for such greetings, but
there was enough unity for the resolutions to be passed virtually unanimously.
Only the presence of the super-patriot seamen's leader, Captain Tupper,
ensured some dissent. The 1,200 delegates passed resolutions welcoming the
revolution, urging the British government to restore civil liberties, and,
remarkably, calling for the formation of workers' and soldiers' councils.[11] This
latter resolution, moved by W. C. Anderson of the ILP, suggested that the
convention aimed to carry into effect the slogan 'Follow Russia!'[12] though
the resolution was given an English and Fabian ring to it, by urging the formation of such councils 'in every town, urban and rural district'.[13] Gallacher
conveys a more accurate impression of the convention, if one takes account
of the general anti-tsarism, and allows for the factual errors and Gallacher's
belief that great opportunities were missed in the years between 1917 and
1919:

> About two thousand delegates packed the hall and were treated to a regular
> orgy of generalities on the beauty and holiness of bourgeois democracy. Mac-
> Donald, Snowden, Lansbury, and others went all out to sing the praises of par-
> liamentary democracy. Russia had got her freedom at last; what they had all
> worked for and prayed for. Soon Russia would have a 'free parliament just like
> us'.[14]

Leeds was not intended by the majority of delegates as the first step in following Russia but as a celebration of the Russian people's taking of the British
left's advice to follow Britain.

But the Russian Revolution did strike a blow at ideas of British liberty and
democracy. The war had seen infringements of civil liberties that the left had
said would destroy any notion of traditional liberties. After the Russian Revolution it could no longer be claimed that Britain was the freest country in the
world. Lansbury wrote of the Russian revolutionary programme:

> We boast of British freedom and boast of the liberty which we enjoy, but
> should the new Russian government carry out the programme ... the political
> condition of affairs in Russia will be very much more liberal and progressive
> than in any other belligerent country and most certainly in advance of the

---

10 Stephen Richards Graubard, *British Labour and the Russian Revolution 1917–1924*, Cambridge, Mass.–London 1956, 36–7.
11 *Herald*, 9 June 1917. In large part the unanimity of Leeds was ensured by the Labour Party's failure to support the convention: Labour Party NEC minutes, 18 July 1917.
12 See, for example, *Labour Leader*, 17 May 1917.
13 Ibid. 7 June 1917.
14 Gallacher, *Revolt on the Clyde*, 149–50. Lansbury was in fact absent due to illness.

conditions prevailing in this country, which was formerly known as the home of civil and religious freedom.[15]

At Leeds, a resolution on civil liberties was passed that urged the British government to imitate Russia by creating a charter of liberties including universal suffrage, freedom of the press and speech, an amnesty for political prisoners, and the end of conscription.[16] Radical ideas claiming an innate democratic spirit for Anglo-Saxon peoples and an innate political backwardness for Slavs lost credibility in 1917, even if they were later to return. In June 1917 the anti-war left appealed for civil liberties not by referring to traditional ideas of British liberty but by reference to another country.[17]

The Russian Revolution also pushed the pro-war left towards a formulation of war aims, and this in itself brought them closer to the anti-war left, which had been campaigning for such a step since early in the war.[18] Thus, in December 1917, a joint Labour Party/TUC conference accepted a memorandum on war aims drawn up by Sidney Webb, and in February 1918 this was used as a basis for discussion at an inter-Allied labour and socialist conference in London.[19] These war aims included making the world safe for democracy, an end to secret diplomacy, international arbitration through a league of nations, and the restoration of Belgian independence. While they depended on the defeat of Germany, they also coincided with the aims of the anti-war left. Hence the latter came to see Labour's war aims as marking a turning point in the war. It is, however, important to recognise the limits of Labour's change of heart.

Henderson's conversion to attendance at the Stockholm conference was not a move into the anti-war camp. He explained to both the House of Commons on 1 August and the Labour Party conference on 10 August that attendance would be better for the Allies than non-attendance, when less moderate forces could predominate.[20] During the German spring offensive of 1918, Henderson declared that 'the latest act of military aggression on the part of the German government placed under temporary suspension the moral, political and diplomatic effort'.[21] His wish for a democratic peace was conditional on Germany's defeat. The Labour Party executive also reaffirmed its commitment to the war effort during April 1918, resolving that:

> The Labour Party places on record its deep sense of gratitude for, and admiration of, the heroic resistance offered by our Armies in the field to the terrible

---

[15] Herald, 24 Mar. 1917.

[16] Ibid. 9 Jun. 1917.

[17] See Pick, War machine, ch. xi for views on the relationship between Slavs, Teutons and civilisation in 1914.

[18] For example, Herald, 8 May 1915.

[19] See Paul U. Kellog and Arthur Gleason, British Labor and the war: reconstructors for a new world, New York 1919, 29–32, 61–73, 343–51, 352–66.

[20] Leventhal, Arthur Henderson, 67, 68.

[21] Wrigley, Arthur Henderson, 125.

onslaughts of the enemy during the recent offensive. Such magnificent courage and resolution – so consistent with the best British traditions – imposes an imperative obligation upon all sections of the country to assist by their skill, energy or substance, to carry on the great work of liberation in which our armies are engaged in order that our joint efforts may eventually result in the final overthrow of militarism and secure for the world a lasting and democratic peace.[22]

The executive also called a halt to all domestic political propaganda.[23] Even Snowden, addressing the April 1918 ILP conference as chairman, decided that, 'The military situation on the Western front has, for the time being, made one indisposed to adopt the critical attitude.'[24] The labour movement after 1917 did become more united, but it was a unity made possible by the patriotic minimum of an Allied victory. What had changed was that discussion of the terms upon which peace could be achieved was becoming widespread. Lord Lansdowne's peace letter was printed in the *Daily Telegraph* at the end of November 1917; before the end of the year, the War Cabinet decided it must make a statement on war aims.[25] In this context, even the pro-war left became more willing to discuss peace terms.

A split in the Labour movement did occur, however, and it was directly related to patriotism. The super-patriotic left was made up of a variety of groups. The Socialist National Defence Committee moved through various names to become the National Democratic Party, but its moving force remained Victor Fisher. Another group consisted of trade unionists who wished to form a trade union party excluding 'the professed friends of Germany' in the ILP.[26] Closely connected to this group was Havelock Wilson, who formed the Merchant Seamen's League. Finally, there were those, such as George Barnes, who refused to leave the coalition government when the Labour conference in November 1918 confirmed that the party would do so. These groups were united in putting their ideas of patriotism before party, a justification used before the war by some Labour MPs to vote against the party on armaments. G. H. Roberts who, as Labour chief whip, had voted against a reduction in the navy estimates in 1912, explained in 1918 that 'he knew that what he was saying might involve him in a parting of the ways [with Labour], but he was a British citizen before he was a politician'.[27]

The super-patriots continued to employ a virulent anti-Germanism. Fisher and Ben Tillett used the slogan 'Bomb the Boches!' to attract support, and it was Barnes who initiated the slogan 'Hang the Kaiser!' in the 1918 general

[22] Labour Party, *Conference report*, June 1918, 18.
[23] Labour Party NEC minutes, 17 Apr. 1918.
[24] ILP, *Conference report*, 1918, 42.
[25] See John Turner, *British politics and the Great War: coalition and conflict 1915–1918*, New Haven–London 1992, 248–9, 265–9.
[26] John Hodge, quoted in Kellog and Gleason, *British Labor and the war*, 225.
[27] Ibid. 226.

election campaign.[28] This was linked with the demand for a boycott of Germany after the war. The Merchant Seamen's League commissioned A. P. Herbert to write 'The seamen's boycott song', one verse of which went:

> O never a Fritz shall sail
> In a ship that sails with me,
> Never a box or bale
> That smells of Germany.
> Never the likes of they
> Shall soil the English shore
> Till the seamen of England say,
> 'You've settled the seamen's score.'[29]

They were resolutely hostile to the ILP and other anti-war groups. Supporters of the Merchant Seamen's League were required to 'pledge . . . to do my best to help Patriotic Labour to fight against the Bolshie labour bosses of the ILP and all their mischievous and un-English activities; and to oppose any defeatist or pacifist candidate for parliament or other public body'.[30]

It was this latter position that brought the super-patriots into conflict with the Labour Party. As long as they were prepared to support Labour candidates in elections, membership of Labour was compatible with membership of a super-patriotic organisation. The National Socialist Party held views similar to other super-patriotic groups; Hyndman, aged seventy-five in 1917, volunteered to investigate 'German spy waiters' but the police declined his offer to dine out for the war effort.[31] The NSP however remained affiliated to the Labour Party, because it only ran candidates under Labour Party auspices. In January 1918, Fisher had announced that BWL policy was 'to challenge the re-election of the pacifist members of the Labour Party, notably Mr Ramsay MacDonald, Mr Philip Snowden, Mr Jowett and others'.[32] This brought the BWL into conflict with the Labour Party and membership of the two bodies became incompatible.[33]

The rejection by the TUC conference in September 1918, by 3.8 million to 567,000 votes, of the formation of a trade union party consigned those around Havelock Wilson to the political margins.[34] Despite the election of nine or ten patriotic labour MPs in December 1918, the end of the war saw the end of any need for super-patriotism, and none of the MPs survived the 1922 election under a patriotic labour banner.[35] But patriotic labour was not

---

28 Douglas, 'The National Democratic Party', 537; C. L. Mowat, *Britain between the wars 1918–1940*, London 1956, 4.
29 Merchant Seamen's League, *The seamen's boycott song*, London 1918.
30 Merchant Seamen's League, *The seamen's crusade*, London n.d. [1918].
31 Tsuzuki, *Hyndman and British socialism*, 243.
32 *Times*, 26 Jan. 1918, in Douglas, 'The National Democratic Party', 539.
33 Labour Party, *Conference report*, Jan. 1918, and Labour Party NEC minutes, 9 Jan. 1918.
34 See Kellog and Gleason, *British labor and the war*, ch. xxi.
35 Douglas, 'The National Democratic Party', 551–2.

simply a wartime phenomenon, for it had its roots in Edwardian Britain, among those Labour MPs who rebelled against the party on armaments, and those like Blatchford and Fisher who put patriotism at the forefront of their socialism. It was Blatchford's slogan, 'Britain for the British', which patriotic labour rallied around, but its message was now aimed against Germany rather than against the British propertied classes.

## 'Now for the enemy at home'[36]

The end of the war in November 1918 did not end the peril to the nation. Instead the threat came from within. Its base was the growth of trade union membership from 4.1 million in 1914 and 6.5 million in 1918, to 8.3 million in 1920. Working days lost to strikes rose from 9.9 million in 1914, 2.9 million in 1915, 5.9 million in 1918, 35 million in 1919, 26.6 million in 1920, to 85.5 million in 1921.[37] At the same time, soldiers rioted and demonstrated to speed up demobilisation.[38] In this situation the language of class swept the language of radical patriotism aside. Socialist and labour activists had always used both vocabularies in unison. For all their denials of class as the motive force in social transformation, it had been recognised that the labour movement's aim was the material advance of the poorest sections of society at the expense of the richest sections. In the years immediately after the First World War, the language of class predominated. A Ministry of Labour official noted in February 1920 'an increasing tendency for trade unionists of one shop works or small districts to act together, irrespective of their divisions into crafts or occupations. What is called "class consciousness" is obliterating the distinction between those who follow different occupations in the same works.'[39] Basil Thomson, Director of Intelligence between 1919 and 1921, warned of 'class hatred aggravated by foolish and dangerous ostentation of the rich, the publication of large dividends, and distrust of a "government of profiteers" '.[40] The use of the language of patriotism by the left was further damaged since such language had been devalued by its use in wartime by employers, politicians and trade union leaders to discourage industrial action. Social patriotism had been used and was found wanting when Lloyd George failed 'to make Britain a fit country for heroes to live in'.

Another blow was struck at notions of Englishness by the perception that Britain was close to revolution in the immediate post-war years. Henderson,

---

36 *The Call*, 21 Nov. 1918.
37 Henry Pelling, *A history of British trade unionism*, 4th edn, Harmondsworth 1987, 298.
38 See Andrew Rothstein, *The soldiers' strikes of 1919*, London 1980.
39 Quoted in James E. Cronin, *Labour and society in Britain 1918–1979*, London 1984, 22.
40 Ibid. 21. See Keith Jeffery and Peter Hennessy, *States of emergency: British governments and strikebreaking since 1919*, London 1983, for government intelligence in the face of industrial unrest. For changes in the language of class see Bernard Waites, *A class society at war: England 1914–1918*, Leamington Spa 1987, chs i, ii.

THE BATTLE FOR BRITISH SOCIALISM

in *The aims of Labour*, claimed that 'barricades and blood' revolution was 'alien to the British character', but he had clearly not even convinced himself, for on the very next page he warned that violence 'will rule the thoughts of the masses of the people', and 'vast numbers of the population [were] skilled in the use of arms, disciplined, [and] inured to danger'.[41] Most historians consider that a revolutionary situation did not exist in 1919.[42] Whatever the chances of a British revolution, the contemporary perception from all points of the political spectrum was not only was it possible, but likely. Gallacher, a founding member of the Communist Party of Great Britain (CPGB), was sure an opportunity had been missed. He later wrote with regret that 'Revolt was seething everywhere, especially in the army. We had within our hands the possibility of giving actual expression and leadership to it, but it never entered our heads to do so. We were carrying on a strike when we ought to have been making a revolution.'[43] Beatrice Webb, in her diaries, recorded the growing fear of revolution. 'The Bolsheviks grin at us from a ruined Russia and their creed, like the plague of influenza, seems to be spreading westwards from one country to another', she wrote in November 1918.[44] Figures outside the labour movement shared Webb's anxiety. Home Office agents sent in worrying reports. One such, from an agent working inside Glasgow BSP, illustrated the various strands that heightened fears:

> The ultimate end of this manoeuvre [a general strike] would be Revolution and a Soviet form of government. The dangers consequent upon even the slightest success of such a scheme must be patent to anyone who has studied the course of events in Russia. The spread of this spirit is alarming, and evidence can be obtained of a determined effort to emulate the Russian Bolshevik movement in this country. It is also highly significant that while the soldiers are openly declaring their objection to being sent to Russia to fight the Bolsheviki, this very gang of agitators are publishing broadcast a pamphlet *Hands off Russia*, while their press is divided between panegyrics of praise of the Bolshevik form of government and frenzied abuse of a government which sends an army to fight 'the first Socialist Republic'.[45]

The contemporary perception that revolution was possible in Britain led to a crisis of legitimacy of notions of national identity that stressed the innate constitutionalism of the British people. The combination of industrial unrest,

[41] Arthur Henderson, *The aims of Labour*, London 1918, 57, 58.
[42] See, for example, Miliband, *Parliamentary socialism*, 66; Chris Wrigley, '1919: the critical year', in Chris Wrigley (ed.), *The British labour movement in the decade after the First World War*, Loughborough 1979, and 'The state and the challenge of labour in Britain, 1917–20', in Chris Wrigley (ed.), *Challenges of labour: central and western Europe 1917–1920*, London–New York 1993.
[43] Gallacher, *Revolt on the Clyde*, 221.
[44] *The diary of Beatrice Webb*, III: *1905–1924: 'the power to alter things'*, ed. Norman MacKenzie and Jeanne MacKenzie, London 1984, 316, entry for 4 Nov. 1918.
[45] R. K. Middlemas, *The Clydesiders*, London 1965, 89.

arguments for direct action for political ends, the threat of Bolshevism, and opposition to intervention in Russia presented a powerful challenge to the established interpretations of the national character held by the mainstream of the British left. The relationship of these different factors will be discussed individually in order to draw out their main features and effects on left-wing discussions of national identity.

## Industrial unrest and direct action

Probably the most immediately threatening force against parliamentary socialism was the argument for direct action, stemming as it did from the massive wave of industrial unrest unleashed by the end of the war. It was almost impossible to argue that strikes were un-British, since they were occurring on such a scale, and nor was there any pre-war golden age to look back to; the years 1910 to 1914 had also seen a high incidence of strikes. In the middle of such a wave of strikes – there were 1,607 separate disputes in 1920 – the claim that strikes were not British could alienate large sections of the organised working class. For Labour and trade union leaders the difficulty was great, for in the last resort they had to support strikes by their supporters and members, however distasteful they might find them.

Labour movement leaders had believed that after the war strikes would prove less necessary. They believed their patriotism would be rewarded, and that wartime state control would be a permanent feature in which they would continue to have a role. The co-option of labour leaders during the war only reinforced pre-war thinking on the state. Henderson explained that the effect of the war had been that 'Methods of state control which would once have been regarded as intolerable infringements of the rights and liberties both of employers and workmen have been accepted without effective protest even from those bred in the individualist tradition of the last century.'[46] Beatrice Webb described 'a steady drift towards government control and responsibility', and with this went 'the full recognition of the producers' organisations as junior partners in this control'.[47] As trade union leaders were drawn into the state's business so they were drawn towards a form of state socialism, expressed by Sidney Webb in *Labour and the new social order*.[48] MacDonald was the key figure in formulating Labour's attitude to the role of the state, and despite his opposition to the war, and hence his exclusion from the machinery of the state, he too believed that due to the war 'Labour has had to be

---

[46] Henderson, *Aims of Labour*, 9.
[47] *Beatrice Webb's diaries 1912–1924*, ed. Margaret I. Cole, London 1952, 69, entry for 27 July 1916.
[48] For the trade unions and the new programme see McKibbin, *Evolution of the Labour Party*, ch. v; for Webb, Henderson and MacDonald and the new programme see Winter, *Socialism and the challenge of war*.

THE BATTLE FOR BRITISH SOCIALISM

made a national co-partner.'[49] Whereas Webb and Henderson favoured the functional participation of labour in the state, MacDonald argued for civic participation. In the post-war years he reiterated that

> The Independent Labour Party begins by taking the great unities of community, nation, and State for granted. It studies functions and functional organisations, but it cannot understand them, and they cannot understand themselves, except in their relation to the whole life of the community which they serve. Thus it cannot hesitate in deciding in favour of a State sovereignty, or in coming to the conclusion that the personality which operates in the community is the citizen, not the industrial personality.[50]

Those favouring functional participation believed they had proved their worth in wartime, and believed that through such bodies as the National Industrial Conference and Whitley Councils the labour/state partnership would continue. Trade union leaders also welcomed continued co-operation with business leaders through the National Alliance of Employers and Employed.[51] The Sankey Commission to investigate nationalisation of the mines was seen as the climax to this partnership; Beatrice Webb wrote that Sidney 'believes that the Coal Commission will be the beginning of a landslide into communal control of industries and services', and had high hopes for the Industrial Conference, which she called 'Soviet Government peacefully incorporated in the British Constitution; a revolution in a fit of absentmindedness, without machine guns or barricades – without even waving the red flag'.[52]

In practice there was little contradiction between the MacDonald and Webb views, for the latter view also accepted state sovereignty over other interests. This was explained by J. H. Thomas, leader of the National Union of Railwaymen, to striking tube workers in February 1919:

> Our union is the strongest in the country. We can demand that unless such a thing is done, we can paralyse the community. That is our power. I want to examine what is our duty in relation to that power. However strong and powerful we may be, the State is more powerful and more important. Citizenship has a stronger claim than any sectional interest.[53]

The state control of industry in wartime reinforced the belief in the state's supremacy over sectional interests. E. H. Carr commented after the Second World War that 'the socialisation of the nation has as its corollary the nation-

---

[49] J. Ramsay MacDonald, *Parliament and revolution*, Manchester 1919, 12.
[50] Idem, *Parliament and democracy*, 1920, in *The social and political thought of the British Labour Party*, ed. Frank Bealey, London 1970, 103.
[51] See Wrigley, 'The state and the challenge of labour in Britain', 275, 282.
[52] *Beatrice Webb's diaries*, 162, 157, entries for 23 June, 27 Mar. 1919.
[53] Blaxland, *J. H. Thomas*, 121. Thomas explained the same point to the House of Commons: *Hansard*, 5th ser. cxii. 13 Feb. 1919, 339.

alisation of socialism'.[54] This was already occurring after the First World War. Trade union leaders in the wake of the war appealed to the patriotism of the government and urged it to make an appeal to the patriotism of the workers in their claims for state control. In the Commons, William Brace pointed out one of the benefits of nationalisation:

> To appeal to workmen in the name of the State is to touch them in their most vital spot, their native patriotism. If you would allow us to appeal to the workmen to withhold doing anything in the form of the industrial action policy because it was the property of the State and on behalf of the State, we should be infinitely more effective than any appeal that can be made to them if the concerns are to be allowed to continue in the hands of and under the control of private individuals.[55]

Direct action posed a threat to the authority of the state. Labour leaders not only accepted that authority, but believed they now had a role in the state, hence they opposed direct action. Indeed, it was argued that the use of direct action by Labour would encourage its opponents to do the same when, in the not too distant future, Labour formed a government.[56] But they were in a position of weakness in relation to the arguments for direct action. First, the result of the 1918 general election was seen widely on the left as fraudulent. Two out of every five of the electorate had not voted, and the *Herald* talked of the 'virtual disfranchisement of the army'.[57] Those on the left were particularly appalled by the baseness of the campaign. Snowden said of Lloyd George that 'never before in the history of this country did a politician sink to such depths of infamy to keep in office'.[58] Labour also saw the 1918 intake of MPs as 'the profiteers' Parliament'.[59] Second, the Parliamentary Labour Party between 1918 and 1922 was largely ineffective. While Labour polled just under a quarter of the votes cast in 1918, only fifty-nine Labour MPs were elected. The House was dominated overwhelmingly by the Coalition. Since those associated with an anti-war stance were defeated, the PLP was manned by trade union MPs, and proved 'a very tame lion . . . led by the respectable but dull-witted Adamson'.[60] That *The Call* condemned the PLP's 'scandalous inactivity' was to be expected, but the Labour conference was also critical, and the ILP NAC formally complained of the PLP's apathy on foreign affairs.[61]

The strength of the direct action impulse in the labour movement is best

[54] E. H. Carr, *Nationalism and after*, London 1945, 19.
[55] *Hansard*, 5th ser. cxii. 13 Feb. 1919, 333–4.
[56] For example, see Clynes in *Times*, 13 Sept. 1919.
[57] Labour Party, *Conference report*, 1919, 28; *Herald*, 21 Dec. 1918.
[58] ILP, *Conference report*, 1919, 34. See also MacDonald, *Parliament and revolution*, 2.
[59] W. C. Anderson, *The profiteers' parliament*, ILP, London 1919. See Mowat, *Britain between the wars*, 4–7, for the election campaign.
[60] *Diary of Beatrice Webb*, iii. 329, entry for 10 Jan. 1919.
[61] *The Call*, 27 Mar. 1919; Labour Party, *Conference report*, 1919, 127–30; Johnson to

illustrated by looking at the response of Labour's most devoted advocate of parliamentarism, MacDonald. He warned against any blanket condemnation of direct action, which could have dire consequences for the Labour Party and parliament. It might lead to the Labour leadership losing its hold over the movement, and hence 'Confidence in Parliament will become less than it now is, and the Parliamentary party will suffer the fate of the Irish Nationalists when they mistook the significance of Sinn Fein.'[62] In his diary he worried that he himself had been guilty of such: 'I feel unhappy lest I have gone too far in the other direction, and have encouraged passive obedience in democracy. That is a bad doctrine. I must do something to make my real position somewhat clearer.'[63] The outcome of this concern was *Parliament and revolution*, in which he attempted to seek the middle ground. He wrote to Johnson, the ILP secretary: 'Could you in view of the agitation in the branches and the action of some like Birmingham draw their attention in the next circular you issue to my book which is to appear on Parliament & Revolution. . . . [It] discusses, from the ILP point of view, the Russian revolution, Dictatorship of the Proletariat, Soviets, Direct Action, Democracy.'[64] 'To the socialist', he wrote, 'the relative merits of industrial and political action must be considered, not for the purpose of abandoning one or the other, but of assigning to each its proper place on a full attack all along the line by democracy upon capitalism.'[65] The proper place for direct action, he considered, was in support of, not in opposition to, constitutionalism: 'Because such action can never come into operation whilst Parliamentary government is fulfilling its functions as representative government: it can only be used to support representative government.'[66] This was a bid to make direct action part of a radical patriotic strategy; labour would defend the constitution against government debasement. But it was also an opportunist bid by MacDonald not to lose control of a movement that was becoming attached to political forms with which he had no sympathy.[67]

To a certain extent, other opponents of direct action used a similar argument, but it lacked MacDonald's sophistication. It remained based on an idea of Britain as essentially formed by its parliamentarianism. Adamson worried that industrial action, 'if not dealt with wisely and quickly will undermine the

Henderson, 17 Apr. 1920, Francis Johnson correspondence, 1920/19, Harvester Press Microforms, Brighton.
[62] *Socialist Review*, Apr.–June 1919, 104.
[63] Ward, *James Ramsay MacDonald*, 102.
[64] MacDonald to Johnson, 3 Sept. 1919, Francis Johnson correspondence.
[65] MacDonald, *Parliament and revolution*, 81.
[66] Ibid. 76.
[67] Robert E. Dowse argues that MacDonald sincerely held this joint action view: 'A note on Ramsay MacDonald and direct action', *Political Studies* ix (1961), 306–8. That MacDonald's only explanations of this view came in 1919 and 1920 supports the argument that opportunism rather than conviction was behind it.

stability of the State and endanger the continued existence of this country'.[68] Likewise Brace believed that 'This island home of ours is face to face with a very serious situation in consequence of industrial unrest.'[69] For them, the threat to parliament was a threat to the nation. As Thomas said, 'I want the authority of parliament recognised as being essential to the future of the country.'[70] The consequence of direct action could only be the destruction of what Britain meant, parliamentary democracy, and its replacement by something unknown and un-British.

The moderate leaders did not win the arguments over direct action. At the 1919 Labour conference, when delegates were warned that direct action was unconstitutional, Robert Williams asked in reply whether the government's war against Russia was constitutional. Another delegate was blunt; he said 'He still had to learn that because a movement was unconstitutional it was wrong.' The majority of the delegates seemed to agree; they voted 1,893,000 to 935,000 to consult the Parliamentary Committee of the TUC on 'the unreserved use of their political and industrial power'.[71] The Triple Alliance also called on the TUC to convene a conference to discuss compelling the government to withdraw from Russia. The Parliamentary Committee decided no such conference was necessary. The September 1919 TUC conference censured the Parliamentary Committee by referring back this section of its report by 2.5 million to 1.8 million.[72] The failure of direct action was, therefore, mainly due to the direct actionists' need to rely on the institutions of the labour movement.

The failure of such reliance was shown in the Mines for the Nation campaign, into which labour leaders diverted the movement in December 1919. It offered a direct alternative to industrial action for political ends by appealing to public opinion. Consequently, it sought a cross-class alliance, stressing the benefits of coal nationalisation to the nation. Coal was 'our national heritage', 'our chief national asset', and the miners performed 'a great national service'.[73] Fifteen million leaflets were issued, as well as tens of thousands of pamphlets, and one hundred demonstrations were held.[74] At the 1920 Labour conference, the chairman, W. H. Hutchinson, of the Amalgamated

---

[68] *Hansard*, 5th ser. cxii. 11 Feb. 1919, 60.

[69] Ibid. 13 Feb. 1919, 355–6.

[70] Ibid. 7 Nov. 1918, 2400.

[71] Labour Party, *Conference report*, 1919, 117, 157, 161, 156.

[72] Graubard, *British labour and the Russian Revolution*, 72–3, 75–6.

[73] Sidney Webb, 'The black tiger', and Leo Chiozza Money, 'Nationalisation as a consumers' policy', in The Mines for the Nation Committee, *The mines for the nation*, London n.d, 21, 13, 16. See also The Mines for the Nation Committee, *Coal nationalisation and the middle classes*, London, n.d.

[74] E. Eldon Barry, *Nationalisation in British politics: the historical background*, London 1965, 243.

Society of Engineers, pointed out that, while the campaign had failed, it had 'had a great educational value'.[75]

In the end it was not the arguments of the opponents of direct action that won, but unemployment and the defeat of the Triple Alliance on Black Friday. MacDonald clearly recognised this. He wrote of the Triple Alliance strike that never happened:

> It not only failed but failed ignominiously. If this disastrous venture is pondered over, and if as a result the Labour movement swings with more vigour and singleness of purpose on to the only profitable lines of steady and consistent advance, we may yet look back upon these dark days with gratitude and regard them as having been necessary for our elementary schooling.[76]

### British socialism and Bolshevism

Leading labour and socialist figures had already defined a 'British socialism' before 1914. It was evolutionary, statist, non-violent and above all parliamentary. Its nature had been reinforced by arguments about both British conditions and the national character. It had been under serious threat from syndicalism in the years 1910 to 1914, but war had brought a temporary end to the industrial unrest upon which syndicalism's strength had been based. While the majority of syndicalists opposed the war, they too had some temporary hesitation. Tom Mann had expressed his regret that 'the workers of the world are at one another's throats', but also stated that 'I prefer not to make any definite pronouncement.'[77] Its lack of organisation meant that syndicalism as a theory could not be combined with practice in any cohesive form. Syndicalism was submerged by the question of the war. Hence 'British socialism' was given a reprieve.

The Bolshevik Revolution renewed the threat in a much more dangerous form for British socialists. Bolshevism's great strength was that it had worked. A socialist government was in place. The moderate British labour leaders recognised the continuities of their fight against revolutionism. MacDonald wrote in 1919, 'Is there a single person who has been in the socialist movement for 20 years who, looking back, is not saddened by the long disrupting controversies raised by mere will-o'-the-wisps who today are forgotten and disgraced, but who in their time distracted the movement, dazzled it with their marsh flares, and misled it by their antics?'[78] The fight against

---

75 Labour Party, *Conference report*, 1920, 114.
76 *Socialist Review*, July–Sept. 1921, in Richard W. Lyman, 'James Ramsay MacDonald and the leadership of the Labour Party, 1918–22', *JBS* ii (1962), 138–9.
77 *Daily Herald*, 27 Aug. 1914, in Chushichi Tsuzuki, *Tom Mann 1856–1941: the challenges of labour*, Oxford 1991, 177–8.
78 MacDonald, *Parliament and revolution*, 3. For MacDonald's view of the ILP's struggle against its own left wing see his pamphlet written for ILP study circles which educated new

Bolshevism was seen as the latest incident in a long-running ideological battle. There had been the revolutionism of the SDF and anarchism, syndicalism, and now, Bolshevism. Henderson had returned from Russia in 1917 determined to avert the threat of revolutionary ideologies in Britain through the framing of a new programme for the Labour Party.[79]

While the war lasted, reactions to the Bolshevik Revolution were determined by attitudes to the war. Anti-war groups saw the Bolsheviks as a force for peace, especially after the publication of the secret treaties. Pro-war Labour delegates sang 'For he's a jolly good fellow' to Kerensky at their June 1918 conference, after he told them that the Bolsheviks represented 'the vanguard of the triumphant German imperialism'.[80] The end of the war allowed the conflict between reformism, or British socialism, and revolutionism into the open, uncomplicated by attitudes to the war. In February 1919 the Second International was re-launched at Berne. Branting, of the Swedish social democrats, moved a resolution on democracy and dictatorship contrasting western parliamentary socialism with Bolshevism. It declared that:

> socialism cannot be realised, much less permanently established, unless it rests upon the triumphs of democracy, and is rooted in the principles of liberty. Those institutions which constitute democracy – freedom of speech, and of the press, the right of assembly, universal suffrage, a government responsible to parliament, with arrangements guaranteeing popular co-operation and respect for the wishes of the people, the right of association, etc., – these also provide the working classes with the means of carrying on the class struggle.[81]

This resolution laid down the basic arguments upon which the British moderates were to defend their own socialism and attack Bolshevism. The significance of the resolution is that it shows that this conflict occurred across Europe, yet British moderates were to frame their own arguments in a British context, despite their leading involvement in the Second International. The weakness of European moderate reformist parties left the British Labour Party as the major anti-Bolshevik socialist party in Europe; the International's secretariat was moved to London in recognition of this fact. Of the August 1920 congress at Geneva, the International's own report declared: 'What distinguishes this Congress clearly from those which have preceded it is the attitude of open combat adopted towards Bolshevism. . . . London and Moscow are henceforth two antagonistic forces struggling for supremacy over the

members in the politics of the leadership: *The story of the ILP and what it stands for*, 3rd edn, London 1924, 10–12.

[79] J. M. Winter, 'Arthur Henderson, the Russian Revolution, and the reconstruction of the Labour Party', *HJ* xv (1972), 753–73. The joint motive of making Labour a party capable of challenging for government is dealt with in ch. 9 below.

[80] Labour Party, *Conference report*, June 1918, 60–1. See also Graubard, *British labour and the Russian Revolution*, 57–62.

[81] ILP, *International socialism and world peace: resolutions of the Berne conference February 1919*, London 1919, 6–7.

working masses: two poles around which the socialist forces will crystallise.'[82] It is this conflict which is examined here, though the emphasis is on the debate inside the British left.

There were major difficulties for the moderates in the fight against Bolshevism. Allied intervention in Soviet Russia meant that the moderates had to take care not to be seen to be siding with the Allied capitalist forces, and many were loathe to attack Bolshevism while Russia was under attack. R. C. Wallhead, chairman of the ILP, explained that 'I am continually being asked whether I have any criticism to offer of the Soviet system of government. My answer is that until an honourable peace with Russia has been duly ratified I do not propose to utter any criticism which could be misconstrued and made use of by the enemies of the Russian people.'[83] Also, the ILP, which had been the main source of ideas about what constituted British socialism was in a state of flux in the years immediately after the war. Membership was rising considerably, but people were joining a party which seemed to have lost touch with its traditional politics. This can be illustrated in three ways. Firstly, the ILP was publishing pamphlets praising the Russian Revolution and Bolshevism. Joseph King wrote two pamphlets giving sympathetic accounts of Bolshevism, pointing out that the Bolshevik Revolution, while it had used force, had been effected largely without bloodshed.[84] The ILP published Lenin on *The land revolution in Russia*, with a foreword by Snowden explaining his 'pleasure in presenting these important documents to British readers on account not only of their historical interest, but because of their practical value'.[85] Secondly, the attitude of Snowden, chairman of the ILP, is illustrative. At the time of the Bolshevik insurrection he said 'The extremists have captured the government', but within a month he decided that 'The Bolsheviks are far more representative of Russian opinion than we had been led to believe from prejudiced reports which have appeared in the British press.'[86] In mid 1918 he explained that 'the expectations of those who believed and declared that the Bolsheviks had usurped authority by force in opposition to the wishes of the Russian people have been falsified by the facts'.[87] Third, ILP conferences voted against accepting the Branting resolution by 290 to 203 votes in 1919, and voted for disaffiliation from the Second International by 529 to 144 votes in 1920. Almost a third of delegates voted for immediate affiliation to the Third International, and two-thirds voted for consultation about affiliation.[88] G. D. H. Cole perhaps best characterised the

[82] Graubard, *British labour and the Russian Revolution*, 199.
[83] *Labour Leader*, 12 Aug. 1920.
[84] Joseph King, *Bolshevism and Bolsheviks*, London 1919, 18. See also idem, *Soviets*, London 1919; A. W. Humphreys, *The allies' crime against Russia: an exposure of a capitalist conspiracy*, London 1919, 4, 11; ILP, *Bolshevism!*, Manchester n.d. [1919].
[85] V. I. Lenin, *The land revolution in Russia: with a foreword by Philip Snowden*, London 1919.
[86] *Labour Leader*, 15 Nov., 6 Dec. 1917.
[87] Ibid. 23 May 1918.
[88] ILP, *Conference reports*, 1919, 68; 1920, 86.

position of the ILP towards the Russian Revolution. 'The ILP was sharply divided', he commented. 'Its best known leaders more and more anti-Bolshevik as the character of the second revolution became more plain, the rank and file somewhat bewildered and for the most part wishful to go left-ward without ceasing to be a parliamentary party working within the Labour Party on constitutional lines.'[89]

Under the twin threats of direct action and sympathy for Bolshevism, the moderates had to reconstruct 'British socialism'. Snowden had, by the late summer of 1919, become anti-Bolshevik, and warned of the effects of Bolshevism on the ILP. He warned that 'unless the NAC takes some steps at once to protect the branches from this insidious propaganda, the disruption of the movement is inevitable'. He recommended sending out a memorandum to branches warning against 'novel and untried theories and experiments', restating the ILP's policy as 'the education of the people in the use of the parliamentary and municipal vote'.[90]

This prompted the ILP to undertake a campaign against Bolshevism in the party. The major argument used was quite negative and quite simple. It was argued that, while revolution was supposedly applicable to all countries, this was not the case, for, while socialism was internationally applicable, 'the political and historical developments and genius of each country will determine the exact form which the transition will take'.[91] From this position, and in a variety of forms, it was argued that Russia was not Britain. One pamphlet pointed out that 'Recent events in Russia have given a new lease of life to the revolutionary idea, for it is asked, "If this success can be achieved in Russia, why not in this country?" ' The writer's answer was simple: 'Conditions are different in this country.'[92] Arthur Ponsonby stressed the Russian-ness of revolution: 'The Russian experiment, apart from the fact that it cannot so far be regarded as an unqualified success, is essentially and absolutely a *Russian* experiment evolved from Russian conditions, carried out by Russian methods, and adapted to the Russian psychology.'[93] Having established that the Russian Revolution was essentially Russian, it was argued that Britain was not Russia. 'Russia is not England', the ILP NAC told members, 'The social and political history of the two countries are different.'[94] The advantage to this line of argument was that it implied no criticism of the Bolsheviks in

[89] G. D. H. Cole, *A history of the Labour Party since 1914*, London 1948, 41.

[90] Snowden to NAC members, 29 Aug. 1919; Memorandum for branches, BLPES, ILP papers 3, NAC minutes, item 11, 113, 114–17.

[91] 'Draft memorandum on socialism and government' (for submission to Geneva conference, Feb. 1920) ILP papers 3, item 11, 166–72.

[92] H. C. Shears, *Socialist policy: reform or revolution?*, London 1919, 3.

[93] *Labour Leader*, 28 Sept. 1920. Original emphasis. See also MacDonald, *Parliament and revolution*, 98.

[94] ILP papers 3, item 11, 160–3.

Russia, but only of the application of their methods to Britain. As Ponsonby put it, 'oranges are excellent fruit, but you can't grow them in England'.[95]

The response of those who called themselves 'British Bolsheviks' was contempt for such arguments. They called them un-socialist. The left wing of the ILP said of the leadership that, 'To argue that what is good for Russia is not good for Britain is not good for China, is the very negation of international socialism which seeks a new international mode of life to replace capitalism which, in its essentials is uniform and universal in all the countries of the world.'[96] They also had a different conception of British history than the moderates. The left wing of the ILP said that the moderates' wish for gradual change stood 'in an evident ignorance of the lessons of our own nation's history', and J. T. Walton-Newbold wondered why a statue of Oliver Cromwell stood outside Westminster Hall if change in Britain had been so peaceful.[97] At the 1920 ILP conference, he claimed that 'he had never founded his revolutionary socialism upon the experience of his Russian comrades, but upon his study of English history'. C. H. Norman supported him saying that both Magna Carta and the Bill of Rights had been won by revolution.[98] Theodore Rothstein wrote in *The Call* that through reading Russian, Austrian, Hungarian and German papers he had concluded that 'The truth is, every country can claim exemption from the operation of social and historical forces on the plea of "peculiarities", since every country is "peculiar".'[99]

There was a general belief that Britain was the most democratic country in the world, and that Labour just needed a parliamentary majority to be representative of the nation. The Webbs, in their contribution to the debate on political methods requested by the Second International, put this belief in their usual unsentimental way. They praised 'the particular advantages of the political institutions of the democracy of Great Britain' and its creators, including Fox and Grey, Cobden and Bright, Gladstone and Chamberlain, 'honest enthusiasts in the cause of liberty'. They explained that 'The British Constitution as it now stands, notwithstanding all its manifold imperfections ... has, in fact, secured a larger participation, a more continuous interest and more widespread influence in Parliamentary elections than can be found in any other great nation.' They noted how parliament had acted upon the national political character, leading to the acceptance by all parties of the

---

95 *Labour Leader*, 28 Sept. 1920.
96 Left Wing of the ILP, 'Explanatory notes on the Second International versus the Third International', ILP papers 3, item 61. See also *The Call*, 14 Feb. 1918.
97 Left Wing of the ILP, 'The call of the Third International', ILP papers 3, item 61; *Labour Leader*, 18 Sept. 1919.
98 ILP, *Conference report*, 1920, 73, 74.
99 *The Call*, 17 Apr. 1919. Rothstein wrote under the name John Bryan. His conclusion about such national differences was that 'underlying all peculiarities are the same social factors – modern industry, capitalism, proletariat, and, now, the world war – which are bound to produce the same effects', that is, revolution.

'public judgement and the public conscience'.[100] George Benson of Salford ILP condemned English Bolsheviks because they wished to destroy 'the whole of the English political system which is rooted in our national life by the tradition of seven centuries, and in its place establish something utterly alien to our experience'.[101] It was this conception of an evolutionary parliamentary Britain that the Labour Party and ILP leaders saw themselves as defending.

## Opposition to intervention in Russia

For the Labour movement the years 1919 to 1921 were dominated by issues of direct action and attitudes to Bolshevism. These issues came together in the opposition to British intervention in the civil war in Soviet Russia. The language of radical patriotism, though not necessarily the ideas behind it, were largely absent from this discourse. The Allied intervention was seen as an attack on socialism by capitalism, even by those on the left who opposed Bolshevism. An ILP pamphlet declared: 'It is the assassination of the Russian Republic which we must prevent. The fall of the Soviet Republic would be the signal for the re-doubling of the effort by the forces of capitalism, imperialism, militarism and monarchism to make the new world a new slavery. Russia is holding up the light. She has put capitalism behind her.'[102] Even MacDonald, a bitter opponent of Bolshevism, declared that 'The crushing of Lenin is not only the destruction of his government (a small thing), but the re-establishment in Russia and in Europe of the old order of exploitation and of the subjection of the working class.'[103] This may have been opportunism on MacDonald's part, but this in itself would suggest the strength of pro-Soviet feeling on the British left. The ILP executive in January and June 1919 urged branches to keep up the agitation against intervention in Russia. Demonstrations were held in July 1919, and a special *Labour Leader* on Soviet Russia was published.[104]

It was the fact that Russia was a socialist country that removed old-style radical patriotic vocabulary, for the left still used such terms in relation to British intervention in Ireland. Vernon Hartshorn moved a resolution condemning British actions in Ireland as a 'stain which is besmirching our reputation'. 'The Labour Party', he said, 'and I hope all Britishers feel, that the state of things which now exists in Ireland is no credit to this country or to

100 Sidney and Beatrice Webb, *A constitution for the socialist commonwealth of Great Britain,* Cambridge 1975, first publ. 1920, 87, 88, 89.
101 *Labour Leader,* 22 Jan. 1920.
102 Humphreys, *The allies' crime against Russia,* 24.
103 *Socialist Review,* July–Sept. 1919, 205.
104 Circular to branches, 15 Jan. 1919; NAC minutes, 22–3 June 1919, ILP papers 3, item 11.

the British government.'[105] Henderson, the following year, showed how radical patriotism and loyalist patriotism had come together in the war, as he spoke of the betrayal of the high feelings of patriotism engendered by war:

> A policy of military terrorism has been inaugurated, which in our opinion, is not merely a betrayal of democratic principles and not only a betrayal of the things for which we claimed to stand during the five years great world war, but is utterly opposed to the best traditions of the British people. Such a policy, it seems to me, can only be characterised as being akin to the policy of frightfulness which was associated with the doings of the Germans, and the doings of him whom we described as the Hun during the War.[106]

The Labour Party stated that the government's policy in Ireland filled 'with burning shame all people, irrespective of party, who have followed the recent course of events in that unhappy country, and is an indelible stain on the fair name of the liberty-loving people of Britain'.[107] Labour were not alone in using such arguments. D. G. Boyce has explained the opposition to the Coalition's repressive policy in Ireland: 'Reprisals hit Englishmen's sense of justice and fair play; they also wounded their pride.'[108] This suggests that two sets of terminology could be held simultaneously and reserved for separate occasions.

It can also be suggested that different sections of the left had different motives but a unity in practice. This was certainly the case in relation to the formation of the Council of Action in August 1920.[109] This brought the spectacle of Thomas, the arch-moderate, calling for 'a challenge to the whole constitution of the country'.[110] But moderates were keen to stress that labour's actions implied no sympathy for the Communist form of government.[111]

The moderates were prepared to go so far in August 1920, advocating a 'down tools' policy, because they felt they were voicing the overwhelming desire of the nation for peace. Clynes told the Council of Action conference on 13 August that 'we have felt that we were acting and speaking not merely for the Labour movement, but that we were moulding and interpreting what we felt to be national opinion'.[112] The moderates felt they were representing

---

105 *Hansard*, 5th ser. cxv. 14 May 1919, 1694–6.
106 Ibid. 5th ser. cxiii. 20 Oct. 1920, 925.
107 *An appeal to the British nation by the Labour Party*, London 1920, 4.
108 D. G. Boyce, *Englishmen and Irish troubles: British public opinion and the making of Irish policy 1918–22*, London 1972, 99.
109 For the events surrounding this see L. J. MacFarlane, ' "Hands off Russia", British labour and the Russo-Polish War, 1920', *P&P* xxxviii (1967), 126–52, and Graubard, *British labour and the Russian Revolution*, ch. v.
110 Council of Action, *Report of the special conference on Labour and the Russian-Polish War*, London n.d.
111 See, for example, Clynes, *Hansard* 5th ser. cxxxiii. 10 Aug. 1920, 281.
112 Council of Action, *Report of the special conference*, 12. See also *Diary of Beatrice Webb*, iii. 363, entry for 20 Aug. 1920.

the people against the government. One expression of this was Henderson's telegram to local Labour Parties calling for '*citizen* demonstrations' on Sunday 8 August. This both avoided an appeal to workers as workers, and prevented immediate strike action.[113] Likewise, MacDonald portrayed the Council of Action as defender of the British constitution: 'Thus when people talk of this council being unconstitutional, they talk nonsense. Everything necessary to protect the constitution is constitutional, if constitutional means anything at all except passive obedience to any outrageous acts done by men who happen to be ministers.'[114] Clynes, too, declared that the Council of Action 'was not challenging the constitution, but requiring our government to conform to it'.[115]

The hypocrisy and duplicity of the government also played a part in both the massive support for labour's position and in the lengths the moderates were prepared to go. The British left, from Radical liberals to socialist revolutionaries, had always been extremely hostile to tsarism. British intervention could only be seen as an attempt at restoration of tsarism and capitalism. Snowden, in early 1919, had said, 'The Allied war upon Russia is not a war against Bolshevik excesses, for the Allied governments were bosom friends of the late tsarist regime, which committed greater diabolical outrages in a day than the Bolsheviks have committed in a year in a state of revolution. But it is a war upon the philosophy of social democracy.'[116] Only a month before the Council of Action was formed, the *Daily Herald* had published a secret document reporting conversations in which Churchill offered a White general 10,000 volunteers for the fight against Bolshevism.[117] Pontypridd Trades and Labour Council had responded to these revelations by calling 'on the government to place [Churchill] on trial for high treason'.[118] Such events, combined with the overwhelming desire to prevent another war, ensured labour would receive massive support. The Communist R. Palme Dutt called the agitation 'simply a popular expression of war-weariness and horror at the prospect of being dragged into another war'.[119]

Graubard has argued that Labour's policy towards Russia, both before, during and after August 1920, was determined by 'an identity of status' as underdogs. Russia stood against the capitalist world and Labour stood against the British capitalist parties, and both were excoriated for their alleged unfitness to govern.[120] However, Stephen White has called this thesis unsustainable. He argues that labour's actions in 1920 had nothing to do with sympathy for

113 Labour Party, *Conference report*, 1921, 11. Emphasis added.
114 MacFarlane, ' "Hands off Russia" ', 147.
115 *Times*, 20 Aug. 1920.
116 Graubard, *British labour and the Russian Revolution*, 70–1.
117 See George Lansbury, *The miracle of Fleet Street: the story of the Daily Herald*, London n.d. 127–32.
118 Pontypridd Labour Party minute book, 30 July 1920, E. P. Microforms, Wakefield 1980.
119 *The Communist*, 19 Aug. 1920, in MacFarlane, ' "Hands off Russia" ', 151.
120 Graubard, *British labour and the Russian Revolution*, 242, 243.

Russia, but were solely about avoiding both the financial burden and loss of life that would result from war. He argues that there was little pro-Soviet feeling on the British left, and that policy towards Russia, including trade and recognition, was based on combating unemployment and on the influence of ex-Liberals on the foreign policy of the Labour Party.[121] It is argued here that it is right to see the Council of Action agitation as dependent on war-weariness, but that an essential ingredient was the 'transferred nationalism' of a significant section of left-wing activists, who were responsible for the establishment of 350 local councils of action.[122] The levels of activity of these local councils varied considerably. At Merthyr Tydfil, the Labour *Pioneer* hailed the local council as 'an important instrument for the emancipation of the workers'. It co-operated with other local radical organisations, and issued a circular to other councils stressing the links between the agitations on Russia, Ireland and unemployment. Aberdeen Trades Council supported a demonstration called by the local 'Hands Off Russia' committee, and sent a telegram to the Prime Minister, foreign secretary and local MPs threatening direct action in the event of war, and demanding 'the immediate raising of the Blockade and resumption of trading relations with "Soviet Russia" '. It then co-operated with other local bodies in forming a council of action. These examples suggest some activity from local councils. Elsewhere activity was more restricted. In Sussex, three local councils were set up, at East Grinstead, where 11s. was collected at an open air meeting, at Uckfield and Haywards Heath, but little was done. In Edinburgh the trades council decided in August that it would act as the council of action until a local conference could be called. In October it was still delaying the calling of such a conference, months after the reasons for its existence had receded. How many of the 350 local councils had only the same level of existence as that in Edinburgh is unclear. But if there is little evidence of unconditional support for the soviet system, neither is there evidence that local councils of action saw themselves as MacDonald's defenders of the constitution.[123]

Certainly, the Communist Party and its predecessors in the BSP, Workers' Socialist Federation, Socialist Labour Party and smaller groups were unconditional in their support for Soviet Russia. The BSP, as early as February 1918, had urged the British working class to 'learn to speak Russian', by setting up a labour convention, 'an anti-parliament, as the great Chartist conventions were, and then we shall soon see how easily Russian can be spoken in these

---

[121] Stephen White, *Britain and the Bolshevik Revolution*, London–Basingstoke 1979, 204–5, 28, 241–3.
[122] The phrase is George Orwell's: 'Notes on nationalism', 1945, in *The Penguin essays of George Orwell*, Harmondsworth 1984, 306–23.
[123] White, *Britain and the Bolshevik Revolution*, 46–7; Aberdeen Trades Council minutes, 8, 11, 15 Aug. 1920, Microform Ltd, Wakefield; Edinburgh Trades Council minutes, 17 Aug., 3 Sept., 3 Oct. 1920, E. P. Microform, Wakefield; Sussex Divisional Labour Party minutes, 16 Aug., 11 Sept. 1920, BLPES, archives collection miscellaneous 488.

islands without the knowledge of grammar or vocabulary'.[124] The membership of the Communist Party, finally united in January 1921, may have only been 3,000, but *The Communist*, its weekly paper, sold about 50,000 copies.[125]

The largest circulation newspaper of the left, the *Daily Herald*, under Lansbury's editorship, gave much support to Soviet Russia. The circulation of over 300,000 was recognised as important by the Russian government. Litvinov, representative of the Russian government in Britain, wrote to Chicherin, the Russian foreign secretary, that 'in Russian questions it acts as if it were our organ', and recommended that finance be supplied to keep it going. The British government exposed this offer of help, and the money (in the form of tsarist jewels) was rejected by a majority of the board of management, despite Lansbury and a majority of the readership recommending acceptance.[126] Lansbury had visited Russia in early 1920 and sent glowing accounts back to the *Herald*, one of whose writers noted that his critics were calling him 'the self-elected Messiah of British Bolshevism'.[127] Lansbury explained why he went to Russia in *What I saw in Russia*, the book he published on his return: 'I did not go to Russia as a cold-blooded investigator seeking to discover what there was of evil; I went as a socialist, to see what a socialist revolution looks like at close quarters; and, above everything else, to look at the faces of those who had made the revolution.'[128]

Lansbury rejected the violence associated with revolution, though like most of the British left, accepted its necessity in the context of tsarism. It was violent revolution in Britain that most of the left opposed. Clifford Allen, another visitor to Russia in 1920, wrote, 'I feel such a profound sympathy for all the experiments and sacrifices which have taken place in Russia', and recommended the ILP's affiliation to the Third International if it could reject violence.[129] The report of the Labour Party delegation to Russia in May 1920 also presented a sympathetic account of Soviet Russia, condemning the capitalist press's 'perversions of the facts'. Hunger and suffering in Russia, they said, were caused not by the Bolsheviks, but by the Allied blockade, which should be lifted at once. That is not to say that they were totally uncritical, for they condemned the lack of personal freedom and the methods of the Communist Party.[130] Ethel Snowden, a member of the delegation, was more critical upon her return. She wrote:

124 *The Call*, 14 Feb. 1918.
125 Morton H. Cowden, *Russian Bolshevism and British Labour 1917–1921*, New York 1984, 156–7.
126 Ibid. 106–7.
127 *Daily Herald*, 3 Apr. 1920.
128 Graubard, *British labour and the Russian Revolution*, 212–13
129 Marwick, *Clifford Allen*, 61; ILP, *Conference report*, 1921, 60.
130 *Report of the British Labour delegation to Russia*, July 1920, in *Social and political thought of the Labour Party*, 8–9. See also Margaret Bondfield, *A life's work*, London n.d., 234. She reprints much of her Russian diary in chs xi, xii.

I am not hostile to the Russian Revolution which the tyrannous regime of the Czars made necessary and inevitable; but I am utterly opposed to the *coup d'état* of the Bolsheviki, as I should be to the seizing of power by any small minority of the people; for out of this action has sprung a large part of the misery the unhappy people of Russia endure.[131]

That Lloyd George quoted her to condemn Bolshevism in the Commons brought much criticism upon her from the left, and at the 1921 ILP conference just under 200 delegates voted against her nomination to the Labour Party executive because 'she had criticised the Russian Republic in an unfair and unfortunate way'. Despite 235 delegates backing her, the opposition was enough to prevent her nomination.[132] An earlier ILP conference had voted 290 to 203 against any criticism of the Bolsheviks.[133]

Undoubtedly ex-Liberals played a major part in framing Labour's foreign policy as White argues, but like Labour, radical Liberals had always shared a hostility towards tsarism.[134] When Edward VII had removed Hardie and Grayson from his 1908 garden party list, Arthur Ponsonby had also been removed.[135] Ex-Liberals like Joseph King and Colonel Malone became champions of Bolshevik Russia. Communists, British and Russian, acknowledged the role of such men with gratitude. Rothstein called E. D. Morel 'better than all the socialists', and Russia's representative in Britain thanked Ponsonby 'personally and in the name of the workers of the Soviet Union, for your sympathy and your efforts'.[136] The foreign policy framed by the ex-Liberals did not meet opposition within the Labour Party; indeed their expertise was welcomed.

Likewise, unemployment clearly played a part in Labour's policy towards Russia, but the enthusiasm with which the idea of trade with Russia was embraced can only be explained by some intangible notion of solidarity. Labour thinkers saw international disunity as the major cause of unemployment, but it was Russia that was continually named as the most victimised country. At a special conference on Ireland, the Labour executive allowed the following resolution to be moved: 'The growing volume of unemployment and under-employment is due in large measure to the interruption in world trading following on the war and the defective peace treaties, in addition to the folly of British and Allied policy in relation to the Soviet government of Russia.' From this resolution came a joint committee on unemployment, which recommended 'the immediate adoption of the policy

---

131 Ethel Snowden, *Through Bolshevik Russia*, London 1920, 11.
132 ILP, *Conference report*, 1921, 100–2. For Lloyd George see *Hansard*, 5th ser. cxxxiii. 266.
133 ILP, *Conference report*, 1919, 68.
134 White, *Britain and the Bolshevik Revolution*, 216–23.
135 Benn, *Keir Hardie*, 240.
136 White, *Britain and the Bolshevik Revolution*, 223.

of unobstructed trade with Russia'.[137] It is hard to believe that such enthusiasm for international trade could have been achieved had Russia not been perceived as a socialist or workers' nation. This was the key point. As Councillor H. Sykes, chairman of Woolwich Labour Party, explained at the time of the Council of Action agitation, 'If we war with Russia we shall be warring with a country that is ruled by the workers.'[138]

The First World War and its aftermath had contradictory but simultaneous effects upon the discourse of the British left. Many Labour and trade union leaders had been drawn into the state, reinforcing their view of its benevolent and neutral role, and of the coincidence of parliament and nation. But the war also made the use of patriotic vocabulary less effective, since the language of class, reflecting the massive industrial unrest, came to the fore, as victory removed the restraints of wartime patriotism.

The notion of patriotism as 'my country, right or wrong' also received a major blow in the post-war years, mainly because of war-weariness, but also because many on the left now believed a workers' state existed. Whereas the Boer War had been opposed using radical patriotic language, and the First World War had been supported using both radical and loyalist patriotism, the threatened war against Russia in the summer of 1920 led to a rejection of radical patriotic language among all except a few Labour leaders who sought not to lose control of the movement. Instead a language of class was used, crossing international frontiers. While MacDonald could claim tortuously that labour was defending the constitution, the view of most of the left was that the British government wanted to reassert the international supremacy of the capitalist class. The strength of such feeling is illustrated by the fact that, even when attacking Bolshevism, its opponents remained 'not unappreciative of the striking achievements of the Russian Bolshevist Party, and the genius and energy they have displayed in grappling with problems of reconstruction during the time of Civil War and foreign invasion'.[139]

The defeat of the Triple Alliance on Black Friday, April 1921, and rising unemployment spelt the end of direct action as a serious force on the left, and allowed the moderates to reassert their traditional parliamentary strategy. The end of civil war and foreign intervention in Russia allowed attacks on Bolshevism to henceforth be conducted with real determination. But, some on the left now had a focus outside of Britain for their loyalty, and transferred their patriotism to Russia.

137 Labour Party, *Conference report*, 1921, 25, 27. See also Joint Committee on Unemployment, *Unemployment: a Labour policy*, London 1921.
138 *Woolwich Pioneer*, 13 Aug. 1920.
139 ILP NAC, 'A message to the members: the principles of the ILP and its policy', Dec. 1919, BLPES, ILP papers 3, item 11, 160–3.

# 9

# *Labour and the Nation, 1917–1924*

Labour leaders were involved in an ideological battle inside the left. They were also concerned with portraying a new image to the world outside their ranks. The war had changed the leadership's view of themselves. Having been invited into the government, they came to see Labour as a potential governing party. But if Labour wanted to be a governing party, they felt it had to act like one; effectively this meant that politics were to be fought solely in the parliamentary arena. Henderson also believed that a new 'outlook for Labour' had been created by the Representation of the People Act and the psychological effect of the war itself. He argued that the Labour Party had to prepare for this new situation.[1] Labour would no longer be the pressure group of the pre-war years; the Liberal split provided Labour with its opportunity. The Labour leaders' view was that this new role could only be achieved by being a party of the nation, and not one in opposition to it. This involved a concentration upon winning parliamentary seats at the expense of socialist propagandising. Hence the emphasis of this analysis moves from left-wing journalists and pamphleteers to the parliamentary leaders of the Labour Party. This chapter concentrates on Henderson, Clynes, Snowden, Thomas and, above all, MacDonald, and the way in which they sought to portray Labour as a national party in the early 1920s. This reveals those leaders' views of what constituted the British nation.

## Building a national party

The first task was to explain that they were not the representatives of a single class or a sectional interest, as the very name, the Labour Party, implied.[2] There was nothing new in this; it had been their claim even before the war. But with improved prospects for the party in the post-war years, the claims became more urgent, and more frequent. The Labour Party, which proclaimed itself a socialist party in 1918, also appealed to the electorate in that year on the basis of not being a class party. Henderson argued that Labour now sought 'the creation of a genuine national party' whose aims were 'to

[1]  Arthur Henderson, 'The outlook for Labour', *Contemporary Review* cxiii (Feb. 1918), 121–30.
[2]  Thomas Jones recorded how, in September 1917, a group of prominent Labour figures, including Henderson, discussed the 'People's Party' as a possible name: *Whitehall diary*, I: *1916–1925*, ed. Keith Middlemas, London 1969, 36–7.

promote the political, social, and economic emancipation of the people, and more particularly of those who depend upon their own exertions by hand or by brain for the means of life'.[3] This phrase shows both the difficulty for Labour, and one of the ways by which it hoped to overcome that difficulty. Labour had to represent the interests of the organisations of the working class, but it also had to deny that this could conflict with its potential role as a governing party. The formula of workers by hand or by brain was supposed to broaden its representation so far that a conflict would no longer arise. Henderson therefore continued: 'The definition of Labour's aim and purpose will serve to remove the idea that the party is the party of the manual wage earners merely, and that its politics is the politics of the trade unions – a purely class conscious demand for specific improvements in wages, hours, conditions of employment.'[4] The opening of the party to individual membership was designed to allow the entry of the workers by brain.

This broadening of the party's appeal was also reflected in the party's manifestos issued in elections from 1918 to 1924 (and beyond). The 1918 and 1922 manifestos were called 'Labour's call to the people', in 1923 this was changed to 'Labour's appeal to the nation'.[5] They stressed the comprehensive nature of Labour's appeal. In 1918, it was emphasised that 'Labour's appeal to the people is not a sectional appeal, unless an appeal which excludes only militarists, profiteers, and place-hunters be regarded as sectional.'[6] This was a view that Labour leaders stressed again and again in speeches. Henderson told a Labour audience in June 1921 that Labour was 'the most comprehensive and only all-inclusive people's party engaged in British politics. . . . We are not a class party.'[7]

The purpose of such claims was explained by Clynes to a university extension meeting in Oxford in August 1919. 'If Labour was ever to think of itself as a controlling force in the nation', he said, 'it must cease to think of itself in the terms of class, as it had done hitherto.'[8] The aim was therefore to show that Labour would not come into conflict with the nation. Philip Snowden, in his election address for the 1922 election, wanted to rebut such accusations: 'You will be told that Labour is a menace. . . . Labour is not a menace to anything which is honest and fair and in the best interests of the nation.'[9] J. H. Thomas, unveiling a war memorial in South London, provided reassurance that this was the case. He was sure that 'there was no

---

3   Henderson, 'The outlook for Labour', 122.
4   Ibid.
5   *British general election manifestos 1918–1966*, ed. F. W. S. Craig, 3rd edn, Chichester 1983, 5, 12, 21.
6   Ibid. 5
7   Labour Party, *What Labour stands for: a restatement of policy*, London 1921, 7–8 (speeches at the annual conference demonstration, 21 June 1921).
8   *Times*, 8 Aug. 1919.
9   *New Leader*, 10 Nov. 1922.

section of men or women in any movement who really desired ill to the old country'.[10]

That Thomas should say this while honouring the war dead was significant, for Labour believed that its war service should already have secured its place in the nation, and the pro-war section of Labour were prepared to remind the nation of its role. It had been suggested during the war that Labour should create a 'National Memorial of Peace and Freedom', a war memorial, 'to commemorate the heroic deeds and unselfish devotion of those members of the British trades unions and other Labour organisations who fell in action . . . in the great struggle for freedom and peace'.[11] The tremendous advantage of the scheme would be that the memorial would take the form of new buildings for Labour and the TUC, which would act as a permanent reminder of Labour's patriotism. The inclusion of such anti-war figures as Robert Smillie and Ramsay MacDonald on the board of trustees that would handle the finances made the endeavour difficult. Union and local Labour Party parsimony, combined with a confusion as to exactly what would be commemorated, made the scheme a failure.[12] It was decided to dissociate the memorial from the building of Labour's new headquarters and Labour's reminders of its wartime patriotism had therefore to be less concrete.

The 1918 Labour manifesto, while calling for 'a peace of reconciliation', declared that 'victory has been achieved, and Labour claims no mean share of its achievement'.[13] The defeat of all prominent anti-war candidates in 1918 gave the party a warning that the war could not immediately be forgotten. Henderson was keen not to repeat defeat at the Widnes by-election in September 1919. His election address quoted both Lloyd George and Asquith on his own 'valuable' role during the war. It included photographs of his two sons, who had both volunteered in 1914, one being killed on the Somme.[14] Henderson also used Labour's war service to respond to Churchill's accusation of Labour's unfitness to govern, pointing out 'that during the war Labour leaders without governmental experience were called on to assume State responsibilities and had assisted in saving the nation in the hour of its dire need'.[15] But in the Woolwich by-election in early 1921, when MacDonald stood for Labour, his opponent, Captain Gee VC, used the slogan 'A traitor for parliament?' to win the safe seat by 700 votes.[16] No doubt Gee's use of his military rank won him votes. Labour candidates likewise were not averse to using their war ranks. The list of Labour candidates for the 1922 election included a brigadier-general (C. B., later Lord, Thomson), three colonels,

10 *Times*, 16 Feb. 1920.
11 Labour Party NEC minutes, 16 Oct. 1917.
12 For the slow death of the plan see Labour Party, *Conference reports*, Jan. 1918, 13–4; June 1918, 90–1; 1919, 155; 1920, 43, 128–9; 1921, 62–3, 149–50.
13 *General election manifestos 1918–1966*, 5.
14 Henderson election address, Labour Party NEC minutes, 1919. Henderson won the seat.
15 *Times*, 9 Jan. 1920.
16 Marquand, *Ramsay MacDonald*, 272–5.

one lieutenant-colonel, three majors (including Clement Attlee), five captains and one commander.[17] As late as 1924, during the debate on Labour's amendment to the Baldwin government's royal address, Thomas described how 'We were not defeated in this late war because Labour contributed its share as well as other people. We were not defeated because Labour showed that patriotism was not the monopoly of one class.'[18]

Anti-war sections of Labour could exhibit a kind of retrospective patriotism, by expressing the demands of ex-servicemen. One could remain anti-war yet demand a fair deal for those who had fought for their country. In 1919 the National Union of Ex-Servicemen was formed, linked explicitly to Labour. Indeed, a party circular to Labour branches instructed them to welcome the affiliation of National Union branches.[19] The National Union linked the experience of war service with radical social demands, such as the claim for 'back pay' to make up the former soldiers' wages to 6s. a day. The National Union failed to survive its isolation by the authorities, and its self-imposed exclusion from the negotiations that led to the founding of the British Legion.[20] Nevertheless the demands of ex-servicemen could allow anti-war figures to make good on the war, especially since they could disclaim responsibility for it and the subsequent peace.[21] MacDonald, in early 1923, received a deputation from Aberdeen British Legion, and told them that 'The Labour Party would not support any unfair advantage being taken of ex-servicemen. . . . He was sorry that since 1919 those great patriots who smote their breasts with a sort of perfervid enthusiasm, and who drank the health of the men in the trenches, had forgotten good deal about them.'[22]

Labour therefore aimed to show that it was a party of the nation with a proven record of service to the nation. But it did not leave it at that. It also sought to make itself the party of all classes, to turn its claim into reality. Labour expanded the number of parliamentary candidates from fifty-six in December 1910 (seventy-eight in January) to 361 in 1918. Whereas before the war the national executive had tried to limit candidacies, Henderson told the June 1918 conference that they 'intended to impose no limit' at the next election. This attempt to expand the geographical spread of the Labour Party

---

[17] Labour Party, *Conference report*, 1922, 254–62. Of course only those commissioned could continue to use their ranks.
[18] *Hansard* 5th ser. clxix. 18 Jan. 1924, 414.
[19] Labour Party circular, *The Labour Party and the National Union of Ex-Servicemen*, Dec. 1919.
[20] Graham Wootton, *The politics of influence: British ex-servicemen, cabinet decisions and cultural change (1917–1957)*, Cambridge, Mass. 1963, 63, 107.
[21] The involvement in the politics of ex-servicemen did not always involve a retrospective patriotism. In 1927 the Communist Party set up the Labour League of Ex-Servicemen. Wootton has observed that it 'consisted not so much of ex-servicemen who incidentally exerted political influence as of political animals who also happened to be ex-servicemen': ibid. 63.
[22] *Times*, 23 Jan. 1923.

was not entirely successful, for the elected Labour MPs were largely restricted to mining divisions and the north. Likewise the PLP remained the preserve of the trade unions, twenty-five from the Miners' Federation, and only eight of the sixty-one MPs were nominated by local parties or the ILP. But if the 1918 election, a khaki election, did not result in the achievement of Labour's hopes, it showed its intention. The reorganisation of the party in 1918 aimed to strengthen the appeal of moderate socialism against revolutionary socialism, but a second objective was to create a party accepting the concept of, and seeking to represent, a homogenous national interest.[23] Thus *Labour and the new social order* stated that nationalisation and the control of prices were in no sense class measures, and that, with its policy of the capital levy, 'the Labour Party claims the support of four-fifths of the whole nation, for the interests of the clerk, the teacher, the doctor, the minister of religion, the average retail shopkeeper and tradesman and all those living on small incomes are identical with those of the artisan'.[24] Labour saw the capital levy as a method of constructing a producers' alliance against *rentiers*.[25] It was designed as a policy that would include much of the nation in support of Labour. Hence F. W. Pethick-Lawrence argued that 'If there is to be no levy [the people] will have a permanent rich class of bond-holders who will sap the life-blood of the country and leave the rest of the citizens poor and burdened with debt.'[26]

It was the ILP during the war which had perceived the benefits of appealing to the middle class, though in wartime it had been the middle-class dissenter they had in mind.[27] After the war, they continued the appeal with, for example, Leo Chiozza Money, himself a middle-class recruit, appealing to a stratum not known for its radicalism, in a front page article called 'The plight of the small shopkeeper'. He sent 'a May Day message to the chemist, the milkman, and the fishmonger', explaining 'how capitalism ruins and socialism would save'.[28] The recruitment of the middle class to Labour became a general aim of the Labour Party after its reorganisation in 1918. Clynes, as party leader, went so far as to defend private enterprise. 'That went down long ago under the weight of craftily organised syndicates, trusts and combines', he explained when Lloyd George accused Labour of wishing its destruction. 'The small trader, the struggling shopkeeper, and the over-burdened middle-

---

[23] McKibbin, *Evolution of the Labour Party*, 53, 106, 111.
[24] Kellog and Gleason, *British labor and the war*, 385, 387, 389–90.
[25] M. J. Daunton, 'How to pay for the war: state, society and taxation in Britain 1917–24', *EHR* cxi (1996), 890–1.
[26] F. W. Pethick-Lawrence, *The capital levy: how the Labour Party would settle the war debt*, London n.d. [1920], 8. See also R. C. Whiting, 'The Labour Party, capitalism and the national debt, 1918–24', in P. J. Waller (ed.), *Politics and social change in modern Britain*, Brighton 1987, 140–60.
[27] See Swartz, *The UDC in British politics*, ch. x, and more generally Catherine Ann Cline, *Recruits to Labour: the British Labour Party 1914–1931*, New York 1963.
[28] *Labour Leader*, 1 May 1919.

class man know better than the Prime Minister how completely private enterprise has been crushed out.'[29] The appeal to such supposed victims of capitalism was also pursued by Thomas. He was prepared to see the middle class as victim not only of big business, but of the trade unions too:

> Today you have a much larger membership of that class which falls between the millstones of the capitalist and organised manual labour. This class has no trades union, no organisation, is invariably the victim of industrial disputes. Whoever is responsible for such upheavals, the middle class man is always the victim, the man with a fixed income, who has to maintain a certain standard of respectability because of his avocation or profession, who has to clothe himself well, who spends more than the worker on the education of his children. Between the capitalist and the trade unionist he is crushed.

He concluded that 'the only future for the middle class man is under the rule of Labour. We welcome him into our ranks.'[30] Snowden too saw the position of the middle class becoming 'increasingly precarious and difficult', which led to 'many of the middle classes . . . turning to the Labour Party'. But he also warned that these new supporters feared 'that the movement had got into the hands of an extreme element who were determined upon violent methods for the overthrow of society'.[31] Individual membership of the Labour Party, the establishment of advisory committees, the new slogan 'producers by hand or brain', and the encouragement of middle-class candidates, were all aimed at widening the scope of membership, to break free from a perceived class representation, and to validate the claims of being a national party. To maintain this perceived middle-class support, to remain a national party, Labour also had to stress its moderation.

There was another aspect of Labour's attempts to become a national party that had a pre-war labour and socialist tradition to put to use. This was the party's aim to expand out from its traditional urban areas of support into rural seats. McKibbin points out that Labour believed mistakenly that it had to win rural seats to form a parliamentary majority, but there was also a belief that such seats ought to be won, 'that it was the party's mission to liberate them from the feudal barons under which they were supposed to languish'.[32] To be a truly national party, Labour felt it must represent the real, rural England.

Labour manifestos from 1918 to 1924 all devoted a section to land and agriculture. These manifestos reveal two developments. First, they show the growing moderation of Labour's demands. The 1918 manifesto unequivocally called for land nationalisation as 'a vital necessity'. In 1922, the party called only for 'a bold policy of re-organisation', and by 1923 they sought only

---

[29] Ibid. 31 Mar. 1921.
[30] J. H. Thomas, *When Labour rules*, London 1920, 60, 62.
[31] Philip Snowden, *Labour and the new world*, London n.d. [1921], 57–8.
[32] McKibbin, *Evolution of the Labour Party*, 151.

'special measures'.[33] When George Edwards, the veteran Norfolk farm labourers' leader, was refused wage subsidies by MacDonald, the newly installed Prime Minister, Thomas Jones noted with sardonic wit 'that we were not going to see just yet the new Jerusalem set up in England's green and pleasant land'.[34] As with all Labour policy, the needs of agricultural labourers gave way to a desire to show Labour's fitness to govern.

Second, the manifestos show a changing attitude to the land. By 1924 the land had become 'the countryside'.[35] This was a change in the image of the land, from working environment to leisure resource, which was much more in tune with Labour's ideal of the country as the depository of Englishness. In the wake of the First World War, and despite the decline in the economic importance of rural economic activity, the countryside became symbolically more important for many versions of national identity in the inter-war years.[36] Thus, while Labour had practical measures – a minimum wage for agricultural labourers, state credit facilities and promotion of co-operative methods[37] – sentimentality is the key to understanding Labour's attitudes to the country. To use Stanley Baldwin's phrase from 1924, Labour had long felt that 'England is the country and the country is England.' MacDonald could even outflank Baldwin in the use of such language in 1923. 'Protect our home market!' was Baldwin's protectionist slogan. MacDonald used images of the countryside, not of industry, to counter this slogan with an alternative economic nationalism:

'Protect our home market!' What an insignificant phrase that is alongside the Labour Party's policy: Develop our own country! (Cheers.) I wish, my friends, I could meet you oftener on tramp. I could take you into the open fields of any county, or stand with you on any hilltop and, pointing to the wastes, say 'There is our case!'. . . If I were to describe our ideal in a phrase, I should say this:- *We are going to develop our own country, we are going to work it for all it is worth, to bring human labour into touch with God's natural endowments, and we are going to make the land blossom like a rose and contain houses and firesides where there shall be happiness and contentment and glorious aspirations.*[38]

Whereas practical proposals for agricultural labourers had only limited attraction, this sort of sentimentality had a much wider appeal, as the middle class

33 *General election manifestos 1918–1966*, 5, 13, 22.
34 Jones, *Whitehall diaries*, 270, entry for 31 Jan. 1924.
35 *General election manifestos 1918–1966*, 35. See also Philip Lowe, 'The rural idyll defended: from preservation to conservation', 117.
36 See Alex Potts, ' "Constable country" between the wars', in Samuel, *Patriotism*, iii, and Lowe, 'The rural idyll defended', 115. For Stanley Baldwin's use of rural imagery and national identity in the construction of a 'new' Conservatism see John Ramsden, *The age of Balfour and Baldwin 1902–1940*, London 1978, 212–13.
37 See, for example, Snowden, *Labour and the new world*, ch. v, 'The land problem'.
38 J. Ramsay MacDonald, *Labour's policy versus protection: the real issues of the general election*, London n.d. [1923], 9. Original emphasis.

climbed into motor cars and the working class mounted their bicycles and rode out to rediscover England. By the early 1930s there were around half a million walkers. While they may have seen rambling as mainly recreational, they were told again and again that the countryside was the real England through guide books such as those produced by Shell.[39] Access to the countryside was becoming a real political issue, and access was linked to anti-landlordism. Even the Communist Party could be drawn into the old radical language when it came to the land. A pamphlet by the infant party echoed exactly the language of Carpenter in the 1880s: 'By force and craft a robber band has grabbed your native land. 'Tis up to you to do your bit to *grab it back again*. Join the Communist Party and help to bring about the day of working class emancipation.'[40] The second Labour government set up a national parks committee in 1929 under Addison, but the depression postponed any action (until Labour returned to the issue after 1945). In 1932 the Communist Party through the British Workers' Sports Federation undertook direct action to extend access in the Peak District with a mass trespass at Kinder Scout, which led to a pitched battle with gamekeepers and police, and the jailing of the organisers. MacDonald involved himself in less confrontational ways of protecting the countryside. In 1925 he put his name to a letter written by G. M. Trevelyan for the National Trust which sought to prevent the sale of the Ashridge estate in Hertfordshire. Other signatories included Baldwin and Asquith. MacDonald supported the Council for the Preservation of Rural England from its foundation in 1925 and strengthened state powers for the protection of historical buildings and ancient monuments.[41] There seemed to be a consensus of intention regarding the countryside, but Labour and the left felt that it was they who had most right to be regarded as the guardians of the rural nature of England. This belief was increased for, as David Cannadine has noted, 'For all his rural rhetoric, Stanley Baldwin had done nothing, as Prime Minister, for the safeguarding of the countryside.'[42]

Socialists continued to link the notion of an organic rural society to the restoration of medieval England. Hence Merrie England fairs continued to be held, though less often than before the war. To raise money for the jailed Poplar councillors, 'Ye Old English Fayre' was held in September 1921. Another, in Lambeth at Christmas 1922 offered 'old English cottages, . . . attendants . . . dressed as Quakeresses, . . . a town crier and a band of strolling minstrels'. MacDonald made another Merrie England fair the opportunity for affirming that socialism meant 'cycling and singing'. 'The socialist movement', he

---

[39] See Angus Calder, *The myth of the Blitz*, London 1991, ch. ix, 'Deep England'.

[40] Frank Tanner, *The land grabbers: a tale of robbery*, London n.d. [1920], 15.

[41] David Cannadine, G. M. *Trevelyan: a life in history*, London 1992, 153; Mandler, *Fall and rise of the stately home*, 271.

[42] Cannadine, *Trevelyan*, 75.

explained, 'must remain a purely mechanical and hard economic thing unless it was inspired by good music.'[43]

The left continued to provide a historiographical base for this rural radicalism. G. D. H. Cole, finding himself removed from political influence with the collapse of guild socialism in the early 1920s, turned his attention to writing a biography of William Cobbett.[44] This was no sterile historical project but a sympathetic journey. Hugh Gaitskell recalled how, walking through southern England with Cole (his tutor at Oxford), they would talk of past radicals:

> His favourite was certainly Cobbett. He loved this brilliant, forthright pamphleteer with his hatred of sham and evasions, his colossal energy, his robust language and his passion for the English countryside. These were qualities which Douglas himself held in the highest esteem. The special edition of *Rural rides* upon which he was working [after completing the Cobbett biography] was a labour of love.[45]

As well as sharing Cobbett's love of southern England, Cole admired his criticism of industrialisation. Cole's biography of Cobbett was a denunciation of the uprooting from the soil of the English 'peasant' by enclosure and the industrial revolution. Cole saw Cobbett as 'the tribune of the transition' when 'the peasant, who had held an independent, though modest, position in the village community, lost his status and came to depend for the means of life solely on wage-labour eked out more and more by poor relief'.[46]

In 1925 MacDonald published a book called *Wanderings and excursions*, which devoted much space to discussion of the British countryside. It may have been published in response to Baldwin's largely successful attempt to appropriate the countryside for the Conservative Party. In the introduction, MacDonald explained his reluctance to reprint articles that had meant to 'fill a corner in ephemeral sheets', but stated that his friends had flattered him that, collected together, these articles might induce 'a few more feet . . . to take to the open road and moor, and a few more thoughts [to be] turned to the rising and the setting sun'.[47] The writings show MacDonald's pride in his Scottishness, and how this could be fitted into an idea of a rural Britain. Thus he could draw on Scottish legend. Writing of the area around Callender, he mused how 'in the hills Rob [Roy] still wanders; in the mists the miserable remnants of his clansmen still gather. . . . [T]he romance that time has woven

---

[43] Schneer, *George Lansbury*, 64; *New Leader*, 13 Oct. 1922; *Daily Telegraph*, 5 Mar. 1923, in Maurice Cowling, *The impact of Labour 1920–1924*, London 1971, 291.
[44] L. P. Carpenter, *G. D. H. Cole: an intellectual biography*, Cambridge 1973, 43.
[45] Hugh Gaitskell, 'At Oxford in the twenties', in Briggs and Saville, *Essays in labour history in memory of G. D. H. Cole*, 11. Cole's edition of *Rural rides* was published in three volumes in 1930.
[46] G. D. H. Cole, *The life of William Cobbett*, London 1924, 12, 6. See also Martin J. Wiener, 'The changing image of William Cobbett', *JBS* xiii (1974), 135–54.
[47] J. Ramsay MacDonald, *Wanderings and excursions*, London 1929, first publ. 1925, 7.

round them makes them desirable companions on a hill tramp'.[48] But he also wrote of walks in England, remembering 'our British predecessors'.[49] The central point for MacDonald was the rural nature of the country, north and south of the border. In the country, one could feel that Bolshevism and direct action were distant and harmless. Rural Britain was a haven of moderation. On going into the Cairngorms he wrote, 'I started, and guided some youthful feet as well, to where the golden age still lingers, despite the worries of Bolshevism, Marxian rebels, and increasing prices.'[50] Of a walking trip in Yorkshire, he decided that socialism was a creed of open spaces:

> Politics in the city is too much a thing of bars and spittoons. Here it is a national spirit. The proper platform of the ILP is a glacial boulder. In the streets it is an affair of wages, hours, grub, housing; on the moors it is a thing of liberty and spirit. Every hill-top is a Pisgah for a democrat.[51]

Rural nostalgia was a sentiment that much of the left shared. Agricultural reorganisation and the hope of winning rural seats was a poor substitute. The latter task was difficult outside Norfolk, where agricultural labourers were unionised.[52] Labour won only one agricultural seat in 1918, two in 1922, five in 1923, one in 1924 and five in 1929.[53] Of the thirty seats in the English counties with no Divisional Labour Party in 1922, twenty-six were agricultural seats.[54] Where little or no union organisation existed, it could be difficult to find candidates and election workers. There were other problems for prospective candidates. The ILP candidate at the Ludlow by-election in March 1923 candidly admitted he had not previously considered agricultural problems, and his 1,400 votes placed him at the bottom of the poll.[55] One estimate was that £600 annually was needed for non-election years for every rural seat and £1,000 for an election. Labour was unable to raise this money locally, and unable to afford it nationally.[56] Even where Labour fought by-elections in rural seats, the outcome was not always satisfactory. *Labour Organiser* noted that 'The results of the Louth election emphasises that however much we may imagine the countryside to be politically awakening, the hopes and enthusiasm engendered by successful village green meetings

[48] Ibid. 43.
[49] Ibid. 81.
[50] Ibid. 57. See also p. 61.
[51] Ibid. 91. Pisgah was the mountain from which Moses looked down on the Promised Land.
[52] Labour won North Norfolk in 1922, 1923 and 1924, and South Norfolk in 1920 and 1924: *British parliamentary election results 1918–1949*, 431–5.
[53] Michael Kinnear, *The British voter: an atlas and survey since 1885*, London 1968, 120. Agricultural seat here means one with more than 30% of its occupied male population over the age of 12 engaged in agriculture; there were only eighty-six of these throughout Britain.
[54] Ibid. 108. By 1924, however, only North Dorset, Rye and Richmond still had no DLP. Hereford had a County Labour Party.
[55] McKibbin, *Evolution of the Labour Party*, 152–3.
[56] Ibid. 154.

dwindle away as the actualities of deficient organisation put them to the test.'[57] Labour's desire to spread into rural areas, increasing the validity of their claims to be a national party and salving their anti-landlord consciences, remained largely unfulfilled in the 1920s.

Labour did have more success in another long-term project, that of integrating town and countryside. Already by 1914, garden city architecture, influenced as it was by Raymond Unwin, had become the model for public housing.[58] Towards the end of the First World War, housing had come to be seen as an insurance against serious political and industrial unrest.[59] This enabled Arts and Crafts and socialist architects such as Unwin and Frank Baines (a pupil of Ashbee) an entry into state counsels. This culminated in the Tudor Walters Report of 1918 that not only recommended the building of 500,000 houses, but declared that they should be of high quality and low density. Unwin's voice, urging open spaces and tree-lined street pictures, could be heard throughout. The impression of the countryside was to be brought to urban areas. As John Burnett has remarked:

> [T]he Tudor Walters proposals were remarkably far-sighted and progressive, yet the external design of the houses themselves – 'cottages' as they were described throughout – was firmly rooted in the vernacular, rural idiom which pictured groups of buildings of traditional appearance dotted about a landscape of winding lanes, trees and gardens. The Report was to give a particular stamp to local authority housing. . . .[60]

The housing programme also allowed a revitalisation of the guild idea. Before the First World War, A. J. Penty, another socialist Arts and Crafts architect, had called for 'the restoration of the gilds system', providing for beauty rather than profit to be the motive behind production.[61] Guild socialism had been side-tracked by syndicalism away from Penty's medievalist ideas, but in the wake of the war, with high demand for housing and a shortage of labour, Penty and others were able to form building guilds. These successfully tendered for local authority housing contracts. 'We shall do work worthy of the Middle Ages', declared Malcolm Sparkes, secretary of the London Builders' Guild.[62] While the decline of trade union power at the end of the post-war boom brought an end to the building programme, Unwin, the Tudor Walters Report and the building guilds brought a pre-industrial aesthetic to public

---

57 *Labour Organiser*, Oct. 1921. Labour came bottom of the poll with 19.5 % of the vote.
58 Swenarton, *Homes fit for heroes*, 47.
59 Ibid, ch. iii.
60 John Burnett, *A social history of housing 1815–1985*, 2nd edn, London–New York, 1986, 225.
61 Swenarton, *Artisans and architects*, ch. vi.
62 Ibid. 183. For the organisation of the building guilds see Frank Matthews, 'The building guilds', in Briggs and Saville, *Essays in labour history 1886–1923*, 284–331. Matthews plays down the medieval origins of the guilds, describing this aspect as 'utopian' (p. 301).

housing between the wars.[63] With Labour advancing on municipal councils throughout the 1920s, this neo-vernacular established itself as the leading tradition in housing.[64]

## Labour and the children of Moscow

If Labour wanted to show that it was a national party, in terms of geography and cross-class representation, it also wished to show that it was a national party in the sense that it accepted the established form of British politics. In the first instance this meant that Labour wanted to distance itself from the Russian experience. In almost any situation, Labour's opponents were prepared to attempt to link Labour and Bolshevism. Winston Churchill, conducting his campaign on Labour's unfitness to govern, accused Labour of being 'in love with these Bolshevist autocrats'. Perhaps the most remarkable of these accusations came from Lord Curzon in the debate on the Labour amendment to the Royal Address, which led to Baldwin's resignation in January 1924:

> It is all very well for the Member for Miles Platting (Mr Clynes) to make such a speech as we have listened to this afternoon, a mild and moderate speech I agree, but behind the forces of Labour such as we see represented on the benches in this House there are far more sinister forces ranged. There are in my constituency [South Battersea] on the register no fewer than 1,000 known members of the IRA. There are behind them again the forces of naked Communism. (Interruption.) I know the hon. Member is well known for his sympathy with the enemies of his country. He goes to Russia and Germany.[65]

Labour knew that such as Curzon could not be convinced of their benignity. They earnestly wished, however, to refute such accusations to calm the fears of the less hysterical. Henderson reported to the national executive of the Labour Party that 'the coquetting with Bolshevism and the "direct action" propaganda have prevented our reaping the full fruits of our promising

---

63 Ken Young and Patricia L. Garside point out that some Labour councillors preferred the European modernist aesthetic. For example K. Adam urged the production of 'giant blocks of flats, worthy of socialist Vienna': 'The government of London 1889–1939', *Fortnightly Review*, Mar. 1939, 333–4, in Young and Garside, *Metropolitan London: politics and urban change 1837–1981*, London 1982, 180.

64 Many council estates, for sake of economy, preferred neo-Georgian styles, though it is significant that these were still based on a pre-industrial model.

65 *Times*, 16 Feb. 1920; *Hansard*, 5th ser. clxix. 17 Jan. 1924, 373. See also David A. Jarvis, 'Stanley Baldwin and the ideology of the Conservative response to socialism 1918–31', unpubl. PhD diss. Lancaster 1991, ch. iii. For the 1924 election campaign which *New Leader* described as 'a carnival of barbaric unreason' see *New Leader*, 31 Oct. 1924, and Chris Cook, *The age of alignment: electoral politics in Britain 1922–1929*, London 1975, ch. xviii.

strategical position'.[66] The best method of soothing fears was seen as total dissociation from the Communist Party of Great Britain.

Not only was Communist affiliation rejected year after year at Labour conferences, but it was made clear as to why this was the case. Speakers against Communist affiliation alleged that the CPGB followed orders from Moscow. This argument was developed by Frank Hodges, secretary of the Miners' Federation, whose visit to conference was not complete without an indignant attack on Communism. Not only were Communists under orders from a foreign power, which was in itself against the best traditions of the British, but the orders came from minds totally alien to western Europe: 'The British Communist Party – and he was sorry to confess it of his countrymen – were the intellectual slaves of Moscow, unthinking, unheeding, accepting decrees and decisions without criticism or comment, taking orders from the Asiatic mind.'[67] In the wake of the Campbell case, which led to the fall of the first Labour government, such views could become openly xenophobic, and even antisemitic.[68] Jack Jones, MP for Silvertown, at the 1924 conference which spanned the fall of the Labour government, rejected completely the idea that 'a certain number of gentlemen in Moscow with unpronounceable names, and of very doubtful nationality . . . should have the right to dictate British policy, and they say that MacDonald was a traitor'.[69]

Also explicit in such arguments was the superiority of western socialism and the connection between Labour and British national history. Hodges made this quite clear:

> Russia had nothing to teach the political democracy of the Western world. British institutions had grown up in accordance very largely with Britain's own peculiar history, and if anyone could show him where Russia could give to Western civilisation ideas better than those that had been adopted by them, he would be delighted for that man to come and state his case, because that would be an intellectual argument. . . . Of all the Labour movements of the world the British was the best . . . He wanted them to be worthy of the British Labour movement, and they could only be worthy as they stood true to their political institutions.[70]

Gradually, Labour made it more and more difficult for Communists to play a role in the party. By 1924 no Communist could stand as a Labour candidate in local or national elections, and in theory no member of the Communist

---

[66] 'Notes on Mr Williams' letter by the secretary [Arthur Henderson]', Labour Party NEC papers, 1921.
[67] Labour Party, *Conference report*, 1922, 198.
[68] The Conservatives wishing to draw attention to Labour's sympathy for Russia wanted the government to fall on the Russian treaties. MacDonald saw that an election on the Campbell case would confuse issues and chose to make it a matter of confidence: Keith Middlemas and John Barnes, *Baldwin: a biography*, London 1969, 273.
[69] Labour Party, *Conference report*, 1924, 128.
[70] Ibid. 1923, 187–8.

Party could be a member of the Labour Party. Palme Dutt, editor of the Communist *Labour Monthly*, saw such moves as part of the 'great transformation which was begun in 1918, when the Labour Party was taken up to cease to be the organ of a class and became the organ of the "community" '. Through expulsions, the renunciation of the class struggle, 'the proclamation of devotion to king and country, . . . the shouldering of the imperial burden', he argued, the Labour Party sought to become 'part and parcel of the great machinery of the capitalist State. As if to symbolise the completion of the transformation, Sidney Webb, his handiwork completed, comes out into the open as not merely the head, but the figure head of the Party'.[71]

### Sidney Webb and British socialism

The Fabian Society had long advocated a distinctive British socialism. That Labour from 1918 seemed to adopt Fabian ideas has been interpreted as the victory of Webb and the Fabian Society over Labour. Historical opinion has echoed Palme Dutt. A. M. McBriar concluded that, after 1918, 'the Labour Party had accepted Fabianism as its doctrinal basis'.[72] Such an interpretation suggests that Labour had different ideas about socialism than the Fabians, that the Fabian Society had long wished to shape the Labour Party in its own image, and that events external to the Labour Party played no part in the formulation of its strategy. This argument is clearly untenable. The ILP, much more influential than the Fabian Society, had also constructed a view of British socialism. The Fabian Society had alienated most of the left over its response to the Boer War, Taff Vale, and even over the central issue of labour representation. It was, indeed, the failure of Fabian permeation and subsequently of their independent campaign for the reform of the Poor Law, that made the Webbs view the Labour Party as crucial for the advancement of socialism. It was only the First World War that ensured Webb a role near the centre of the Labour Party. His patriotism meant agreement with the majority of the Labour leadership on the central issue of the day, and his work on the War Emergency Workers' National Committee brought him into daily co-operation with that leadership. Hence, J. M. Winter, who rightly sees the 'Fabianism' as an inappropriate blanket description of Labour's socialism, better explains the position of Webb: 'Webbian socialism, with its emphasis on institutional, administrative action, emerged from the war as a far more potent force in large part because of the war itself and the nature of the demands it made on the Labour movement.'[73] It was the war, not Webb, that made Labour leaders so aware of the state, and its potential role in their plans

[71] *Labour Monthly*, Aug. 1922, 71.
[72] McBriar, *Fabian socialism and English politics*, 345. See also MacKenzie and MacKenzie, *The first Fabians*, 398.
[73] Winter, *Socialism and the challenge of war*, 277, 6.

for social change. Webb joined the national executive in 1915. He drafted the new constitution and *Labour and the new social order*; he became president of the party in 1922; but Henderson and MacDonald were certainly more important than Webb. He was there on terms set by the Labour Party.

Presiding over the 1923 Labour conference, Webb's speech was what the Labour leadership wanted to hear: 'First, let me insist on what our opponents habitually ignore, and indeed, what they seem intellectually incapable of understanding, namely the inevitable gradualness of our scheme of change.' He then spoke of 'our practical British way', and privileged this approach with the claim that it formed a distinct set of ideas, which could be called British socialism: 'We must always remember that the founder of British socialism was not Karl Marx but Robert Owen, and that Robert Owen preached not "class war" but the ancient doctrine of human fellowship – a faith and a hope reaffirmed in the words of that other great British socialist – William Morris.'[74]

Webb may have felt that British socialism needed clarifying after the House of Commons debate initiated by Snowden. Snowden noted in his autobiography that 'socialism' did not figure on the party executive's list from which MPs might choose should they win the private members' ballot[75] and MacDonald was not pleased at the prospect of drawing attention to Labour's socialism.[76] Snowden ensured that the members opposite were aware of the moderation of his motion, by stressing that 'We propose no revolution, and we do not propose, and I certainly will resist any proposal of confiscation. . . . There is no analogy between socialism and Bolshevism. Socialism and Bolshevism are antitheses.'[77] When the motion was debated again, because Bonar Law allowed it a further day, Clynes came forward to claim socialism as the work of the patriot. 'Who is the good patriot?' he asked. 'Surely he who wants property not for himself but for his country.' And Henderson drew attention to 'the conservative character of the British people', which he said, Labour 'do not ignore'.[78] Labour were seeking to replace the Liberals as the main anti-Conservative party, and their socialism aimed to distinguish them from the Liberals. But at the same time they wanted it known, and widely, that their socialism was British.

---

[74] Labour Party, *Conference report*, 1923, 178, 179, 180. It is not quite unnecessary to draw attention to Morris's *News from nowhere*, ch. xvii, 'How the change came': 'Tell me one thing, if you can', said I. 'Did the change, the "revolution" it used to be called, come peacefully?' 'Peacefully?' said he; 'what peace was there amongst those poor confused wretches of the nineteenth century? It was war from beginning to end: bitter war, till hope and pleasure put an end to it.' 'Do you mean actual fighting with weapons?' said I, 'or strikes and lock-outs and starvation of which we have heard?' 'both, both', he said.

[75] Snowden, *Autobiography*, ii. 581.

[76] Cross, *Philip Snowden*, 186.

[77] *Hansard*, 5th ser. clxi. 20 Mar. 1923, 2482.

[78] Ibid. 5th ser. clxvi. 16 July 1923, 1914.

## Socialism of the Privy Council

In the Snowden debate, the Communist MP, J. T. Walton Newbold, called Labour's socialism 'the socialism of the Privy Council'.[79] Supporters of Communist affiliation to Labour had contrasted Labour leaders' willingness to swear the oath of allegiance as Privy Councillors with their unwillingness to admit entry to Communists who gave their allegiance to the world's only workers' state.[80] They defined this contrast as loyalty to the British state rather than solidarity with the international working class. Yet Labour leaders were unapologetic. Henderson said that it was an honour to be a Privy Councillor, the only honour Labour members should accept.[81] In the years after the First World War, Labour leaders sought to show both Labour's moderation and its attachment to the institutions of the British state. Membership of the Privy Council was one such method of doing so.

In the immediate post-war years, the major threat to this image of Labour had come from direct action and industrial unrest. J. H. Thomas denied that the actions of a minority were representative of Labour as a whole:

> Despite all these wild and alarming statements, the fact remains that Labour forms the second largest party in the State; its history proves that it is not the inexperienced stripling some people would have us believe, and demonstrates that it possesses as great a sense of responsibility as any body of men which has ever claimed the right and ability to administer the affairs of the nation.[82]

When the wave of strikes was brought to an end by increasing unemployment and Black Friday, Labour leaders' claims of moderation, responsibility and respectability became easier to make and defend. In 1923 Snowden wrote a series of articles for the Conservative *Morning Post* called 'If Labour rules', in which he argued that 'The majority of the electors of this country will never vote for the Labour Party unless they are assured that a Labour government will be controlled by common sense and moderation.'[83]

This is what Labour leaders set out to achieve. Here three themes will be examined, all intimately linked to the concept of British nationhood: monarchy, parliament and empire. When Thomas said Labour wished no harm to the 'old country', he meant not a radical idea of the nation, but the traditional idea held by Conservatives and Liberals.

In 1922, as leader of the Labour Party, Clynes was invited to the wedding of King George V's only daughter, Princess Mary. His acceptance was greeted

---

[79] Ibid. 1982.
[80] For example, Robert Williams at Labour Party, *Conference report*, 1921, 164.
[81] Ibid. 1922, 213. The resolution under discussion declared that 'no useful service can be served by any member of the Labour Party becoming a Privy Councillor'. It was defeated by 3,694,000 to 386,000 votes.
[82] Thomas, *When Labour rules*, 33.
[83] Cross, *Philip Snowden*, 175.

with some criticism from within the labour movement. Clynes explanation for his acceptance was that 'I considered the invitation an honour, not to me so much as to the Party I led in Parliament. . . . In 1922 I felt that the vast majority of Labour voters throughout Great Britain would like to be represented at the wedding to which they obviously offered their good wishes.'[84] This explanation helped Clynes to maintain the idea of himself as representative of ordinary people, but it also showed his acceptance of monarchy as symbol of the nation. Later, Clynes, with Thomas and Snowden, was invited by Lady Astor to a dinner party at which the king and queen would be present. It was expected that guests would wear knee-breeches. Thomas already owned a pair, Snowden was excused because of lameness, but Clynes showed his deference by wearing a pair lent by Lord Astor upon which many safety pins had to be used to hold them up.[85] Again, criticism came from within the movement. But Thomas had an answer: 'I would like to know when, or in what way', he demanded, 'we as a party ever declared ourselves for a republican constitution.'[86] A Labour conference had never declared in favour of a republic, but neither had it declared for a monarchy. But Labour leaders, in these years, framed an attitude to monarchy that not only accepted it, but actively endorsed the monarchy. MacDonald, in 1919, had written that

the Labour Party has to save itself from chastisement; it cannot allow hand-bills to be issued against its candidates, headed: 'The Labour Party condones an insult to our Gracious Sovereign'. . . . With its eye upon a Parliamentary majority won by retaining the confidence of all sorts and conditions of opinion, it must avoid scares amongst the flock, and it must keep their minds placid and trustful as regards itself.[87]

It is, however, important to understand that Labour's attitude to the monarchy was not simply about winning or losing votes at elections. In *When Labour rules*, Thomas had adopted a position that seemed to be abstentionism, however benevolent. 'Our King', he wrote, 'has proved himself during many political crises, to be an essentially constitutional monarch, and I have no hesitation in saying that while such an attitude is adopted by the King, the question of Republic versus Monarchy will not arise.'[88] Linda Colley has shown that these limits on the monarch were the accepted outcome of the Protestant Glorious Revolution, accepted by all British monarchists.[89] Thomas's qualification, therefore, included no desire to see the end of the monarchy. Indeed, once Labour was invited to the Palace to kiss hands, once the

84 Clynes, Memoirs 1869–1924, 326.
85 Snowden, Autobiography, ii. 661.
86 Blaxland, J. H. Thomas, 164.
87 Socialist Review, Oct.–Dec. 1919, 308.
88 Thomas, When Labour rules, 45–6. Thomas's attitude to the monarchy is better expressed in his autobiography; see the chapter entitled 'Some cherished memories of the Royal House': My story, London 1937.
89 Colley, Britons, 46–7.

king had proved himself to be acting constitutionally, Thomas praised the monarchy for its 'recognition that patriotism, love of empire, service and duty were not the gift or monopoly of a class or creed'.[90] The Webbs advanced from this admiration for monarchy, seeing it as an important element in their socialist constitution, though they too stressed that the monarch must not be involved in politics:

> The national organisation herein proposed does not involve the abolition of the ancient institution of an hereditary monarch. The common decision that is both necessary and desirable that the titular head of State should not be charged with any part of the actual government or administration of the community may certainly be accepted in the Socialist commonwealth.[91]

Moderate Labour accepted the idea of the British empire, and argued from this that a monarch was necessary. For Labour, yearning to be a national party, acceptance of national institutions became inevitable.

There were critics of Labour's monarchism, but they were relatively easily deflected. George Lansbury was excluded from the first Labour cabinet for saying publicly that the king ought to remember Cromwell and Charles I rather than hesitate to call on Labour to form a government.[92] Yet it was Lansbury, earlier in 1923, whom the national executive had chosen to deflect a resolution at conference asking for a statement on the attitude of the party to the monarchy. Lansbury told the delegates that capitalism, not the monarchy, was the source of poverty, and that they should not 'fool about with a question of no vital importance'.[93] 'This was the more surprising', exclaimed the *Workers' Weekly*, 'because Lansbury in his speech declared that he was a republican.'[94] To republicans within their own ranks, Labour monarchists called the issue irrelevant; to monarchists outside their ranks, Labour monarchists called the monarch's survival 'a question of the highest importance not only to Great Britain, but to the whole Empire'.[95] And it was this latter view that dominated in the Labour Party. When Stephen Walsh, Secretary of State for War in Labour's first government, chaired his first meeting of the Army Council, he felt confident enough to appeal to the generals' patriotism. 'Gentlemen', he began, 'always remember that we must be loyal to the King.'[96]

One reason Labour gave for the need for an apolitical monarch was that he provided the British empire with the only possible head of state. This was

---

90 Blaxland, *J. H. Thomas*, 170.
91 Webb and Webb, *A constitution for the socialist commonwealth of Great Britain*, 108.
92 Raymond Postgate, *The life of George Lansbury*, London 1951, 224–5; Sidney Webb, 'The first Labour government', *Political Quarterly* xxxii (1961), 13.
93 Labour Party, *Conference report*, 1923, 251.
94 *Workers' Weekly*, 7 July 1923.
95 Thomas, *When Labour rules*, 45.
96 Hugh Dalton, *Call back yesterday: memoirs 1887–1931*, London 1953, 147.

important, since the majority of prominent Labour policy-makers wanted to see the continued existence of the empire. The party's attitude towards empire was summarised by a sentence from *Labour and the new social order*: 'The Labour Party stands for its maintenance and progressive development on the lines of local autonomy and "Home Rule All Round".'[97] Labour stood, therefore, for reform of the empire, and was critical of imperial abuses, such as repression in Ireland and the massacre at Amritsar, but this criticism implied no wish to bring about the end of empire.[98] Labour chose to call the empire by less distasteful names, for example, 'a Britannic Alliance', or 'the British Commonwealth of Free Nations', and this helped to reinforce their belief that empire was good both for Britain and the rest of the world.[99] Expressing the former, Clynes, speaking on 'Labour and the Commonwealth' in 1919, said that 'The War . . . had taught the nation the unmistakable lesson that it had to rely more than ever upon the resources of the Empire if it was to maintain its place of authority among the nations of the world.' On the latter, Thomas explained that 'Labour's aim will be to civilise, not to exploit.'[100]

Labour leaders, therefore, shared the dominant view of the British as the most fit nation to hold an empire. 'A proud boast of the British is that they have no equals as colonisers', Thomas wrote in his autobiography: 'I think it is true.'[101] Belief in Britain's essential fitness to govern an empire led directly to simple statements in support of the empire. Thus, at a British Empire Exhibition luncheon for trade union leaders, Thomas declared, 'We love our Empire. We are proud of the greatness of our Empire.' Clynes explained that 'We on the Labour side want as fervently as any class to see the British Empire well developed.'[102]

There was a limit to Labour's 'anti-imperialism' and even its plans for imperial reform. First, all that Labour was prepared to concede was 'freedom *in* the Empire'.[103] Second, if Britain was to bring its native liberty to the empire it was at a pace to be set by the imperial parliament. Thomas claimed that 'Labour says it is not right that these human beings should have their lives directed by strings pulled in Whitehall', and 'India ought to become a self-governing dominion within a British Commonwealth, and under Labour it would be given every opportunity of development to this end.' But he continued, 'I know it could not happen quickly. I am not suggesting that, if a

97 Kellog and Gleason, *British Labor and the war*, 392.
98 For Amritsar see Ben Spoor, *Hansard*, 5th ser. cxxxi. 8 July 1920, 1739–42.
99 Kellog and Gleason, *British Labor and the war*, 392; *General election manifestos 1918–1966*, 5 (1918 manifesto). This was noticed by the Communist Party: CPGB, *The Labour movement at the crossroads: an open letter to the Labour Party conference*, London n.d. [1924], 5.
100 *Times*, 8 Aug. 1918; Thomas, *When Labour rules*, 135.
101 Idem, *My story*, 81.
102 *Workers' Weekly*, 19 Oct. 1923.
103 The title of the section on the empire in Labour's 1922 manifesto: *General election manifestos 1918–1966*, 12. Emphasis added.

Labour government be elected tomorrow, the government of India would cease the next day. One has to educate.'[104] Likewise, Sydney Olivier, Labour's first secretary of state for India, proclaimed in the House of Lords that 'The programme of constitutional democracy . . . was not native to India. . . . It was impossible for the Indian people of Indian politicians to leap at once into the saddle and administer an ideal constitution.' The similarity of such statements to those of traditional imperialists was pointed out by the Indian Communist, M. N. Roy, who said: 'The Indian people did not require the advent of a Labour government to hear all those stock arguments of imperialism . . . . Such a speech could have been expected from a Curzon – but it fell instead from the lips of a Fabian socialist, a Labour lord.'[105]

Labour's attitudes to Ireland show that the party was not united over the empire, and that the leadership was prepared to ignore conference if it interfered with attempts to establish Labour as a party fit to govern. As Ireland moved towards rebellion, the Labour Party was forced to take the issue seriously after years of neglect. At the June 1918 conference, Ireland was debated in detail for the first time. A resolution was passed declaring 'that the conference unhesitatingly recognises the claim of the people of Ireland to Home Rule and to self-determination in all exclusively Irish affairs'. An amendment to remove the last phrase was defeated.[106] But, as the war for independence escalated, the contradiction between self-determination and any qualification to it became apparent. The view of the leadership was expressed by Thomas: 'Ireland is a nation, and the Irish should decide their own destiny. . . . If they had to wait until Labour comes into power, they will have to wait only that long before they get their freedom. I do not think a republic would be right. I believe that it is not a necessary part of the granting of freedom to that country.'[107] The party as a whole, however, rejected the latter part of this at the 1920 conference, when an executive amendment reinstating the 'exclusively Irish affairs' clause was defeated by 1,191,000 to 945,000 votes. Despite this, within a month, Thomas told the Commons that Labour demanded only dominion status for Ireland. The leadership attempted to justify the contradiction. Adamson explained that while 'the great bulk of the Irish people in the south and west are, undoubtedly, demanding complete independence . . . I do not believe in their heart of hearts they really want a republic; they are simply putting forward, in my opinion, their maximum demand'. The Labour leadership therefore limited their support of self-determination to that which did not conflict with the British national interest. Hence, when the treaty allowed the Royal Navy access to five Irish ports

---

104 Thomas, *When Labour rules*, 126, 138.
105 CPGB, *The record of the Labour government*, London n.d. [1924], 12–13. For Olivier see *Sydney Olivier: letters and selected writings*, ed. Margaret Olivier, London 1948, 152–3, and Francis Lee, *Fabianism and colonialism: the life and political thought of Lord Sydney Olivier*, London 1988.
106 Bell, *Troublesome business*, 38–9.
107 Thomas, *When Labour rules*, 143.

and forced the southern parliament to swear an oath of allegiance to the monarch, Clynes welcomed it as 'a triumph of national patriotism, a victory for enduring national spirit over every obstacle and every form of force'.[108] This could have been applied equally to either Irish or British patriotism. Hence while Labour were prepared to mount an impressive campaign of 500 meetings against the government's Irish policy, it continued to support Home Rule rather than accept the decisions of the Irish. The Labour leadership, therefore, judged questions of the empire chiefly in relation to a perceived British national interest. In such a context, Thomas's alleged declaration upon his meeting his civil servants at the Colonial Office that 'I've been sent here to see that there's no mucking about with the British Empire', becomes less surprising.[109]

Clynes, in a speech to the annual meeting of the Empire Parliamentary Association in 1921, said that the resources of the empire, which he believed were moral as well as economic, 'could only effectively find expression through Parliamentary institutions', and that 'if the struggle for Parliamentary institutions had been a long one . . . it was [also] a successful one'.[110] Here Clynes was drawing out the third element in the British national trinity. It was, for Labour, the most important one, for whereas monarchism and imperialism were difficult to defend from a socialist point of view, they had few such problems with parliamentary democracy after the defeat of the direct actionists.

One argument that parliamentary socialists had used against direct action was that if Labour acted unconstitutionally when in opposition, they would have provided the opposition to a future Labour government with the justification of unconstitutional action.[111] This was not an ephemeral argument. Labour leaders, however moderate, could not be entirely sure that even if they won an election, they would be allowed into office. Those on the left could threaten drastic measures, such as Lansbury's reminder to the king of the fate of Charles I. Moderates were more temperamentally inclined to hope their moderation would not provoke any unconstitutional action from their opponents, and were also keen not to provide these opponents with the moral right to do so, on the grounds that Labour, while in opposition, had themselves acted unconstitutionally.

Labour continued to stress that its aim of social change was peaceful. Thus C. R. Buxton, standing for Accrington in 1922, stated in his election address that, 'The Labour Party believes in changing this system, by gradual and constitutional means, into a Co-operative Commonwealth under which the worker shall enjoy the fruits of his work, and have some voice in the carrying on of industry. That is what socialism means and this is the socialism I stand

---

108 Bell, *Troublesome business*, 57, 63, 62, 67.
109 Blaxland, *J. H. Thomas*, 170.
110 *Times*, 3 Nov. 1921.
111 See, for example, *Hansard* 5th ser. cxii. 12 Feb. 1919, 168–9.

for. It is not "revolution" but sober common sense.'[112] But Labour's constitutionalism did not stop there. Many, if not most, Labour MPs also held a deep affection for the peculiar British constitution, its conventions and procedures. They enjoyed 'taking part in the game', as James Sexton called it.[113] This covered the spectrum of the party. It is no surprise that Thomas should write that 'Correct procedure . . . is absolutely essential in the conduct of British politics: there must be no deviation from precedent in constitutional matters.'[114] Still less that MacDonald in 1922 should explain that the Commons' 'ceremonial part is its inheritance from a rich history of conflict to establish liberty'.[115] But even left-wing figures found themselves admiring the British parliament and its ways. Lansbury in 1912 made a name for himself shaking his fist in Asquith's face at the Treasury bench over the plight of imprisoned suffragettes. After the war, he took children around the House of Commons. He would tell them 'the thing they most obstinately refuse to believe, which is that this "venerable pile" is not venerable at all. It is very recent', but he left these children

> with great reluctance, and with a strong feeling that all we members of Parliament should take every opportunity of showing our children all there is to see in the stone and bricks and mortar of Parliament, but above everything else make them understand that Parliament is their birthright, their safeguard against tyranny, and should be cared for and preserved for further service on behalf of people in the days to come.[116]

Also on the left of the PLP were the Clydesiders, authors of the most famous scene of the inter-war years, in which Maxton and other Clyde MPs were suspended for calling the Conservative government murderers.[117] At the general election of 1922, a phalanx of Scottish Labour MPs, ten from Glasgow's fifteen constituencies, were returned. David Kirkwood announced their intention to do well for their nation, and the method by which they would achieve it. He warned that the MPs from the Clyde had arrived to 'smash' the House's 'atmosphere of indifference':

> There will be no tranquillity as long as there are children in Scotland starving. . . . No child ought to starve. It should be utterly impossible in this land of the brave and free. Do you think that we, who come from Scotland . . . from that

---

112 New Leader, 10 Nov. 1922.
113 Hansard, 5th ser. xii. 13 Feb. 1919, 361.
114 Thomas, My story, 74.
115 New Leader, 29 Dec. 1922.
116 George Lansbury, Looking backwards – and forwards, London–Glasgow 1935, 137, 148–9. For Lansbury's parliamentary scene see Postgate, Life of George Lansbury, 124–6.
117 See Middlemas, The Clydesiders, 127–30. That parliamentary scenes became famous shows how few there were, or in other words how often Labour MPs have not made them.

hardy and intelligent race whom the Romans could never defeat, are going to allow those nincompoops who sit on those benches to efface us?[118]

Kirkwood was not present during the 'murderers' episode, but the *Times* parliamentary correspondent remarked 'how the member for Dumbarton Burghs must regret his absence'.[119] Yet Kirkwood became an admirer of parliament and its procedure; he noted that 'the "conventions" of the Commons are strong to bind. At first I thought they were nothing more than surface politeness. They are not. They are the foundation of the Parliamentary system.'[120] Middlemas has remarked that 'a disrespect for parliamentary methods [was] wholly alien to Maxton and the old Clydesiders'.[121] Even those of the Labour left who did not so wholeheartedly embrace parliamentary procedure still accepted the legitimacy of parliament.

The majority of the British left looked at the old country and liked what they saw. The monarchy, empire and parliament were historical components of Britain and Britishness which were overwhelmingly accepted. Indeed, MacDonald liked to draw attention to the oldness of such institutions, and the great value of the 'unity of historical nationality', for, 'To associate the living generations with those whose actions still throw a glamour over history, and to make the association not merely of accident but of spirit, is of inestimable advantage in the education of a democracy.'[122] MacDonald's argument was that an attachment to an historic national identity was not only good for democracy but also for socialism.

### The English game – Labour after the 1923 general election

In the autumn of 1923, Baldwin, looking for a way to reunite the Conservative Party and to outflank Labour, adopted the idea of protection, and called a general election for 6 December.[123] The Conservatives fought a dull campaign attempting to link protection, empire and patriotism to the fight against unemployment.[124] They also attempted to brand Labour as linked to foreign organisations, particularly through the 'Socialistche [sic] Arbeiter International'.[125] However, it would seem that less use was made of this than in previous or subsequent elections. Whereas nearly a quarter of Conserva-

[118] Mowatt, *Britain between the wars*, 154.

[119] *Times*, 28 June 1923.

[120] Kirkwood, *My life of revolt*, 203.

[121] Middlemas, *The Clydesiders*, 246.

[122] J. Ramsay MacDonald, *Socialism: critical and constructive*, rev. edn, London 1924, 239.

[123] See Middlemas and Barnes, *Baldwin*, ch. x, and Robert Self, 'Conservative re-union and the general election of 1923', *Twentieth Century British History* iii (1992).

[124] Richard W. Lyman, *The first Labour government 1924*, New York 1957, ch. ii.

[125] See the National Union leaflet reproduced in full in Robert MacKenzie and Allan Silver, *Angels in marble: working class Conservatives in urban England*, London 1968, 64–5.

tive election addresses used the theme in 1922 and 1924, only 5 per cent did so in 1923.[126] This was probably because Conservative candidates spent more time on the defensive about protectionism.

Protection presented Labour with a problem, for it could potentially lead to a revival of the reunited Liberal Party. On 13 November, Asquith and Lloyd George had agreed to fight a united campaign. All Liberals would stand as Liberals without an additional label. In a free trade versus protection contest the Liberals were fighting on their 'home ground'.[127] Labour therefore had to attempt to be distinctive while also appearing moderate. MacDonald declared that 'The fight we are in now is not Protection versus Free Trade; the fight we are in now is Protection versus the Labour programme.'[128] But the Labour manifesto offered a very moderate programme. While it described a 'Labour programme of national work', it did not include nationalisation. Indeed it asked voters to raise the election above party fractiousness, 'to refuse to make this general election a wretched partisan squabble about mean and huckstering policies'.[129] Again Labour stressed its special attachment to the constitution. MacDonald, at Neath, asked

> What political party had ever fought a more finely constitutional battle than the Labour Party had ever done? . . . What party had ever done a greater service to the constitutional mind and the constitutional habit than the Labour Party, bringing all those people together and instilling in their hearts a firm belief in Parliamentary government and legislation?[130]

Only the capital levy provided Labour with a distinctive programme; it was described by the manifesto as 'a non-recurring, graduated war debt redemption levy', for reducing the National Debt only, which would offer 'relief for the taxpayer'.[131]

While some in the Labour Party forecast accurately the number of seats Labour would win, they did not forecast the significance of these wins.[132] Labour won 191 seats, up from 144 at the dissolution. What made the election so significant was that the Liberals won forty-four extra seats, and thanks to Labour and Liberal gains, the Conservatives were reduced to 258 seats. While still the largest party, the Conservatives could claim no victory for protection.

126 Jarvis, 'Baldwin and the Conservative response to socialism', 119.
127 Chris Cook, A short history of the Liberal Party 1900–1976, London–Basingstoke 1976, 91–4.
128 Lyman, First Labour government, 53.
129 General election manifestos 1918–1966, 21–3. See also Margaret Bondfield's election address in Northampton, in her autobiography, A life's work, 251.
130 Times, 3 Dec. 1923.
131 General election manifestos 1918–1966, 23, 22. See Dalton, Call back yesterday, 143, and Daunton, 'How to pay for the war', 896, for MacDonald's misgivings and retreat from the capital levy.
132 See, for example, Beatrice Webb's diaries 1912–1924, 250, 253.

MacDonald claimed this advance as a victory for moderation, explaining that

> The Labour Party had entered into the affections of the better sections of labour, and had gained the trust of many of the middle and professional classes. . . . It had acquired a character which rendered it scatheless against all forms of attack which implied meanness, dishonour or dishonesty – like 'Labour is after your savings', or 'Labour is in the pockets of foreigners', and such like.[133]

Nevertheless, there was an outburst of hysteria, as the peculiar constitutional situation presented the possibility of the first Labour government. Churchill forecast 'a serious national misfortune such as has usually befallen great States only on the morrow of defeat in war'.[134] The *Saturday Review* attacked Labour on a number of fronts: it had 'left the Communists in organized gangs to intimidate men and maul women'; it was not a party of labour at all, 'but one of international socialists in all their ramifications'; and 'it is in essence town-bred, and its experiments in land-expropriation for its favourites could never breed yeomen'. It concluded that MacDonald believed in his cause, 'but we . . . deny that he believes in patriotism'.[135] The *English Review* saw 'the sun of England . . . menaced with final eclipse'. The *National Review* regretted 'the unspeakable humiliation of an anti-national government'.[136]

If some were hysterical, the leaders of the Conservative and Liberal parties were more realistic. Both Baldwin and Asquith realised that to keep Labour out of power through a coalition would weaken both their parties and leave Labour much strengthened. Baldwin believed that, constitutionally, His Majesty's Opposition had a right to govern and he took the view that Labour would benefit from a period in office, becoming more responsible. He wanted, however, the responsibility for putting Labour into office to rest with the Liberals.[137] Asquith also rejected the idea of coalition. He wished to assert the independence of the Liberals, and believed that a Liberal government might follow a discredited Labour administration.[138]

A joint meeting of the Labour national executive and the General Council of the TUC on 13 December had decided that Labour would form a government if they were 'called upon'.[139] Some on the left wanted a Labour government to present a radical programme and then fight an immediate

---

133 *Socialist Review*, Jan. 1924, 2.
134 Quoted by Thomas, *Hansard*, 5th ser. clxix. 18 Jan. 1924, 414.
135 *Saturday Review*, 136, 15 Dec. 1923, 648
136 Lyman, *First Labour government*, 81.
137 See Middlemas and Barnes, *Baldwin*, 253, and Ramsden, *Age of Balfour and Baldwin*, 182.
138 Cook, *Short history of the Liberal Party*, 95, 97.
139 Miliband, *Parliamentary socialism*, 100

election on its defeat.[140] Had Labour decided to take this course, the king would have been acting constitutionally if he called on either the Conservative or Liberal leaders to form a government. He had certainly received advice from Asquith to this effect.[141] This would have meant that Labour either had to accept this decision, or rebel against the constitution. The Labour leadership, however, decided on a moderate line. As Snowden recalled, 'I urged very strongly to this meeting [at the Webb's house] that we should not adopt an extreme policy. . . . We must show the country that we were not under the domination of wild men.'[142] MacDonald, Henderson, Clynes, Webb and Thomas, all present at the meeting, were unlikely to have needed convincing of this; since 1917 (and before) they had pursued the aim of creating Labour as a moderate and national party. It was decided that Mac-Donald would, following constitutional practice, pick his own government. Even the left of the party accepted this decision. Webb noted that 'The responsibility of so sudden and unexpected assumption of office gave the Party a shock which sobered even the wildest shouters.'[143]

Having decided that they were ready to form a government, Labour leaders appealed for the chance to do so. They sought a reciprocal agreement. Labour offered moderation; in return they asked for fair play. This was the crucial phrase in the period from 6 December 1923 to 21 January 1924. 'Fair play' had a long history as a political phrase, and it was inextricably linked to notions of Englishness.[144] MacDonald, having returned from Lossiemouth to choose his cabinet, made a speech at Elgin, in which he made clear Labour's right to political justice:

> He would appeal to the nation very solemnly and seriously, not only for the forms of the constitution, but for the spirit of the constitution, for fair play and plain dealing. Had it not been for the constitutional action of the Labour Party again and again in the face of all sorts of demagogic and revolutionary temptations the nation would not have been able, perhaps, in tranquillity and joy, to enjoy Christmas and the New Year recess. He told them plainly that the price of the continuation of that tranquillity was gentlemanly and honest politics.[145]

In return for fair play, Labour offered moderation and an avoidance of class politics. Again and again they stressed that Labour in government would act in the national interest. At the Albert Hall victory demonstration on 8 January, both MacDonald and Clynes explained this. MacDonald said, 'I am not

---

[140] See, for example, Clifford Allen, *New Leader*, 14 Dec. 1923, in Cook, *Age of alignment*, 209.

[141] See Harold Nicolson, *King George the Fifth: his life and reign*, London 1952, 400n.

[142] Snowden, *Autobiography*, ii. 595–6.

[143] Webb, 'The first Labour government', 9.

[144] See, for example, McWilliam, 'Radicalism and popular culture: the Tichborne case', and Joyce, *Visions of the people*, 52, 117, 252.

[145] *Times*, 24 Dec. 1923.

thinking of party. I am thinking of national well-being. . . . I want a Labour government so that the life of the nation can be carried on.' Clynes made the same point, but he remembered that Labour was the party of the working class. He argued, therefore, that any government should act as Labour would do:

> Labour, if entrusted with the power of government, would not be influenced by any consideration other than that of national well-being. No class or sect or party could govern the British nation on narrow class lines, but any party having the responsibility would fail in its first duty if it did not give ready aid to the class numbering millions of the poorest in the country.[146]

Labour's promises and the awareness of Labour's minority position had a calming effect. The *Spectator*, noting that 'the profound knowledge and devastating logic of the permanent official' would prove 'a terrible and salutary experience for any visionary', decided that 'When . . . the Labour Party demand fair play, we can say with our hand on our heart that they must certainly receive it.'[147] The *Saturday Review* was converted, though with some qualification. After MacDonald's Albert Hall speech, it said, 'We also desire to see fair play; but we do not regard the conflict of our own ideas and those of the Socialist Party as a cricket match.'[148]

It was in a much calmed situation, therefore, that Labour moved an amendment to the Royal Address of the Baldwin government. Labour MPs assured the House of Commons of their good intentions towards the nation. Thomas reasserted Labour's role in the war and said that 'In spite of differences, we shall work with a single minded desire to make this country worthy of the citizens who showed their patriotism during its most troubled time.'[149] Labour had at least convinced Oswald Mosley, an Independent. 'It is about time', he said, 'that hon. Gentlemen realised that any government formed in this country will be composed of British men and women.'[150] On 21 January, Labour won its amendment by 328 to 256 votes. Shortly after mid-day, MacDonald was sworn into the Privy Council, and at 4.30 he met the king and constitutionally accepted the prime ministership of Great Britain.

The first Labour government saw its task as providing the climax to six years of Labour showing that it could be trusted with the government of the

---

146 Ibid. 9 Jan. 1924. MacDonald also gave private assurances that a Labour government would act sensibly. In a letter dated 24 Dec. 1923, referring to panic in the City, he asked Thomas 'to see one of your financial advisers and ask him if anything can be done to stop this sort of thing'. He added a postscript: 'Could you possibly get conveyed to the King a statement that I am very much concerned about his peace of mind in the present crisis': Blaxland, *J. H. Thomas*, 166–7.
147 *The Spectator*, 132, 5 Jan. 1924, 7.
148 *Saturday Review*, 137, 12 Jan. 1924, 29.
149 *Hansard*, 5th ser. clxix. 18 Jan. 1924, 424.
150 Robert Skidelsky, *Oswald Mosley*, London–Basingstoke 1975, 126.

British empire.[151] Even in its first days it began this process. The Labour ministers displayed all the constitutional niceties. Returning from Windsor where they had received the seals of office, the moderates laughed 'over Wheatley – the revolutionary – going down on both knees and actually kissing the King's hand'.[152] MacDonald's choice of cabinet and junior ministers had been made with an eye to the approval of all political parties. Only Wheatley and Jowett were on the left. Lansbury was excluded. As Sidney Webb later recorded, 'No one could pretend that a cabinet containing Haldane, Parmoor and Chelmsford were either contemptible, or likely to ruin the Empire.'[153] MacDonald had relied more on Lord Haldane, Liberal imperialist and framer of the pre-war army reforms, in forming his cabinet than on any Labour figure. Baldwin also urged Haldane to offer his services to MacDonald.[154] MacDonald also did his best to reassure the king of Labour's intentions. According to Lord Stamfordham, MacDonald 'assured the King that, though he and his friends were inexperienced in governing and fully realised the great responsibilities which they would now assume, nevertheless they were honest and sincere and his earnest desire was to serve his King and Country'.[155] Part of this reassurance came in Labour's attitude to court dress. George V saw such details as the fabric of the monarchy and had been concerned about Labour's attitude.[156] 'Fortunately Mr MacDonald proved to be a reasonable man', the king's son later recorded, 'the new prime minister and his cabinet in due course made their debut at Court colourfully clad in the uniform of ministers of the Crown – a blue, gold-braided tailcoat and white knee-breeches with sword – a courtesy that went far to reassure my father.'[157]

The Labour leaders, and indeed the majority of their supporters, came to share a view of a single nation to which they owed loyalty. Labour's advance to power meant that their patriotism was not in opposition to the governance of Britain, even when they again became His Majesty's Opposition. Both publicly and privately Labour ministers expressed their admiration for a country where 'the strange turn of fortune's wheel . . . had brought MacDonald the starveling clerk, Thomas the engine-driver, Henderson the foundry labourer, and Clynes the mill hand, to this pinnacle beside the man whose forbears had been Kings for so many splendid generations'.[158] Thomas said, 'A constitution which enables an engine cleaner of yesterday to be a

151 See Lyman, *First Labour government*, particularly ch. xii, for the conflict between this and socialism.
152 *The diary of Beatrice Webb*, IV: *1924–1943: 'the wheel of life'*, ed. Norman Mackenzie and Jeanne MacKenzie, London 1985, 10, entry for [28?] Jan. 1924.
153 Webb, 'The first Labour government', 13.
154 Lyman, *First Labour government*, 100–1.
155 Nicolson, *King George the Fifth*, 384.
156 Kenneth Rose, *King George V*, London 1983, 331.
157 Quoted in Dalton, *Call back yesterday*, 146n.
158 Clynes, *Memoirs 1869–1924*, 343.

Secretary of State today is a great constitution.'[159] MacDonald recorded the events of 23 January in his diary: 'At noon there was a Privy Council at Buck. Pal.; the seals were handed to us – and there we were Ministers of State. At 4 we held our first cabinet. A wonderful country.'[160]

Labour's social patriotism would henceforth be state-sponsored. Labour accepted a consensual view of Britain, and its political behaviour. Hence they used a language of Englishness to appeal for fair play. Labour accepted that British politics were like a game, and they were prepared to play by the rules. They simply asked that their political opponents did the same. A week before Labour took office in 1924, MacDonald expressed this sentiment perfectly:

> The nation's government – the King's government [this was due to an interruption] – must be carried on and whoever carries it on, under these circumstances, is entitled to appeal for fair play, is entitled to appeal to the sportsmanlike instincts of Englishmen and Englishwomen so long as they are doing their duty.[161]

159 *Times*, 8 Mar. 1924, in Miliband, *Parliamentary socialism*, 93.
160 Marquand, *Ramsay MacDonald*, 305.
161 *Hansard*, 5th ser. clxix. 15 Jan. 1924, 99.

# Epilogue and Conclusion

The late nineteenth and early twentieth centuries held turbulent decades for Britain. International and imperial rivalries broke in upon its mid century confidence. The same period saw the growth of an urban and industrial working class, and from within it the foundation of the modern British labour movement. To meet these developments, patriotism and its necessary partner, the making of a national identity, became increasingly important to Britain's ruling elites. As Hugh Cunningham has explained:

> The ruling class sought in patriotism a means of defusing the consciousness of the working class. The call for loyalty to the state rather than to any section of it was seen as a way both of reducing conflict and of facilitating the imposition of greater demands on the citizen by the state. Patriotism, that is, became a key component in the ideological apparatus of the imperial state.[1]

The British left in its formative years, with the rest of the population, was faced with a bombardment of images of patriotism and Englishness/ Britishness. But it would be simplistic to say that left-wing expressions of patriotism were only formed in response to this bombardment. The incidence of left patriotism was too widespread and recurs too often over a long period of time for this to be the case. Naturally there were some responses to accusations by the right of being unpatriotic, particularly in the House of Commons, where the right knew that some Labour leaders could be embarrassed. But the fact that much of the left voluntarily chose patriotism as a theme of propaganda and as a tool in internal strategic debates stands in the way of calling the British left reluctant patriots. From their reading of English history and from their radical forbears, the British left took up patriotism and ideas of national identity with a vitality that survived at least until 1914.

But at no time during this period were the conditions right for the left to dominate patriotism. Perhaps the moment the left came closest was in its opposition to the 'foreign yoke' of conscription, where the language meshed with a traditional dislike of compulsion and militarism. Significantly, opposition to conscription widened the constituency of the left. Many middle-class Liberals went over to Labour when their party acquiesced in demands for compulsory military service. But with the nation at war against another major industrial power, the majority of the labour movement chose not to turn their opposition to conscription into action against it. A compromise between radical and loyalist patriotism had already been reached. The belief that the

---

1  Cunningham, 'Language of patriotism', 77.

First World War was being fought against Prussianism, the antithesis of Englishness, brought about this merger. Some on the left, such as Hyndman and Blatchford, had made the connection a decade earlier. In 1914 the majority of the British left accepted the shared sources of their patriotism and ideas of Englishness with those of their political opponents. The anti-war left's reliance on the War Emergency Workers' National Committee for the defence of workers' interests, and their belief in national defence meant that the compact between the state and labour would not be seriously challenged. The majority of the British left had subordinated itself to the state as the representative of the nation. But it was also expected that in return for offering their services to the state/nation, advances in the position of the working class would be gained. Radical, oppositional patriotism gave way to social patriotism: reform would come through the state, not in opposition to it.

Events outside Britain also made a major impact upon the left's patriotism. The Russian Revolution, whatever its shortcomings, presented to many labour activists an object of devotion outside their own country, a focal point for their internationalism. In the wake of the First World War when Labour leaders realised that government was in their sights, they were determined to prove that they accepted the rules of British politics, indeed that they were fit to preside over those rules in government. Therefore, to them, the Russian Revolution presented not a model to be emulated, but an embarrassment from which they wanted to distance themselves. They drew again from the vocabulary of Englishness that had been used to brand anarchism, Marxism and syndicalism as foreign. At the core of the British socialism they argued for was parliament, which they claimed was the acceptance of English history and traditions. It involved a further compromise with traditional views of Englishness which were given renewed vigour by Stanley Baldwin in the inter-war years. Hence, as Tom Nairn has pointed out, 'Westminster's courtly institutions furnished . . . the spine for an entirely Parliament-oriented opposition.'[2]

The inter-war years presented no major challenge to this dominant view of Englishness framed in radical patriotic vocabulary. Indeed such language became less attractive for the left of the labour movement. Radical patriotic language found a home not in Englishness, but in Scottish and Welsh nationalisms. Plaid Cymru was formed in 1925. Socialists gave support to Scottish nationalist groups, until the Scottish National Party was formed in a merger with the conservative Scottish Party in 1934.[3] Wales and Scotland contained local strongholds of the left of the labour movement. There was a belief that the English working class was more conservative than those of Scotland and Wales. The Clydeside Labour MPs were seen as being moulded by their Scottishness. James Leatham wrote in 1923 that

2 Nairn, *Enchanted glass*, 289.
3 Morgan, *Rebirth of a nation*, 206–8; Keith Webb, *The growth of nationalism in Scotland*, Harmondsworth 1978, 74.

Scotland is nowhere more Scots, in the sense of being turbulent, than in the second city: 'Scenes' at Westminster are the natural, spontaneous expression of the national character, and never had more legitimate reason for flaring up than it has in these days of governmental ineptitude and frank reaction, with oddly enough, a Glasgow representative [Bonar Law] at the head of it.[4]

The impact of mass unemployment in traditional heavy industries hit Scotland and Wales with greater severity than England as a whole, and this encouraged national feeling. The Scottish Labour Party maintained a strong commitment to Home Rule in the 1920s. The Communist Party was deeply embedded in the 'Little Moscows' of Wales and Scotland. It too lent support to expressions of Celtic nationalism, particularly in the Popular Front period. In 1938 the central committee of the CPGB declared its support for Welsh self-determination and the Welsh language.[5]

Events within the labour movement also discouraged reference to ideas of the unity of the nation. MacDonald's betrayal in 1931 seemed to show what an over-concern for the national interest led to. The minute of the penultimate cabinet meeting of the crisis records that, 'In conclusion, the Prime Minister said that it must be admitted that the proposals as a whole represented the negation of everything that the Labour Party stood for, and yet he was absolutely satisfied that it was necessary in the national interest to implement them if the country was to be secured.'[6] When a large minority in the Cabinet led by Henderson realised that the dominant idea of the national interest conflicted to such an extent with their role as the political representatives of the trade union movement, MacDonald left them behind to form a 'National' government.[7]

Labour's post-1931 leadership did not believe that a major rethink on strategy was required. But there were those in the party who questioned its direction. Some in the party asked the same question as Stafford Cripps: 'Can socialism come by constitutional methods?' This took the left of the labour movement further away from the traditional Labour view of Englishness. But it was not Labour's constitutionalism that was threatened, but rather its gradualism. Cripps wrote that ' "revolutionary" action such as we have in

[4] James D. Young, *The rousing of the Scottish working class*, London 1979, 189.
[5] Ian S. Wood, 'Hope deferred: Labour in Scotland in the 1920s', in Ian Donnachie, Christopher Harvie and Ian S. Wood (eds), *Forward! Labour politics in Scotland 1888–1988*, Edinburgh 1989, 35–6; Stuart Macintyre, *Little Moscows: Communism and working-class militancy in inter-war Britain*, London 1980; Calder, *Myth of the Blitz*, 68–9.
[6] Marquand, *Ramsay MacDonald*, 634.
[7] For the crisis see R. Bassett, *Nineteen thirty-one: political crisis*, Aldershot 1986; Robert Skidelsky, *Politicians and the slump: the Labour government of 1929–1931*, Harmondsworth 1970; and especially, Philip Williamson, *National crisis and national government: British politics, the economy and the empire 1926–1932*, Cambridge 1992. Williamson rejects (p. 17) the notions of 'national interest' and 'patriotism' as leading explanations for responses to the 'national crisis', since what constituted the 'national interest' was the subject of controversy.

mind can be taken within the walls of the constitution'.[8] As the 1930s pro-gressed unemployment in Britain was contrasted with the planned economy of Soviet Russia, and the fight against fascism found its symbol in the Spanish Civil War. Grainger has commented that the left of the labour movement could raise a glow only for foreign *patriae*.[9] Left-wing young men went off to fight in Spain, and the Webbs, who had done so much to build a British socialism, visited Russia and declared it 'a new civilisation'.[10]

The Labour leadership, often with the support of the majority of the party, continued to see politics as confined to parliament. Ellen Wilkinson, a newly-elected Labour MP, was rebuked by the 1936 Labour conference for organising the 'Jarrow crusade'. Arthur Pugh decried calls for extra-parliamentary activity against the unemployment benefit cuts of 1931; 'That has not been the method of the British trades union movement', he declared. 'Whether it is on the political side or on the industrial side', he continued, 'the British trade union movement throughout the struggles of the past cen-tury has been gradually building, building and building.'[11] Clement Attlee, elected leader in 1935, could still write that the Labour Party was 'an expres-sion of the socialist movement adapted to British conditions', and that Brit-ish socialism was not influenced by Marx since it 'is not the creation of a theorist. It does not propagate some theory in another country. It is seeking to show the people of Britain that the socialism which it preaches is what the country requires in order in modern conditions to realise the full genius of this nation.'[12]

The expulsion of Cripps, the leading Labour rebel, from the party in 1939, shows that the politics he represented, questioning the political strategy of gradualism and arguing for a Popular Front, were never official Labour poli-cies.[13] Nevertheless the dominant popular mythology of the 1930s is of a left, flirting with Communism, in opposition to the National government, and concerning itself with the fight against fascism and unemployment. Labour left and Communist politics did not lend themselves easily to an oppositional Englishness,[14] and it is only the popular survival of the myth of the 'Red

8  See Miliband, *Parliamentary socialism*, ch. vii.
9  Grainger, *Patriotisms*, 329.
10  See Royden Harrison, 'Sidney and Beatrice Webb', in Levy, *Socialism and the intelligent-sia*, 35–89. For British socialists' 'grand illusions' in Stalin's Russia see A. J. Davies, *To build a new Jerusalem: the British labour movement from the 1880s to the 1990s*, London 1992, ch. vii.
11  John Stevenson and Chris Cook, *The slump: society and politics during the depression*, Lon-don 1977, 185; Miliband, *Parliamentary socialism*, 187.
12  Harris, *Attlee*, 130.
13  For relations between leaders and rebels, particularly over the Popular Front, see Ben Pimlott, *Labour and the left in the 1930s*, London 1986.
14  Popular Frontism did however find the CPGB trying to claim oppositional Englishness for their own. In 1936 it organised a 'March of English history' in Hyde Park. The pro-gramme described the English as 'a people proud of their instinct for fair play, for the rule of law and justice': Kevin Morgan, *Against fascism and war: ruptures and continuities in British Communist politics 1935–41*, Manchester–New York 1989, 41–2.

Decade' that makes the dominance of patriotism by the left in the Second World War appear surprising. The apparent failure of appeasement and the inadequacies of the appeasers once war was declared led to the entry of the Labour Party into the coalition government in May 1940. This combined with a popular radicalism to enable the left to appropriate patriotism.[15] But it is important to understand that the left had in fact found its way back into a long tradition of oppositional Englishness and social patriotism, which provided a vocabulary ideally suited to fighting a 'people's war'. The combination of British socialism and patriotism in evidence after 1939 did not spring from nowhere, but from a version of patriotism that the left had long held.

The transition back to the language of patriotism had also been eased by one outcome of the 1930s. This was the leftward shift of middle-class intellectuals (for want of a better description), those very people George Orwell had described as 'boiled rabbits of the left' who failed to appreciate the meaning of patriotism.[16] Interest in left-wing causes led these middle-class radicals to investigate the common people, from whom, in wartime, they were to draw the materials for a democratic view of Englishness. J. B. Priestley, whose radio broadcasts in 1940 were second only in popularity to those of Churchill, had in 1933 made his 'English journey'.[17] The documentary film movement, though restricted in its radicalism by government and commercial sponsorship, went in search of the working class in 1930s Britain, producing such films as Night Mail (1936) and Spare Time (1939).[18] Humphrey Jennings, the maker of the latter film, was also co-founder of a related movement, Mass Observation. As Raphael Samuel has commented, 'Cultural nationalism is an inescapable sub-text in 1930s literature and leitmotif of the documentary in writing and film.'[19]

Towards the end of the 1930s, Labour had found its way to supporting the National government's rearmament programme. In 1937 the Parliamentary Labour Party did not vote against the military estimates, though its decision not to do so had been opposed by Attlee, Morrison and Greenwood. Bevin and Dalton were vocal advocates of rearmament, and by the time of the Czechoslovakian crisis, Labour was demanding that the government change policy. Through the failure of the government Labour gained the approbation of Tory rebels. Hence on 2 September 1939, after a confused speech by Chamberlain, Leo Amery called on Greenwood, acting as Labour leader, to

---

[15] Paul Addison, The road to 1945: British politics and the Second World War, London 1975; Field, 'Social patriotism and the British working class'.

[16] The collected essays, journalism and letters of George Orwell, I: An age like this 1920–1940, ed. Sonia Orwell and Ian Angus, Harmondsworth 1970, 592.

[17] Chris Waters, 'J. B. Priestley (1894–1984): Englishness and the politics of nostalgia', in Pedersen and Mandler, After the Victorians, 208–26.

[18] Paul Swann, The British documentary film movement 1926–1946, Cambridge 1989.

[19] Samuel, 'Introduction: exciting to be English', in his Patriotism, i, p. xxiii. See also Addison, The road to 1945, ch. v.

'Speak for England!'[20] The turning point came, however, in 1940 rather than in 1939. Patriotism was not without its problems for Labour. In April 1939, Chamberlain had announced the government's intention to reintroduce conscription, to which the Labour Party remained vigorously opposed. The arguments of 1915 and 1916 were renewed. Attlee, also foreshadowing one aspect of wartime propaganda, declared that, 'The voluntary efforts of a free people are more effective than any regimentation by dictatorships.' Another Labour MP, E. G. Hicks, asked, 'Is the spirit of the volunteer now beneath the military jack-boot? . . . The British tradition of freedom has been dealt a severe blow by this proposal for conscription.'[21] The left did not trust Chamberlain's government, hence while it remained in office, the left would remain wary. Blitzkrieg and Dunkirk, however, made 'guilty men' of Chamberlain and his accomplices.[22] In 1940, the 'people's war' began. The moderate Socialist Clarity Group expressed this perception of change: 'This war', it argued in June 1940, 'which originated in capitalist and imperialist conflicts and began under capitalist leadership, is now assuming the character which was implicit in it from the outset – that of a people's war for liberty and social progress against the forces of reaction and monopoly power.'[23] It was a combination of the left's belief in national defence, the cultural nationalism of the 1930s, the inadequacies of the appeasers, and a tradition of radical patriotism from the 1880s, that allowed the left to take patriotism for itself in 1940. As Addison says of Labour's entry into government in 1940, so of patriotism: 'Labour were not in reality *given* office: they broke in and took it.'[24]

There were, however, limits. Churchill was prime minister. The Britain of the 'why we fight' mode, as Churchill liked to point out, had a long history. As Angus Calder has remarked, Dunkirk was about 'reiteration, retrenchment, history-as-made'.[25] It was a shared history, but in 1940 the left had a stronger claim to it.

The Second World War left-wing patriots rarely acknowledged that their oppositional patriotism had its origins inside the left. Orwell acknowledged that one source of his patriotism was his middle-class upbringing, mocking himself that 'a time comes when the sand of the desert is sodden red and what have I done for thee, England my England'.[26] But he was deeply critical of what he perceived as the lack of patriotism of British socialists. This failure to acknowledge a debt was based on a memory of the 1930s when much of the left was seen as calling for 'arms for Spain' but not for Britain. Longer term

---

20 A. J. P. Taylor, *English history 1914–1945*, Harmondsworth 1975, 552.
21 *Hansard*, 5th ser. cccxlvi. 27 Apr. 1939, 1361, 1397. See also Greenwood, col. 1440, and H. B. Lees-Smith, col. 2113 (4 May 1939).
22 See Addison, *The road to 1945*, ch. iv.
23 Calder, *The myth of the Blitz*, 80.
24 Addison, *The road to 1945*, 62.
25 Calder, *The myth of the Blitz*, 8.
26 Michael Shelden, *Orwell: the authorised biography*, London 1992, 347. See also Orwell, 'My country right or left', in *Collected essays*, 587–92.

memories were of the 'betrayal' by the left in 1914, when it had supported a war that, in the popular view of the 1930s, had been a massive waste of life, which resulted in the betrayal of the hopes to build a land fit for heroes.

In the general election of 1945 Labour won its first overall parliamentary majority. Its victory marked a triumph of social patriotism, of improving the condition of the people as patriotic endeavour, over traditional patriotism. Churchill's allegations that Labour's socialism would require some form of Gestapo, were swept aside. Attlee replied that the prime minister's memory was short, since he had 'forgotten that socialist theory was developed in Britain long before Karl Marx by Robert Owen'. He reiterated Labour's patriotism, both in traditional and inward-looking terms:

> We are proud of the fact that our country in the hours of its greatest danger stood firm and united, setting an example to the world of how a great democratic people rose to the height of the occasion and saved liberty and democracy. . . . We have to preserve and enhance the beauty of our country to make it a place where men and women may live finely and happily, free to worship God in their own way, free to speak their minds, free citizens of a great country.[27]

Labour went to the polls with an alternative democratic interpretation of Britishness,[28] but it shared many characteristics with more traditional views. Parliament was placed at the core of a Whiggish national history of the gradual advancement to political liberty. Socialisms that did not accept this view were branded as foreign. Despite the wartime alliance with Russia, the un-Englishness of Soviet Communism was to play a major role in the prevalence of support in the Labour Party for the anti-Russian slant of Bevin's foreign policy.[29] In office Labour fulfilled its promises of guardianship of the countryside as depository of a true Englishness. Again it showed that Labour was integrated into the nation as established. Dalton as chancellor of the exchequer agreed to match with government money pound for pound the National Trust's jubilee appeal, accepting that organisation's links with landowners and its role of preserving stately homes as heritage. He also established the National Land Fund of £50m. as a memorial to the men and women who had fought for Britain during the Second World War. This fund would on the one hand show Labour's commitment to national defence, its memorialisation of those who had stood in defence against its external enemies, but at the same time was designed to add a democratic edge through its championing of

---

[27] Harris, *Attlee*, 256–7.

[28] Friendship with Soviet Russia was also important in 1945. Ernest Bevin had talked of 'left speaking to left in comradeship and confidence', and the Labour conference that year had sung the 'Internationale' as well as 'The Red Flag' and 'Auld Lang Syne': Kenneth O. Morgan, *Labour in power 1945–1951*, Oxford 1984, 240; Labour Party, *Conference report*, 1945, 152.

[29] Morgan, *Labour in power*, 239–61.

access to the real Britain. It did not challenge notions of national identity shared with more conservative forces. When it came to the creation of the National Parks in 1949, the countryside was not nationalised but remained in private hands.[30] Labour's shared view of the Britain formed an important part of the partnership between Labour and the nation. It made the nation's existence possible, if, to quote a French commentator on nationalism writing at the time of modern British socialism's emergence,

> A nation is a soul, a spiritual principle. Two things, which in truth are but one, constitute this soul or spiritual principle. One lies in the past, one in the present. One is the possession in common of a rich legacy of memories; the other is present-day consent, the desire to live together, the will to perpetuate the value of the heritage that one has received in an undivided form.[31]

Most of the left shared memories of British, mainly English, history with the wider nation, and gave its consent to perpetuate the value of this heritage. The left's consent is only understandable because of its development since the 1880s. It was a development deliberately shaped to make a British socialism, a process largely completed by 1924. British socialism must take its place alongside other 'invented traditions'.

30 Mandler, *Fall and rise of the stately home*, 355. See also Richard A. J. Weight, 'Pale stood Albion: the formulation of English national identity', unpubl. PhD diss. London 1995, ch. iii.
31 Ernest Renan, 'What is a nation?' (1882), in Homi K. Bhabha (ed.), *Nation and narration*, London 1990, 19.

# Bibliography

## Unpublished primary sources

**Liverpool University, Sydney Jones Library**
J. Bruce Glasier papers

**London, British Architectural Library**
Raymond Unwin papers

**London, London School of Economics, British Library of Political and Economic Science**
British Socialist Party collection, archives collection miscellaneous 155
George Lansbury papers
Independent Labour Party, members' papers, c. 1908–38, archives collection miscellaneous 496
Independent Labour Party, National Administrative Council papers
Sussex Divisional Labour Party minute books, archives collection miscellaneous 488

**Manchester, Central Library**
Robert Blatchford papers, MS F 920.5 B27

**Microfilm/Microform**
*Brighton, Harvester Microfilm*
Labour Party National Executive Committee minutes

*Brighton, Harvester Microform*
Francis Johnson correspondence

*Wakefield, E. P. Microfilms*
Edinburgh Trades Council minute books, 1920
Pontypridd Labour Party minute books, 1920

*Wakefield, Microform Ltd*
Aberdeen Trades Council minute books, 1920

## Official documents and publications

Hansard parliamentary debates, House of Commons, 4th, 5th series
Royal Commission on Alien Immigration, Parliamentary papers, Cd. 1741, Cd.
  1742, 1903
The Tudor Walters report, Cd. 9191, 1918


## Reports

British Socialist Party, *Conference reports*, 1912–14, 1916
Communist Party, *Communist unity convention, London 31 July and 1 Aug.
1920, official report*, 1920
Council of Action, *Report of the special conference on Labour and the Russo-Polish
  War, Friday 13 Aug. 1920*, London 1920
Independent Labour Party, *Conference reports*, 1893–1924
—— *Nominations for officers and NAC and resolutions for the agenda 1903
  conference*
Labour Party, *Conference reports*, 1906–
Labour Representation Committee, *Conference reports*, 1900–5
*National labour and socialist conference on our food supply: official report*, London
  1909
Social Democratic Federation, *Conference report*, 1901


## Newspapers and periodicals

*The Call*
*Clarion*
*Commonweal*
*Daily Herald/ Herald*
*Fabian News*
*ILP News*
*Industrial Syndicalist*
*Justice*
*Labour Leader*
*Labour Monthly*
*Labour Organiser*
*Labour Party Bulletin* (from 1920)
*Labour Prophet* (Jan. 1892–Jan. 1893)
*New Age*
*New Leader*
*New Statesman*
*Saturday Review* (Nov. 1923–Nov. 1924)
*The SDP News* (Aug. 1910–Aug. 1911)
*Social-Democrat*
*The Socialist* (1888–9)
*Socialist Review*
*The Spectator* (Nov. 1923–Nov. 1924)

*The Times*
*To-day*
*Woolwich Pioneer* (1920 only)
*Workers' Weekly*

## Contemporary books and articles

### Articles in non-labour periodicals

Hardie, J. Keir, 'Labour at the forthcoming election', *Nineteenth Century and After*, Jan. 1906, 12–24
———— 'The Labour Party: its aims and policy', *National Review* xlvi (Feb. 1906), 999–1008
———— and J. R. MacDonald, 'The Independent Labour Party's programme', *Nineteenth Century*, Jan. 1899, 20–38
Henderson, Arthur, 'The outlook for Labour', *Contemporary Review* cxiii (Feb. 1918), 121–30
———— 'The industrial unrest: a new policy required', *Contemporary Review*, Apr. 1919, 361–8
———— 'Parties and programmes: the Labour Party', *Contemporary Review*, Mar. 1922, 300–3
Hyndman, H. M., 'The dawn of a revolutionary epoch', *Nineteenth Century*, Jan. 1881, 1–18
MacDonald, J. Ramsay, 'The Labour Party and its policy', *Independent Review* xlvi (Mar. 1906), 261–9
———— 'The trade union unrest', *English Review*, Nov. 1910, 728–39
Stead, W. T., 'The Labour Party and the books that helped to make it', *Review of Reviews* xxxiii (June 1906), 568–82
Webb, Sidney, 'Lord Rosebery's escape from Houndsditch', *Nineteenth Century* l (Sept. 1901), 366–86

### Memoirs, autobiographies, published letters and diaries

Barnes, George N., *From workshop to war cabinet*, London 1924
Bax, E. B., *Reminiscences and reflexions of a mid and late Victorian*, London 1918
*Beatrice Webb's diaries 1912–1924*, ed. Margaret I. Cole, London 1952
Blatchford, Robert, *My eighty years*, London 1931
Bondfield, Margaret, *A life's work*, London n.d. [1948]
Brockway, Fenner, *Inside the left: thirty years of platform, press, prison and parliament*, London 1947
Carpenter, Edward, *My days and dreams*, London 1916
Clynes, J. R., *Memoirs 1869–1924*, London 1937
———— *Memoirs 1924–1937*, London 1937
*The collected essays, journalism and letters of George Orwell*, I: *An age like this 1920–1940*, ed. Sonia Orwell and Ian Angus, Harmondsworth 1970
Crane, Walter, *An artist's reminiscences*, London 1907
Dalton, Hugh, *Call back yesterday: memoirs 1887–1931*, London 1953
*The diary of Beatrice Webb*, III: *1905–1924: 'the power to alter things'*; IV: *1924–1943: 'the wheel of life'*, ed. Norman MacKenzie and Jeanne MacKenzie, London 1984, 1985

Gallacher, William, *Revolt on the Clyde*, London 1978
Hamilton, Mary Agnes, *Remembering my good friends*, London 1944
Hobson, S. G., *Pilgrim to the left: memoirs of a modern revolutionist*, London 1938
Hyndman, H. M., *The record of an adventurous life*, London 1911
—— *Further reminiscences*, London 1912
Jones, Thomas, *Whitehall diary*, I: *1916–1925*, ed. Keith Middlemas, London 1969
Kirkwood, David, *My life of revolt*, London 1935
Lansbury, George, *Looking backwards – and forwards*, London–Glasgow 1935
*The letters of Sidney and Beatrice Webb*, III: *Pilgrimage 1912–47*, ed. Norman MacKenzie, Cambridge 1978
*The letters of William Morris to his family and friends*, ed. Philip Henderson, London 1950
Mann, Tom, *Memoirs*, London 1967
Salt, Henry S., *Seventy years among savages*, London 1921
Sanders, William Stephen, *Early socialist days*, London 1927
Snowden, Philip, *An autobiography*, I: *1864–1919*; II: *1919–1934*, London 1934
*Sydney Olivier: letters and selected writings*, ed. Margaret Olivier, London 1948
Thomas, J. H., *My story*, London 1937
Thorne, Will, *My life's battles*, London 1989
Tillett, Ben, *Memories and reflections*, London 1931
Webb, Beatrice, *Our partnership*, ed. Barbara Drake and Margaret I. Cole, Cambridge 1975


**Books, pamphlets, leaflets and other ephemera**
**[P] = pamphlet; [L] = leaflet**
Allen, Clifford, *Why I still resist*, London n.d. [L]
Bax, E. B., *The ethics of socialism*, London 1889
—— *Essays in socialism old and new*, London 1907
Blatchford, Robert, *The new religion*, Manchester n.d.
—— *Merrie England*, London 1894
—— *The Clarion ballads*, London 1896 [P]
—— *Britain for the British*, 3rd edn, London 1910
—— *Dismal England*, New York–London 1984
Brailsford, H. N, *Belgium and 'the scrap of paper'*, London 1915 [P]
Brockway, A. Fenner, *Is Britain blameless?*, Manchester–London n.d. [P]
Burns, John, *The man with the red flag*, London n.d. [1986] [P]
—— *Trafalgar Square: speech for the defence*, London n.d. [1888] [P]
Carpenter, Edward (ed.), *Chants of labour: a song book of the people*, London 1888
—— *England's ideal*, London 1895
—— *Towards democracy*, London 1949
—— *Civilisation: its cause and cure*, 5th edn, London 1897
Cole, G. D. H., *The life of William Cobbett*, London 1924
—— *Robert Owen*, London 1925
Communist Party, *The record of the Labour government*, London n.d. [1924] [P]
—— *The Labour movement at the crossroads: an open letter to the Labour Party conference*, London n.d. [1924] [P]
Copland, Elijah, *Guarantees against unlawful war*, Newcastle-upon-Tyne 1884 [P]
Crane, Walter, 'England to her own rescue', in Andrew Reid (ed.), *Vox clamantium: the gospel of the people*, London 1894, 162–5

———— *William Morris to Whistler: papers and addresses on Art and Craft and the commonweal*, London 1911

———— *Cartoons for the cause: designs and verses for the socialist and labour movement 1886–1896*, London 1976

Dalton, Hugh, *Hitler's war*, Harmondsworth 1940

Davidson, Morrison, *Anarchist socialism v. state socialism*, London n.d. [1896] [P]

Desmond, Shaw, *Labour: the giant with the feet of clay*, London 1921

Fabian Society, *Fabian essays in socialism*, London 1920

———— *What socialism is*, London 1890 [P]

———— *Report on Fabian policy*, London 1896 [P]

———— *Fabianism and the empire*, London 1900

Glasier, J. Bruce (ed.), *Socialist songs*, Glasgow 1893

———— *On strikes*, Glasgow–Manchester n.d. [1897?] [P]

———— *Militarism*, Manchester 1915 [P]

———— *The peril of conscription*, London 1915 [P]

———— *William Morris and the early days of the socialist movement*, London 1921

Hall, Leonard and others, *Let us reform the Labour Party*, Manchester n.d. [1910] [P]

Hardie, J. Keir, *Young men in a hurry*, 3rd edn, London–Glasgow n.d. [1896] [P]

———— *From serfdom to socialism*, London 1907

———— *India: impressions and suggestions*, London 1909

———— *My confession of faith in the labour alliance*, London n.d. [1909] [P]

Henderson, Arthur, *The aims of Labour*, London 1918

Hobson, J. A., *The war in South Africa: its causes and effects*, London 1900

———— *Imperialism: a study*, London 1902

Hyndman, H. M., *England for all: the text book of democracy*, Brighton 1973

———— *The historical basis of socialism in England*, London 1883

———— *The coming revolution in England*, London n.d. [1883] [P]

———— *The social reconstruction of England*, London n.d. [c. 1884] [P]

———— and William Morris, *A summary of the principles of socialism*, London 1884

Independent Labour Party, *The socialist state*, London n.d. [L]

———— *How the war came*, London 1915 [P]

———— *Persia, Finland and our Russian alliance*, London 1915 [P]

———— *Against conscription*, Manchester 1915 [L]

Joynes, J. L., *Socialist rhymes*, London 1885 [P]

Kahan, Zelda, *The principles of socialism*, London n.d. [P]

*Keir Hardie's speeches and writings (from 1888–1915)*, ed. Emrys Hughes, Glasgow n.d.

Kirkup, Thomas, *A history of socialism*, 5th edn, rev. Edward R. Pease, London 1920

Kneeshaw, J. W., *How conscription works*, Manchester n.d. [P]

———— *Profits and patriotism*, Manchester n.d. [P]

*The Labour Church hymn book*, Manchester 1892 [P]

*The Labour Church hymn and tune book*, n.p. n.d. [P]

Labour Party, *Labour work in parliament Feb. to Jun. 1914*, London 1914 [L]

———— *Labour and the new social order*, London 1918

———— *The Labour Party and the National Union of Ex-Servicemen*, London 1919 [L]

——— *Report of the commission of inquiry into present conditions in Ireland*, London 1920 [P]

——— *An appeal to the British nation by the Labour Party*, London 1920 [P]

——— *What Labour stands for: a restatement of policy*, London 1921

——— *Labour's climb to power! Help it 'over the top'*, London n.d. (1922) [L]

Lansbury, George, *My England*, London 1934

Lee, H. W. and E. Archbold, *Social-democracy in Britain*, London 1935

MacDonald, J. Ramsay, *Labour and the empire*, Hassocks 1974

——— *Socialism*, New York 1970

——— *Socialism and government*, 2 vols, London 1909

——— *The socialist movement*, London 1911

——— *Syndicalism: a critical examination*, London 1912

——— *The social unrest: its cause and solution*, London–Edinburgh 1913

——— *Margaret Ethel MacDonald*, 4th edn, London 1913

——— *War and the workers: a plea for democratic control*, London n.d. [P]

——— *Patriots and politics*, Manchester–London n.d. [P]

——— *The conscription of wealth*, Manchester–London n.d. [P]

——— *Parliament and revolution*, Manchester 1919

——— *Labour's policy versus protection: the real issues of the general election*, London n.d. [1923] [P]

——— *Socialism: critical and constructive*, rev. edn, London 1924

——— *Wanderings and excursions*, London 1929

Masterman, J. H. B., *The House of Commons: its place in national history*, London 1908

Merchant Seamen's League, *The seamen's boycott song*, London n.d. [1918] [L]

——— *The seamen's crusade*, London n.d. [L]

*Merrie England Fayre programme*, Liverpool 1895 [P]

Mines for the Nation Committee, *The mines for the nation*, London n.d. [P]

——— *Coal nationalisation and the middle classes*, London n.d. [L]

Morris, May, *William Morris, artist, writer, socialist*, Oxford 1936

Morris, William, *Chants for socialists*, London 1892 [P]

——— *Communism*, London 1903 [P]

——— *News from nowhere*, London 1908

——— *The collected works of William Morris*, xxii, xxiii, London 1915

——— *Stories in prose, stories in verse, shorter poems, lectures and essays*, ed. G. D. H. Cole, London 1934

——— and E. Belfort Bax, *Socialism: its growth and outcome*, London 1893

Nesbit, Edith, *Ballads and lyrics of socialism*, London 1908

Orwell, George, *The Penguin essays of George Orwell*, Harmondsworth 1984

Paul, William, *Communism and society*, London 1922

Pease, Edward R., *The history of the Fabian Society*, London 1916

Pethick-Lawrence, F. W., *The capital levy: how the Labour Party would settle the war debt*, London n.d. (1920)

Priestley, J. B., *English journey*, London 1934

Quelch, H., *Social-democracy and the armed nation*, London 1900 [P]

Quelch, Tom, *The crimes of Liberalism and Toryism*, London n.d. [P]

Shaw, Bernard, *The impossibilities of anarchism*, London 1893 [P]

——— *Plays pleasant*, Harmondsworth 1946

Snowden, Ethel, *Through Bolshevik Russia*, London 1920

Snowden, Philip, *The Christ that is to be*, London n.d. [1905] [P]
—— *Socialism and syndicalism*, London–Glasgow 1912
—— *The game of party politics*, London 1913 [P]
—— *Labour in chains: the peril of industrial conscription*, Manchester–London 1917 [P]
—— *Labour and the new world*, London n.d. [1921]
—— and Sir William Bull, *Socialism – yes or no*, n.p. n.d. [1907] [P]
Socialist National Defence Committee, *Socialists and the war: manifesto of the Socialist National Defence Committee*, n.p. 1915 [L]
Tanner, Frank, *The land grabbers: a tale of robbery*, London n.d. [1920]
Thomas, J. H., *When Labour rules*, London 1920
Thompson, A. M., *That blessed word – liberty*, London n.d. [P]
—— *Patriotism and conscription*, London n.d. [P]
Tillett, Ben, 'The need for labour representation', in Frank W. Galton (ed.), *Workers on their industries*, London 1895
—— *Is the Parliamentary Labour Party a failure?*, London n.d. [1910] [P]
TUC/Labour Party, *Unemployment: a Labour policy*, London 1921
Union of Democratic Control, *The Union of Democratic Control: what it is and what it is not*, London n.d. [L]
Unwin, Raymond, *Nothing gained by overcrowding: how the garden city type of dwelling may benefit both owner and occupier*, London 1912 [P]
Varon, *Fair play: England for the English*, Manchester 1891 [P]
Ward, John, *England's sacrifice to the God Mammon*, 3rd edn, London n.d. [P]
Webb, Sidney, 'The first Labour government', *Political Quarterly* xxxii (1961), 6–44
—— *Socialism in England*, Aldershot 1987
—— and Beatrice Webb, *A constitution for the socialist commonwealth of Great Britain*, Cambridge 1975

## Pamphlets and leaflets of the Independent Labour Party (Harvester microforms, Brighton)

1894/10 Independent Labour Party, *Labour cartoons: picture studies for the workers*, Manchester 1894 [P]
1895/4 Edward Carpenter, *St George and the dragon: a play in three acts*, Manchester 1895
1895/9 Katherine St John Conway and J. Bruce Glasier, *The religion of socialism: two aspects*, Glasgow–Manchester n.d. [P]
1895/12 Tom Mann, *What the ILP is driving at*, Glasgow–Manchester n.d. [P]
1897/16 J. Bruce Glasier, *On strikes*, Glasgow–Manchester n.d. [P]
1897/19 Harry Henshall (ed.), *The ILP song book*, London n.d. [P]
1898/7 Jim Connell, *Brothers at last: a centenary appeal to Celt and Saxon*, London–Glasgow n.d. [P]
1899/8 Leonard Hall, *Land, labour and liberty, or the ABC of reform*, London 1899 [P]
1900/13 C. A. Glyde, *Liberal and Tory hypocrisy during the 19th century*, Bradford n.d. [P]
1900/16 ILP City branch, *Imperialism: its meaning and tendency*, London n.d. [P]
1900/24 Philip Snowden, *Election address*, Blackburn 1900 [P]
1902/5 T. D. Benson, *A socialist's view of the Reformation*, London–Glasgow n.d.

1902/8 J. Ernest Jones, *The case for progressive imperialism*, 2nd edn, London 1902

1902/36 ILP, *Mock loyalty*, London 1902 [L]

1902/47 ILP, *On royalty*, London 1902 [L]

1903/15 J. Bruce Glasier, *Labour: its politics and ideals*, London n.d. [P]

1905/34 Ashton-under-Lyne ILP, *'No English need apply': why did we go to war in South Africa?*, Ashton-under-Lyne n.d. [P]

1906/24 *Programme for the reception of Labour MPs, 15 Jan. 1906, Royal Horticultural Hall, Westminster*, London n.d. [P]

1906/64 H. Snell, *The foreigner in England: an examination of the problem of alien immigration*, London n.d. [P]

1907/3 William C. Anderson, *Socialism, the dukes and the land*, Manchester–London n.d. [P]

1907/10 T. D. Benson, *Socialism*, London n.d. [P]

1907/16 'Casey', *Who are the bloodsuckers?: with a list of the principle ones*, 2nd edn, London n.d. [P]

1907/28 Richard Higgs, *Socialism and agriculture*, London n.d. [P]

1908/19 Isabella O. Ford, *Women and socialism*, London n.d. [P]

1908/22 J. Bruce Glasier, *Who owns the land?*, London 1908 [P]

1908/23 *Handbook of the great international bazaar, Exchange Hall, Blackburn, Mar. 1908*, Blackburn n.d. [P]

1908/32 J. Keir Hardie, *Socialism the hope of Wales/Socialeth gabaith Cymru*, London n.d. [P]

1908/72 *Souvenir of the welcome home demonstration to greet J. Keir Hardie MP on his return from his world tour, Royal Albert Hall, 5 Apr. 1908*, London n.d. [P]

1909/4 William C. Anderson, *Hang out our banners*, Manchester n.d. [L]

1909/8 George N. Barnes, *Karl Marx*, London n.d. [P]

1909/13 H. Brockhouse, *The curse of the country: the land monopoly*, London n.d. [P]

1909/14 ILP, *By order of the Czar: death and imprisonment*, London 1909 [L]

1909/28 Victor Grayson, *The appeal for socialism*, Stockport n.d. [P]

1909/69 ILP, *Socialism for shopkeepers*, London 1909 [L]

1910/9 Bradford ILP, *Yearbook 1910*, Bradford 1910

1910/16 J. R. Clynes, *Has the Labour Party failed? The reply suppressed by the Clarion*, London n.d. [L]

1910/21 T. Gavan Duffy, *The Labour Party in parliament – what it is: what it does: what it wants*, London n.d. [P]

1910/40 J. Keir Hardie, *Karl Marx: the man and his message*, Manchester n.d. [P]

1910/53 *Programme of the international demonstration, Royal Albert Hall, 10 Dec. 1910*, London n.d. [L]

1911/4 William C. Anderson, *What means this labour unrest?*, Manchester n.d. [P]

1911/19 J. A. Fallows, *The story of German and English relations*, Manchester–London–Birmingham n.d. [P]

1911/32 J. M. McLachlan, *Democracy and foreign policy*, Manchester n.d. [P]

1911/42 G. H. Perris, *Hands across the sea: Labour's plea for international peace*, Manchester n.d. [P]

1911/43 ILP, *The power of parliament*, London n.d. [L]

1912/1 Norman Angell, *War and the workers*, Manchester–London n.d.

1912/4 ILP, *The battle of the ballot*, London n.d. [L]

1913/13 Harry Dubery, A *Labour case against conscription*, Manchester– London n.d. [P]

1913/28 J. T. Walton-Newbold, *The war trust exposed*, Manchester–London n.d. [P]

1914/9 Bradford ILP, *Yearbook 1914*, Bradford 1914

1914/33 ILP, *Resist the foreign yoke of conscription!*, Manchester–London n.d. [L]

1914/15 ILP NAC, *Circular to branches 2 Sept. 1914*, London n.d. [L]

1915/16 Clive Bell, *Peace at once*, Manchester–London n.d.

1915/54 ILP, *The ILP attitude*, Manchester–London n.d. [L]

1915/67 C. H. Norman, *British militarism: a reply to Robert Blatchford*, Manchester–London 1915 [P]

1915/70 C. H. Norman, *Nationality and patriotism*, Manchester–London 1915 [P]

1915/88 Robert Williams, *Un-common sense about the war*, London n.d. [P]

1916/2 Clifford Allen, *Conscription and conscience*, London n.d. [P]

1916/25 J. W. Kneeshaw, *Conscription enters the workshops*, Manchester–London n.d. [P]

1916/38 Philip Snowden, *British Prussianism: the scandal of the tribunals*, Manchester–London n.d. [P]

1917/53 Will Crooks, *The truth about the war makers: a reply to the Independent Labour Party pamphlet*, London n.d. [P]

1919/1 W. C. Anderson, *The profiteers' parliament*, London 1919 [P]

1919/4 ILP, *Bolshevism!*, Manchester n.d. [L]

1919/24 A. W. Humphreys, *The allies' crime against Russia: an exposure of a capitalist conspiracy*, London 1919 [P]

1919/28 ILP, *International socialism and world peace: resolutions at the Berne conference Feb. 1919*, London 1919 [P]

1919/32 Joseph King, *Bolshevism and Bolsheviks*, London 1919 [P]

1919/35 Joseph King, *Soviets*, London 1919 [P]

1919/36 Joseph King, *Three bloody men*, Glasgow n.d. [P]

1919/39 Lenin, *The land revolution in Russia*, with a foreword by Philip Snowden, London 1919 [P]

1919/42 *The manifesto of the Moscow International*, Manchester n.d. [P]

1919/66 H. C. Shears, *Socialist policy: reform or revolution?*, London 1919 [P]

1920/13 J. Bruce Glasier, *Socialism and strikes*, Manchester n.d. [P]

1920/19 ILP, *The ILP and the Third International*, Manchester–London 1920

1922/9 ILP, *Bunkum v. fact*, London 1922 [L]

1922/10 ILP Information Committee, *The capital levy*, London 1922 [L]

1923/10 National 'Hands Off Russia' Committee, *For Labour and socialist speakers*, London 1923 [L]

1923/31 ILP Information Committee, *Weekly notes for speakers*, London 1923 [L]

1923/54 Bradford ILP, *Pocket handbook 1923–1924*, Bradford n.d.

1924/38 J. Ramsay MacDonald, *The story of the ILP and what it stands for*, 3rd edn, London 1924 [P]

**Pamphlets and leaflets of the Social Democratic Federation and the British Socialist Party (Harvester microforms, Brighton)**

1892/5 H. M. Hyndman, *Socialism and slavery*, 3rd edn, London n.d. [P]

1893/8 *Report presented by the Social Democratic Federation to the International socialist congress, Zurich, Aug. 1893*, London n.d. [P]

1894/1 James Leatham (ed.), *Labour's garland, being poems for socialists*, London n.d. [P]

1897/2 Arthur Hickmott, *Socialism and agriculture*, London 1897 [P]

1899/2 Arthur Hickmott, *Songs by the wayside*, London n.d. [P]

1899/7 F. Reginald Statham, *The South African crisis: the truth about the Transvaal*, London 1899

1900/3 H. W. Lee, *The First of May: international labour day*, London 1900

1901/1 SDF, *The Boer War and its results*, London 1901 [L]

1901/3 James Leatham, *What is the good of empire?*, Peterhead–London 1901 [P]

1902/1 E. Belfort Bax and Harry Quelch, *A new catechism of socialism*, 2nd edn, London 1902

1902/3 Harry Quelch (ed.), *How I became a socialist*, London n.d.

1902/8 SDF, *The right of free speech*, London n.d. [L]

1904/1 H. W. Humphreys, *The case for universal military training as established in Australia*, London 1912 [P]

1906/4 James Leatham, *The settling of Britain: some neglected historical origins*, Peterhead–London n.d. [P]

1907/2 SDF, *The child's socialist reader*, London 1907

1907/18 H. Quelch, *The Social Democratic Federation: its objects, its principles and it work*, London n.d. [P]

1908/2 Robert Edmondson, *An exposition and exposure of Haldane's Territorial Forces Act 1907*, London 1908 [P]

1909/5 A. P. Hazell and W. Cook, *Work for the unemployed!: a national highway for military and motor traffic*, London n.d. [P]

1911/9 George Whitehead, *Socialism and eugenics*, London n.d. [P]

## Published collections of documents

*British general election manifestos 1900–1970*, ed. F. W. S. Craig, London– Basingstoke 1975

*British general election manifestos 1918–1966*, ed. F. W. S. Craig, Chichester 1983

*British socialism: socialist thought from the 1880s to the 1960s*, ed. Anthony Wright, London 1983

*The challenge of socialism*, ed. Henry Pelling, London 1954

*Chartism and society: an anthology of documents*, ed. F. C. Mather, London 1980

*The early Chartists*, ed. Dorothy Thompson, London–Basingstoke 1971

*The Labour Party: 1881–1951 a reader in history*, ed. Keith Laybourn, Gloucester 1988

*Labour's turning point 1880–1900*, ed. E. J. Hobsbawm, 2nd edn, Brighton 1974

*The left and war: the British Labour Party and World War I*, ed. Peter Stansky, London–New York 1969

*The pro-Boers: the anatomy of an anti-war movement*, ed. Stephen Koss, Chicago–London 1973

*The social and political thought of the British Labour Party*, ed. Frank Bealey, London 1970

## Secondary sources

Adams, R. J. Q. and Philip P. Poirier, *The conscription controversy in Great Britain, 1900–18*, Basingstoke–London 1987

Addison, Paul, *The road to 1945: British politics and the Second World War*, London 1975

Anderson, Benedict, *Imagined communities: reflections on the origin and spread of nationalism*, London 1983

Anderson, Perry, 'Origins of the present crisis', in Perry Anderson and Robin Blackburn (eds), *Towards socialism*, Ithaca 1966

Arnot, R. Page, *The impact of the Russian Revolution in Britain*, London 1967

Bagehot, Walter, *The English constitution*, Glasgow 1963

Baker, Bill, *The Social Democratic Federation and the Boer War*, London 1974

Barker, Rodney, 'Socialism and progressivism in the political thought of Ramsay MacDonald', in Morris, *Edwardian radicalism 1900–1914*, 114–30

Barnett, Anthony, 'After nationalism', in Samuel, *Patriotism*, i. 140–55

Barrow, Logie, 'Determinism and environmentalism in socialist thought', in Raphael Samuel and Gareth Stedman Jones (eds), *Culture, ideology and politics*, London 1982, 194–214

—— 'White solidarity in 1914', in Samuel (ed.), *Patriotism*, i. 275–87

Barry, E. Eldon, *Nationalisation in British politics: the historical background*, London 1965

Bassett, R., *Nineteen thirty-one: political crisis*, Aldershot 1986

Bauman, Zygmunt, *Between class and elite: the evolution of the British labour movement: a sociological study*, Manchester 1972

Bealey, Frank and Henry Pelling, *Labour and politics 1900–1906: a history of the Labour Representation Committee*, London 1958

Bell, Geoffrey, *Troublesome business: the Labour Party and the Irish question*, London 1982

Benn, Caroline, *Keir Hardie*, London 1992

Bevir, Mark, 'H. M. Hyndman: a re-reading and a reassessment', *History of Political Thought* xii (1991), 125–45

—— 'British socialism and American romanticism', *EHR* cx (1995), 878–901

Biagini, Eugenio F. and Alistair J. Reid (eds), *Currents of radicalism: popular radicalism, organised labour and party politics in Britain 1850–1914*, Cambridge 1991

Blaxland, Gregory, *J. H. Thomas: a life for unity*, London 1964

Blewett, Neal, 'The franchise in the United Kingdom, 1885–1918', *P&P* xxxii (1965), 27–56

—— *The peers, the parties and the people: the general elections of 1910*, London–Basingstoke 1972

Boyce, D. G., *Englishmen and Irish troubles: British public opinion and the making of Irish policy 1918–22*, London 1972

Briggs, Asa, 'The language of "class" in early nineteenth-century England', in Briggs and Saville, *Essays in labour history in memory of G. D. H. Cole*, 43–73

—— *Saxons, Normans and Victorians*, Hastings–Bexhill 1966

—— and John Saville (eds), *Essays in labour history in memory of G. D. H. Cole*, London–Basingstoke 1960

—— and John Saville (eds), *Essays in labour history 1886–1923*, London 1971

Brock, Michael, *The great Reform Act*, London 1973

Brockway, Fenner, *Socialism over sixty years: the life of Jowett of Bradford (1864–1944)*, London 1946

Buder, Stanley, *Visionaries and planners: the garden city movement and the modern community*, New York–Oxford 1990

Burnett, John, *A social history of housing 1815–1985*, 2nd edn, London–New York 1986

Burrow, J. W., *A liberal descent: Victorian historians and the English past*, Cambridge 1981

Bush, Julia, *Behind the lines: East London labour 1914–1919*, London 1984

Calder, Angus, *The myth of the Blitz*, London 1991

Cannadine, David, 'The context, performance and meaning of ritual: the British monarchy and the "invention of tradition", c. 1820–1977', in Hobsbawm and Ranger, *The invention of tradition*, 101–64

——— *G. M. Trevelyan: a life in history*, London 1992

Carpenter, L. P., *G. D. H. Cole: an intellectual biography*, Cambridge 1973

Carpenter, Niles, *Guild socialism: an historical and critical analysis*, New York–London 1922

Carr, E. H., *Nationalism and after*, London 1945

Carsten, F. L., *War against war: British and German radical movements in the First World War*, London 1982

Challinor, Raymond, *The origins of British Bolshevism*, London 1977

Claeys, Gregory, 'The lion and the unicorn, patriotism, and Orwell's politics', *Review of Politics* xlvii (1985), 186–211

Clark, David, *Victor Grayson: Labour's lost leader*, London 1985

Clarke, Peter, *Liberals and social democrats*, London 1978

Cline, Catherine Ann, *Recruits to Labour: the British Labour Party 1914–1931*, New York 1963

Coates, David, *The Labour Party and the struggle for socialism*, London 1975

Coetzee, Frans, *For party and country: nationalism and the dilemmas of popular Conservatism in Edwardian England*, Oxford–New York 1990

Cole, G. D. H., *A history of the Labour Party since 1914*, London 1948

Colley, Linda, 'The apotheosis of George III: loyalty, royalty and the British nation 1760–1820', *P&P* cii (1984), 94–129

——— 'Whose nation?: class and national consciousness in Britain 1750–1830', *P&P* cxiii (1986), 97–117

——— 'Radical patriotism in eighteenth century England, in Samuel, *Patriotism*, i. 169–87

——— *Britons: forging the nation 1707–1837*, New Haven–London 1992

Colls, Robert, 'Englishness and the political culture', in Colls and Dodd, *Englishness*, 29–61

——— and Philip Dodd (eds), *Englishness: politics and culture 1880–1920*, London 1986

Cook, Chris, *The age of alignment: electoral politics in Britain 1922–1929*, London–Basingstoke 1975

——— *A short history of the Liberal Party 1900–1976*, London–Basingstoke 1976

Cottrell, Stella, 'The devil on two sticks: Franco-phobia in 1803', in Samuel, *Patriotism*, i. 259–74

Cowden, Morton H., *Russian Bolshevism and British Labour 1917–1921*, New York 1984

Cowling, Maurice, *The impact of Labour 1920–1924: the beginning of modern British politics*, London 1971

Craig, F. W. S. (ed.), *British parliamentary election results 1918–1949*, 3rd edn, Chichester 1983

Crawford, Alan, *C. R. Ashbee: architect, designer and romantic socialist*, New Haven–London 1985

Cronin, James E., *Labour and society in Britain 1918–1979*, London 1984

Cross, Colin, *Philip Snowden*, London 1966

Crump, Jeremy, 'The identity of English music: the reception of Elgar 1898–1935', in Colls and Dodd, *Englishness*, 164–90

Culler, A. Dwight, *The Victorian mirror of history*, New Haven–London 1985

Cunningham, Hugh, 'Jingoism in 1877–78', VS xiv (1971), 429–53

—— *The Volunteer force: a political and social history 1859–1908*, London 1975

—— 'The Conservative Party and patriotism', in Colls and Dodd, *Englishness*, 283–307

—— 'The language of patriotism', in Samuel, *Patriotism*, i. 57–89

—— 'The nature of Chartism', *Modern History Review* i (1990), 21–3

Daunton, M. J., 'How to pay for the war: state, society and taxation in Britain 1917–24', EHR cxi (1996), 882–919

Davey, Arthur, *The British pro-Boers 1877–1902*, Cape Town 1978

Davies, A. J., *To build a new Jerusalem: the British labour movement from the 1880s to the 1990s*, London 1992

*Dictionary of labour biography*, 8 vols, ed. Joyce Bellamy and others, London–Basingstoke 1972–87

Diller, Hans-Jurgen and others (eds), *Englishness*, Heidelburg 1992

Dodd, Philip, 'Englishness and the national culture', in Colls and Dodd, *Englishness*, 1–28

Dose, Gerd, ' "England your England": George Orwell on socialism, gentleness and the English mission', in Diller and others, *Englishness*

Douglas, Roy, 'Voluntary enlistment in the First World War and the work of the Parliamentary Recruiting Committee', JMH xlii (1970), 564–85

—— 'The National Democratic Party and the British Workers' League', HJ xv (1972), 533–52

—— 'Labour in decline, 1910–14', in Kenneth D. Brown (ed.), *Essays in anti-labour history: responses to the rise of labour in Britain*, London–Basingstoke 1974, 105–25

—— *Land, people and politics: a history of the land question in the United Kingdom, 1878–1952*, London 1976

Dowse, Robert E., 'A note on Ramsay MacDonald and direct action', *Political Studies* ix (1961), 306–8

—— *Left in the centre: the Independent Labour Party 1893–1940*, London 1966

Doyle, Barry M., 'Who paid the price of patriotism?: the funding of Charles Stanton during the Merthyr Boroughs by-election of 1915', EHR cix (1994)

Elliott, Gregory, *Labourism and the English genius: the strange death of Labour England?*, London–New York 1993

Elton, Lord, *The life of James Ramsay MacDonald (1866–1919)*, London 1939

Emsley, Clive, *British society and the French wars 1793–1815*, London 1979

Epstein, James, 'Understanding the cap of liberty: symbolic practice and social conflict in early nineteenth century England', P&P cxxii (1989), 75–118

Etherington, Norman, 'Hyndman, the Social-Democratic Federation and imperialism', *Historical Studies* xvi (1974), 89–103

Feldman, David, *Englishmen and Jews: social relations and political culture 1840–1914*, New Haven–London 1994

Field, Geoffrey, 'Social patriotism and the British working class: appearance and disappearance of a tradition', *International Labour and Working Class History* xli (1992), 20–39

Finn, Margot, *After Chartism: class and nation in English radical politics, 1848–1874*, Cambridge 1993

Foote, Geoffrey, *The Labour Party's political thought: a history*, 2nd edn, London 1986

Gaitskell, Hugh, 'At Oxford in the twenties', in Briggs and Saville, *Essays in labour history in memory of G. D. H. Cole*, 6–19

Galbraith, John S., 'The pamphlet campaign on the Boer War', *JMH* xxiv (1952), 6–19

Garrard, John A., *The English and immigration 1880–1910*, London 1971

Gilbert, Martin, *Winston S. Churchill, IV: 1916–1922*, London 1975

Glass, S. T., *The responsible society: the ideas of the English guild socialists*, London 1966

Gordon, Michael R., *Conflict and consensus in Labour's foreign policy 1914–1965*, Stanford, Ca. 1969

Gorman, John, *Images of labour: selected memorabilia from the National Museum of Labour History*, n.p. 1985

Gott, Richard, 'Little Englanders', in Samuel, *Patriotism*, i. 90–102

Gould, Peter C., *Early green politics: back to nature, back to the land, and socialism in Britain 1880–1900*, Brighton 1988

Grainger, J. H., *Patriotisms: Britain 1900–1939*, London 1986

Graubard, Stephen Richards, *British labour and the Russian Revolution 1917–1924*, Cambridge, Mass.–London 1956

Green, E. and M. Taylor, 'Further thoughts on Little Englandism', in Samuel, *Patriotism*, i. 103–9

Groh, Dieter, 'The "unpatriotic" socialists and the state', *JCH* i (1966), 151–77

Gupta, Partha Sarathi, *Imperialism and the British labour movement 1914–1964*, London–Basingstoke 1975

Guttsman, W. L., *The British political elite*, London 1968

Hamilton, Mary Agnes, *Sidney and Beatrice Webb*, London 1933

—— *Arthur Henderson: a biography*, London 1938

Harcourt, Freda, 'The queen, the sultan and the viceroy: a Victorian state occasion', *London Journal* v (1979), 35–56

—— 'Disraeli's imperialism, 1866–1868: a question of timing', *HJ* xxiii (1980), 87–109

—— 'Gladstone, monarchism and the "new" imperialism, 1868–74', *JICH* xiv (1985), 20–51

Harker, Dave, 'May Cecil Sharp be praised?', *HW* xiv (1982), 44–62

Harris, José, 'Political thought and the welfare state 1870–1940: an intellectual framework for British social policy', *P&P* xxxv (1992), 116–41

—— *Private lives, public spirit: Britain 1870–1914*, London 1994

Harris, Kenneth, *Attlee*, London 1982

Harrison, Royden, 'The War Emergency Workers' National Committee 1914–1920', in Briggs and Saville, *Essays in labour history 1886–1923*, 211–59
—— 'Sidney and Beatrice Webb', in Levy, *Socialism and the intelligentsia*, 35–89
Haste, Cate, *Keep the home fires burning: propaganda in the First World War*, London 1977
Haupt, Georges, *Socialism and the Great War: the collapse of the Second International*, Oxford 1973
Hill, Christopher, 'The Norman yoke', in his *Puritanism and revolution: studies in the interpretation of the English Revolution of the 17th century*, Harmondsworth 1986, 58–125
Hinton, James, *Labour and socialism: a history of the British labour movement 1867–1974*, Brighton 1983
Hobsbawm, E. J., *Labouring men: studies in the history of labour*, London 1968
—— *Worlds of labour*, London 1984
—— *Nations and nationalism since 1780: programme, myth, reality*, Cambridge 1990
—— and Terence Ranger (eds), *The invention of tradition*, Cambridge 1983
Holmes, Colin, *Anti-Semitism in British society 1876–1939*, London 1979
Holroyd, Michael, *Bernard Shaw*, I: *1856–1898 the search for love*; II: *1898–1918 the pursuit of power*, London 1988, 1989
Holton, Bob, *British syndicalism 1900–1914: myths and realities*, London 1976
Howard, Christopher, *Splendid isolation*, London 1967
—— 'MacDonald, Henderson and the outbreak of war, 1914', *HJ* xx (1977), 871–91
Howe, Stephen, 'Labour patriotism 1939–1983', in Samuel, *Patriotism*, i. 127–39
Howell, David, *British workers and the Independent Labour Party 1888–1906*, Manchester 1983
—— *A lost left: three studies in socialism and nationalism*, Manchester 1986
Howkins, Alun, 'The discovery of rural England', in Colls and Dodd, *Englishness*, 62–88
—— 'Greensleeves and the idea of national music', in Samuel, *Patriotism*, i. 89–98
Howorth, Jolyon, 'The left in France and Germany, internationalism and war: a dialogue of the deaf 1900–1914', in Eric Cahm and V. C. Fisera (eds), *Socialism and nationalism in contemporary Europe (1848–1945)*, ii, Nottingham 1979, 81–100
Hynes, Samuel, *A war imagined: the First World War and English culture*, London 1990
James, David, Tony Jowitt and Keith Laybourn (eds), *The centennial history of the Independent Labour Party*, Halifax 1992
Jeffery, Keith and Peter Hennessy, *States of emergency: British governments and strikebreaking since 1919*, London 1983
Jenkins, Brian and Gunter Minnerup, *Citizens and comrades: socialism in a world of nation states*, London 1984
Joll, James, *The Second International 1889–1914*, London 1955
Jones, Barry and Michael Keating, *Labour and the British state*, Oxford 1985
Jones, Gareth Stedman, *Languages of class: studies in English working class history 1832–1982*, Cambridge 1983
Jowitt, Tony, 'Philip Snowden and the First World War', in Keith Laybourn and

David James (eds), *Philip Snowden: the first Labour chancellor of the exchequer*, Bradford 1987, 39–57

—— and Keith Laybourn, 'War and socialism: the experience of Bradford ILP 1914–18', in James and others, *Centennial history of the ILP*, 95–115

Joyce, Patrick, *Work, society and politics: the culture of the factory in later Victorian England*, London 1982

—— *Visions of the people: industrial England and the question of class, 1848–1914*, Cambridge 1991

Kaarsholm, Preben, 'Pro-Boers', in Samuel, *Patriotism*, i. 110–26

Keating, Michael and David Bleiman, *Labour and Scottish nationalism*, London–Basingstoke 1979

Kellog, Paul U. and Arthur Gleason, *British Labor and the war: reconstructors for a new world*, New York 1919

Kendall, Walter, *The revolutionary movement in Britain 1900–21: the origins of British Communism*, London 1969

Kennedy, Paul M., *The rise of the Anglo-German anatagonism 1860–1914*, London–New York 1987

Kinnear, Michael, *The British voter: an atlas and survey since 1885*, London 1968

Lambourne, Lionel, *Utopian craftsmen: the Arts and Crafts movement from the Cotswolds to Chicago*, London 1980

Lansbury, George, *The miracle of Fleet Street: the story of the Daily Herald*, London n.d.

Lawrence, Jon, 'Popular radicalism and the socialist revival in Britain', *JBS* xxxi (1992), 163–86

Laybourn, Keith, *Philip Snowden: a biography 1864–1937*, Aldershot 1988

—— and Jack Reynolds, *Liberalism and the rise of Labour 1890–1918*, London 1984

Lee, Francis, *Fabianism and colonialism: the life and political thought of Sydney Olivier*, London 1988

Lenin, V. I., *Selected works in three volumes*, Moscow 1963

Leventhal, F. M., *Arthur Henderson*, Manchester–New York 1989

Levy, Carl (ed.), *Socialism and the intelligentsia 1880–1914*, London–New York 1987

Lowe, Philip, 'The rural idyll defended: from preservation to conservation', in G. E. Mingay (ed.), *The rural idyll*, London 1989, 113–31

Luttman, Stephen, 'Orwell's patriotism', *JCH* ii (1967), 149–58

Lyman, Richard W., *The first Labour government 1924*, New York 1957

—— 'James Ramsay MacDonald and the leadership of the Labour Party 1918–22', *JBS* ii (1962), 132–60

McBriar, A. M., *Fabian socialism and English politics 1884–1918*, London 1962

McCarthy, Fiona, *The simple life: C. R. Ashbee in the Cotswolds*, London 1981

MacFarlane, L. J., ' "Hands off Russia", British labour and the Russo-Polish War, 1920', *P&P* xxxviii (1967), 126–52

Macintyre, Stuart, *Little Moscows: Communism and working-class militancy in inter-war Britain*, London 1980

MacKenzie, J. M., *Propaganda and empire: the manipulation of British public opinion, 1880–1960*, Manchester 1984

—— *Imperialism and popular culture*, Manchester 1986

MacKenzie, Norman and Jeanne MacKenzie, *The first Fabians*, London 1977

McKenzie, Robert and Allan Silver, *Angels in marble: working class Conservatives in urban England*, London 1968

McKibbin, Ross, *The evolution of the Labour Party 1910–1924*, Oxford 1974

McLean, Iain, *Keir Hardie*, London 1975

McWilliam, Rohan, 'Radicalism and popular culture: the Tichborne case and the politics of "fair play" 1867–1886', in Biagini and Reid, *Currents of radicalism*, 44–64

Maccoby, S., *English radicalism 1786–1832*, London 1955

Mandler, Peter, *The fall and rise of the stately home*, New Haven–London 1997

Marquand, David, *Ramsay MacDonald*, London 1977

Marsh, Jan, *Back to the land: the pastoral impulse in England, from 1880 to 1914*, London 1982

Marwick, Arthur, *Clifford Allen: the open conspirator*, Edinburgh–London 1964

––––––– 'Working-class attitudes to the First World War', *BSSLH* xiii (1966), 9–12

––––––– *The deluge: British society and the First World War*, 2nd edn, Basingstoke–London 1991

Marx, Karl and Frederick Engels, *Correspondence 1846–1895: a selection*, London 1934

––––––– *Selected works in one volume*, London 1968

Matthews, Frank, 'The building guilds', in Briggs and Saville, *Essays in labour history 1886–1923*

Meacham, Standish, 'Raymond Unwin (1863–1940): designing for democracy in Edwardian England', in Pedersen and Mandler, *After the Victorians*, 78–102

Mendilow, Jonathan, *The romantic tradition in English political thought*, London 1986

Michels, Robert, *Political parties: a sociological study of the oligarchical tendencies of modern democracy*, trans. Eden Paul and Cedar Paul, New York 1962

Middlemas, Keith, *The Clydesiders*, London 1965

––––––– *Politics in industrial society: the experience of the British system since 1911*, London 1979

––––––– and John Barnes, *Baldwin: a biography*, London 1969

Miliband, Ralph, *Parliamentary socialism*, 2nd edn, London 1972

Moore, Roger, *The emergence of the Labour Party 1880–1924*, London 1978

Morgan, Austen, J. *Ramsay MacDonald*, Manchester 1987

Morgan, Kenneth O., *Keir Hardie: radical and socialist*, London 1975

––––––– *Rebirth of a nation: Wales 1880–1980*, Oxford 1982

––––––– *Labour in power 1945–1951*, Oxford 1984

––––––– 'Edwardian socialism', in Read, *Edwardian England*, 93–111

Morgan, Kevin, *Against fascism and war: ruptures and continuities in British Communist politics 1935–41*, Manchester–New York 1989

Morris, A. J. A., *Radicalism against war, 1906–1914*, London 1972

––––––– (ed.), *Edwardian radicalism 1900–1914: some aspects of British radicalism*, London–Boston 1974

––––––– *The scaremongers: the advocacy of war and rearmament 1896–1914*, London 1984

Mowat, C. L., *Britain between the wars, 1918–1940*, London 1956

Nairn, Tom, 'The nature of the Labour Party', in Anderson and Blackburn, *Towards socialism*, 159–217

—— The break-up of Britain: crisis and neo-nationalism, 2nd edn, London 1981

—— The enchanted glass: Britain and its monarchy, London 1988

Newman, Gerald, 'Anti-French propaganda and British liberal nationalism in the early nineteenth century: suggestions toward a general interpretation', VS viii (1975), 385–418

—— The rise of English nationalism: a cultural history 1740–1830, New York 1987

Newton, Douglas J., British Labour, European socialism and the struggle for peace 1889–1914, Oxford 1985

Nicolson, Harold, King George the Fifth: his life and reign, London 1952

Offer, Avner, Property and politics 1870–1914: landownership, law, ideology and urban development in England, Cambridge 1981

The Oxford dictionary of English proverbs, 3rd edn, Oxford 1970

Pedersen, Susan and Peter Mandler (eds), After the Victorians: private conscience and public duty, London–New York 1994

Pelling, Henry, The origins of the Labour Party 1880–1900, 2nd edn, Oxford 1966

—— A short history of the Labour Party, 8th edn, London–Basingstoke 1985

—— A history of British trade unionism, 4th edn, Harmondsworth 1987

Pick, Daniel, War machine: the rationalisation of slaughter in the modern age, New Haven–London 1993

Pierson, Stanley, Marxism and the origins of British socialism: the struggle for a new consciousness, Ithaca–London 1973

—— British socialism: the journey from fantasy to politics, Cambridge, Mass. 1979

Pimlott, Ben, Labour and the left in the 1930s, London 1986

Poirier, Philip P., The advent of the Labour Party, London 1958

Porter, Bernard, Critics of empire: British radical attitudes to colonialism in Africa 1895–1914, London 1968

Porter, Roy (ed.), Myths of the English, Cambridge 1992

Postgate, Raymond, The life of George Lansbury, London 1951

Potts, Alex, ' "Constable country" between the wars', in Samuel, Patriotism, i. 160–86

Price, Richard, An imperial war and the British working class: attitudes and reactions to the Boer War 1899–1902, London 1972

Prynn, David, 'The Clarion clubs, rambling and holiday associations in Britain since the 1890s', JCH xi (1976), 65–77

Quail, John, The slow burning fuse: the lost history of the British anarchists, London 1978

Quinault, Roland, 'Westminster and the Victorian constitution', Transactions of the Royal Historical Society, 6th series ii (1992), 79–104

Radice, Giles and Lisanne Radice, Will Thorne: constructive militant, London 1974

Ramsden, John, The age of Balfour and Baldwin 1902–1940, London 1978

Read, Donald (ed.), Edwardian England, London 1982

Reid, Christopher, 'Patriotism and rhetorical contest in the 1790s: the context of Sheridan's Pizarro', in Elizabeth Maslen (ed.), Comedy, London 1993, 232–47

Reid, F., 'Socialist Sunday schools in Britain, 1892–1939', International Review of Social History x (1966), 18–47

—— Keir Hardie: the making of a socialist, London 1978

Renan, Ernest, 'What is a nation?', in Homi K. Bhabha (ed.), Nation and narration, London 1990, 8–22

Robbins, Keith, *Nineteenth–century Britain: England, Scotland and Wales: the making of a nation*, Oxford 1989

Rose, Kenneth, *King George V*, London 1983

Rothstein, Andrew, *The soldiers' strikes of 1919*, London 1980

Rowbotham, Sheila and Jeffrey Weeks, *Socialism and the new life: the personal and sexual politics of Edward Carpenter and Havelock Ellis*, London 1977

Russell, A. K., *The Liberal landslide: the general election of 1906*, Newton Abbot–Hampden, Conn. 1973

Russell, Dave, *Popular music in England, 1840–1914: a social history*, Manchester 1987

Samuel, Raphael, 'British Marxist historians 1880–1980', *New Left Review* cxx (1980), 21–96

———— (ed.), *Patriotism: the making and unmaking of British national identity*, I: *History and politics*, III: *National fictions*, London 1989

Saville, John, 'Henry George and the British labour movement: a select bibliography with commentary', *BSSLH* v (1962), 18–26

Schneer, Jonathan, *Ben Tillett*, Chicago–London 1982

———— *George Lansbury*, Manchester 1990

Schorske, Carl E., *German social democracy 1905–1912: the development of the great schism*, New York 1972

Schwarz, Bill, 'The language of constitutionalism: Baldwinite Conservatism', in *Formations of nation and people*, London 1984, 1–18

Schwarzmantel, John, 'Nationalism and the French working-class movement 1905–14', in Eric Cahm and V. C. Fisera (eds), *Socialism and nationalism in contemporary Europe (1848–1945)*, ii, Nottingham 1979, 65–80

———— *Socialism and the idea of the nation*, Hemel Hempstead 1991

Searle, G. R., *The quest for national efficiency: a study in British politics and political thought, 1899–1914*, Oxford 1971

Self, Robert, 'Conservative re-union and the general election of 1923', *Twentieth Century British History* iii (1992), 249–73

Semmel, Bernard, *Imperialism and social reform: English social–imperial thought 1895–1914*, London 1960

Shelden, Michael, *Orwell: the authorised biography*, London 1992

Shpayer-Makov, Haia, 'Anarchism in British public opinion 1880–1914', *VS* xxxi (1988), 487–516

Siederer, N. D., 'The Campbell case', *JCH* ix (1974), 143–62

Skidelsky, Robert, *Politicians and the slump: the Labour government of 1929–1931*, Harmondsworth 1970

———— *Oswald Mosley*, London–Basingstoke 1975

Smith, Anthony D., *National identity*, London 1991

Smith, R. J., *The gothic bequest: medieval institutions in British thought, 1688–1863*, Cambridge 1987

Steele, E. D., *Palmerston and Liberalism 1855–1865*, Cambridge 1991

Stevenson, John and Chris Cook, *The slump: society and politics during the depression*, London 1977

Stubbs, J. O., 'Lord Milner and patriotic labour, 1914–1918', *EHR* lxxxvii (1972), 717–54

Summers, Anne, 'Edwardian militarism', in Samuel, *Patriotism*, i. 235–56

Swann, Paul, *The British documentary film movement 1926–1946*, Cambridge 1989

Swartz, Marvin, *The Union of Democratic Control in British politics during the First World War*, Oxford 1971

Swenarton, Mark, *Homes fit for heroes: the politics and architecture of early state housing*, London 1981

────── *Artisans and architects: the Ruskinian tradition in British architectural thought*, Basingstoke–London 1989

Tanner, Duncan, *Political change and the Labour Party 1900–1918*, Cambridge 1990

────── 'The development of British socialism, 1900–1918', in E. H. H. Green (ed.), *An age of transition: British politics 1880–1914*, Edinburgh 1997, 48–66

Taylor, A. J. P., *English history 1914–1945*, Harmondsworth 1975

────── *The trouble makers: dissent over foreign policy 1792–1939*, Harmondsworth 1985

Taylor, Miles, 'Patriotism, history and the left in twentieth-century Britain', *HJ* xxxiii (1990), 971–87

────── 'Imperium et libertas? Rethinking the radical critique of imperialism during the nineteenth century', *JICH* xix (1991), 1–23

────── 'John Bull and the iconography of public opinion in England *c.* 1712–1929', *P&P* cxxxiv (1992), 93–128

Thompson, E. P., 'Homage to Tom Maguire', in Briggs and Saville, *Essays in labour history in memory of G. D. H. Cole*, 276–316

────── *William Morris: romantic to revolutionary*, 2nd edn, London 1977

────── *The poverty of theory and other essays*, London 1978

────── *The making of the English working class*, Harmondsworth 1980

Thompson, Laurence, *Robert Blatchford: portrait of an Englishman*, London 1951

────── *The enthusiasts: a biography of John and Katherine Bruce Glasier*, London 1971

Townshend, Jules, J. A. *Hobson*, Manchester–New York 1990

Trentmann, Frank, 'Wealth versus welfare: the British left between free trade and national political economy before the First World War', *Historical Research* lxx (1997), 70–98

Tsiang, Tingfu F., *Labour and empire: a study in the reaction of British labor . . . to British imperialism since 1880*, New York 1923

Tsuzuki, Chushichi, H. M. *Hyndman and British socialism*, London 1961

────── *Tom Mann 1856–1941: the challenges of labour*, Oxford 1991

Turner, John, *British politics and the Great War: coalition and conflict 1915–1918*, New Haven–London 1992

Waites, Bernard, *A class society at war: England 1914–1918*, Leamington Spa 1987

Ward, Stephen R., *James Ramsay MacDonald: low born among the high brows*, New York 1990

Warwick, Peter (ed.), *The South African War: the Anglo-Boer War of 1899–1902*, Harlow 1980

Waters, Chris, *British socialists and the politics of popular culture, 1884–1914*, Manchester 1990

────── 'J. B. Priestley (1894–1984): Englishness and the politics of nostalgia', in Pedersen and Mandler, *After the Victorians*, 208–26

Watson, Ian, *Song and democratic culture in Britain*, London 1983

Webb, Keith, *The growth of nationalism in Scotland*, Harmondsworth 1978

Weinroth, Howard, 'Left-wing opposition to naval armaments in Britain before 1914', *JCH* vi (1971), 93–120

Weinstein, Harold R., *Jean Jaurès: a study of patriotism in the French socialist movement*, New York 1936

Wertheimer, Egon, *Portrait of the Labour Party*, 2nd edn, London–New York 1930

White, Joseph, *Tom Mann*, Manchester 1991

White, Stephen, *Britain and the Bolshevik Revolution*, London–Basingstoke 1979

Whiting, R. C., 'The Labour Party, capitalism and the national debt, 1918–24', in P. J. Waller (ed.), *Politics and social change in modern Britain*, Brighton 1987, 140–60

Wiener, Martin J., 'The changing image of William Cobbett', *JBS* xiii (1974), 135–54

—— *English culture and the decline of the industrial spirit 1850–1980*, Cambridge 1981

Wilkins, M. S., 'The non-socialist origins of England's first important socialist organisation', *International Review of Social History* iv (1959), 199–207

Williams, Raymond, *Culture and society 1780–1950*, London 1958

—— *The country and the city*, London 1973

—— *Orwell*, London 1984

Williamson, Philip, *National crisis and national government: British politics, the economy and the empire 1926–1932*, Cambridge 1992

Winter, J. M., 'Arthur Henderson, the Russian Revolution, and the reconstruction of the Labour Party', *HJ* xv (1972), 753–73

—— *Socialism and the challenge of war: ideas and politics in Britain 1912–18*, London–Boston 1974

Wood, Ian S., 'Hope deferred: Labour in Scotland in the 1920s', in Ian Donnachie, Christopher Harvie and Ian S. Wood (eds), *Forward! Labour politics in Scotland 1888–1988*, Edinburgh 1989, 30–48

Wootton, Graham, *The politics of influence: British ex-servicemen, cabinet decisions and cultural change (1917–57)*, Cambridge, Mass. 1963

Wright, Patrick, *On living in an old country: the national past in contemporary Britain*, London 1985

Wrigley, Chris, *Arthur Henderson*, Cardiff 1990

—— (ed.), *The British labour movement in the decade after the First World War*, Loughborough 1979

—— (ed.), *Challenges of labour: central and western Europe 1917–1920*, London–New York 1993

Yeo, Stephen, 'Socialism, the state and some oppositional Englishness', in Colls and Dodd, *Englishness*, 308–69

—— 'A new life: the religion of socialism in Britain 1883–1896', *HW* iv (1977), 5–56

Young, James D., *The rousing of the Scottish working class*, London 1979

—— *Socialism and the English working class: a history of English labour 1883–1939*, Hemel Hempstead 1989

—— 'A very English socialism and the Celtic fringe 1880–1991', *HW* xxxv (1993), 136–52

Young, Ken and Patricia L. Garside, *Metropolitan London: politics and urban change 1837–1981*, London 1982

## Unpublished theses

Barrow, Logie, 'The socialism of Robert Blatchford and the Clarion 1889–1918', unpubl PhD diss. London 1975

Jarvis, David A., 'Stanley Baldwin and the ideology of the Conservative response to socialism 1918–31', unpubl. PhD diss. Lancaster 1991

Weight, Richard A. J., 'Pale stood Albion: the formulation of English national identity', unpubl. PhD diss. London 1995

# Index

Socialist Labour Party, 104n., 108, 128, 163–4
Socialist League, 32, 46, 56, 72
Socialist National Defence Committee, 124–5, 146. *See also* British Workers' League, National Democratic Party
Socialist Party of Great Britain, 108
South African general strike (1914), 99–100
sports, 14, 52
Stanton, C. B., 129
state, the, 5, 8, 136, 197; left-wing theories of, 4, 76–9, 92, 100, 150–2, 166
Storey, Hedley V., 108
strikes, *see* industrial unrest
super-patriotism, super-patriots: Edwardian, 108–10; First World War, 124–6, 144, 146–8
syndicalists, syndicalism, 89–93, 96, 155

Thistle of Scotland, 15
Thomas, J. H., 3, 123, 141, 154, 161, 168–9, 170, 172, 182, 188, 193, 194; and imperialism, 185–6, 187; and monarchy, 183–4; opposition to conscription, 138–9
Thompson, A. M., 35, 109, 110, 111, 114; and First World War, 124, 130
Thorne, Will, 85, 112, 120
Thorold Rogers, James, 22, 24
Tichborne agitation, the, 19, 21
Tillett, Ben, 42, 54, 55, 146
Trade Union Congress, 47, 121, 138, 139, 145, 147, 154, 191
trade unions, trade unionism, 42, 43, 55–6, 57, 76, 89, 93, 133–4, 136, 139, 146, 148, 171, 199
trades councils, 139–40, 162
tradition, invention of, 6, 203
Triple Alliance, 155, 166
tsarism, hostility to, 97, 120, 143–4, 162

Tudor Walters Report, 177

Union Jack, 99
Union of Democratic Control, 121, 128, 128–9
Unwin. Raymond, 32–3, 177
urban society and industrialism, rejection of, 5, 28–9, 33, 66

Victoria, 17, 73

Wales, Welshness, 3, 44, 48, 51, 71, 91, 197–8
Wallhead, R. C., 157
Walsall anarchists, 41–2
Walsh, Stephen, 124, 184
Walton Newbold, J., 115, 159, 182
war dead, 168–9, 202
Wardle, George, 124, 130, 143
War Emergency Workers' National Committee, 133–4, 135–6, 180, 197
wars, 1, 2, 12, 196 . *See also* French Revolutionary and Napoleonic Wars, Falklands War, Boer War, First World War, Second World War
Webbs, Beatrice and Sidney, 31, 94, 159–60, 184, 199; Beatrice, 149, 150; Sidney, 39, 80, 145, 150–1, and 'British socialism', 39–40, 180–1, and formation of Labour government (1924), 192, 194
Wells, H. G., 124
Wheatley, John, 194
Wilkes, John, 11, 12
Williams, Jack, 21, 109
Williams, Robert, 120, 122, 154
Wilson, Havelock, 146–7
Woodcraft Folk, 2n.

xenophobia, 5, 41, 125, 130–1